Oral Health–Related Quality of Life

Oral Health–Related
Quality of Life

Edited by

Marita Rohr Inglehart, Dr phil habil
Associate Professor
Department of Periodontics, Prevention, and Geriatrics
School of Dentistry
Adjunct Associate Professor
Department of Psychology
University of Michigan
Ann Arbor, Michigan

Robert A. Bagramian, DDS, DrPH
Professor
Department of Periodontics, Prevention, and Geriatrics
School of Dentistry
University of Michigan
Ann Arbor, Michigan

quintessence
books

Quintessence Publishing Co, Inc
Chicago, Berlin, Tokyo, Copenhagen, London, Paris, Milan, Barcelona,
Istanbul, São Paulo, New Delhi, Moscow, Prague, and Warsaw

This book is dedicated with love and gratitude to our parents, Karl and Rita Rohr and Armen and Isabel Bagramian; our spouses, Ronald and Linda; and to our children, Ronald, Marita, and Sara, who bring quality to our lives.

Library of Congress Cataloging-in-Publication Data

Oral health-related quality of life / edited by Marita Rohr Inglehart, Robert A. Bagramian.
    p. ; cm.
Includes bibliographical references and index.
  ISBN 0-86715-421-7 (pbk.)
  1. Oral medicine. 2. Quality of life.
  [DNLM: 1. Oral Health. 2. Quality of Life. WU 113 O6053 2002] I.
Inglehart, Marita Rohr, 1951- II. Bagramian, Robert.
  RC815 .O675 2002
  617.5'22—dc21

                                      2002005595

©2002 Quintessence Publishing Co, Inc

Quintessence Publishing Co, Inc
551 Kimberly Drive
Carol Stream, IL 60188
www.quintpub.com

Editor: Kathryn O'Malley
Production and Design: Dawn Hartman

Printed in the USA

Table of Contents

Foreword

While clinical measurements of oral health continue to reflect how oral health care providers view patient and community well-being, the unique perspective of the public has become increasingly important in assessments of how well an oral health care system functions at the individual or societal level. Oral conditions can have a significant impact, whether positive or negative, both on an individual's sense of personal well-being and on the function of a society as a whole. Such issues are at the heart of this volume, *Oral Health–Related Quality of Life*.

How consumers view their own well-being strongly impacts oral health care systems. This fact became very evident to our research team involved in both of the World Health Organization (WHO) international collaborative studies of oral health systems.[1,2] Particularly startling were the clinical results generated from data collection in the seven nations that participated as part of the first international collaborative study.[3] One of the most significant of those findings was the difference in edentulism among national samples. The highest level of edentulism existed among residents of one particular nation in which there were more extractions than the disease level would indicate, resulting in edentulism in almost 40% of 35- to 44-year-old individuals.

At the time of this preliminary report, analyses available on satisfaction with the condition of one's mouth revealed that the more edentulous a population, the more satisfied they appeared to be. The notion that the profession might condone this tooth loss and the public's satisfaction levels with tooth loss was disconcerting to researchers and administrators and prompted policy makers at the national level to reassess and repeat the study on a national basis. This national study showed that tooth loss was occurring at even earlier ages, in the mid- to late 20s. As a result of cultural beliefs and values, there appeared to be incentive, in both the publicly supported incremental dental care program and in the private practice of dentistry, to promote restorative rather than preventive dentistry. Decision leaders began to institute changes in the national oral health policies and delivery system characteristics.[4] By the time the second international collaborative study took place, that country's interventions, which targeted both providers and consumers, had clearly served to enhance both clinical and sociodental indicators of well-being.[5]

This volume addresses a range of issues predicated on obtaining the patient's or public's perspectives and integrating those with clinical indicators. The public has more to say about whether they ever physically appear for care, or whether they choose to accept all that is suggested for them, than most policy makers are willing to recognize. Therefore, to achieve a more balanced perspective on personal oral health prevention, treatment regimens, and community-based programs, more emphasis must be placed on the public's perceptions and concerns. Whether derived from children, adolescents, adults, patients with special health care needs, women, men, or individuals of varying racial and ethnic identities, these assessments are addressed and brought into focus by the authors and editors.

These reviews of the literature are targeted at a range of health care providers: clinicians, educators, administrators, patient advocates, policy makers and researchers, from basic science to the translational, clinical, sociobehavioral, and public health sciences. This material also helps in the understanding of what is involved in the measurement of oral health–related quality of life. Such an understanding is important because how oral health impacts the global concept of quality of life—how satisfied an individual actually is with his or her ability to function—is the essential outcome measure and indicator of success of any oral health strategy.

This book explores issues such as how clinicians can treat patients as whole people and integrate oral health services appropriately into the life domains of patients, how an educator can convey to future clinicians how they might accomplish such objectives, how administrators can institutionalize incentives to incorporate patient satisfaction into their calculus on payments, and how researchers can measure quality-of-life outcomes. Policy makers are also advised to read this book because public policies that enhance the quality of life of individuals and protect the quality of life of communities are undoubtedly healthy ones.

This volume has served to move this developing field of research forward by convening these expert authors, who have provided translations of what is known about the state-of-the-science to user audiences while mapping out new and logical extensions for researchers. While the majority of the collection is based on US data, there is much to be learned from globally testing many of the ideas and concepts in other cultural settings. In 1876, Louis Pasteur stated, "Science knows no country because knowledge belongs to humanity, and it is the torch which illuminates the world." This quote underlies the need for international collaborations that can advance the science base for important issues such as oral health–related quality of life. Comparing and contrasting results should lead to sharper images of how oral health–related quality of life is defined in different populations. Once this is clarified, it might be easier to design interventions, perhaps borrowing from cultures experiencing success in the enhancement of oral health–related quality of life. A single country therefore might ultimately reduce the disparities and inequities apparent within its national context while also providing instructive guidance for other national systems yet to attempt such change. It is because of this far-reaching potential that oral health–related quality of life is such an important issue that requires immediate attention and action.

Lois K. Cohen, PhD
Associate Director for International Health
Director, Office of International Health
National Institute of Dental and Craniofacial Research
National Institutes of Health
Bethesda, Maryland

References

1. Arnljot HA, Barmes DE, Cohen LK, Hunter PBV, Ship II (eds). Oral Health Care Systems: An International Collaborative Study. Geneva: World Health Organization, 1985.
2. Chen M, Andersen RM, Barmes DE, Leclercq M-H, Lyttle CS. Comparing Oral Health Care Systems: A Second International Collaborative Study. Geneva: World Health Organization in collaboration with Center for Health Administration Studies, Univ of Chicago, 1997.
3. Cohen LK. Dental care delivery in seven nations. In: Ingle JT, Blair P (eds). International Dental Care Delivery Systems: Issues in Dental Health Policies. Cambridge, MA: Ballinger, 1978:201–214.
4. Hunter PBV, Davis PB. The International Collaborative Study of Dental Manpower Systems: The Canterbury Study. Wellington, New Zealand: Department of Health, 1982.
5. Hunter PBV, Kirk R, de Liefde B. The Study of Oral Health Outcomes: The 1988 New Zealand Section of the WHO Second International Collaborative Study. Wellington, New Zealand: Department of Health, 1992.

Preface

Improved quality of life has been the driving force behind dental care since the first person sought relief from oral pain, resolution of biting- or chewing-related problems, or improvement in oral esthetics. Most patients still seek dental treatment for these basic reasons, all of which stem from a desire for good oral health–related quality of life: to be free of pain, to be able to eat and speak without impediment, and to have a nice smile. In the same way, the work of most dental researchers began as a response to patients' quality-of-life concerns. Understanding what causes dental pain and how it can be optimally treated, which materials are most effective for treatment, and how problems in the oral cavity can affect the entire body are quality-of-life issues that have been at the heart of dental research since its beginning.

The implicit centrality of quality-of-life concerns to the field of dentistry is rarely explicitly acknowledged. When dental clinicians, researchers, and educators overlook the person while concentrating solely on the oral cavity itself, the ultimate result is unsatisfied patients. Clinicians and researchers must not look only at patients' oral cavities. They must consider the patient as a person and how treatment decisions will affect overall health and quality of life.

This book grew out of a multidisciplinary workshop on oral health–related quality of life that took place in May 2000 at the University of Michigan School of Dentistry in Ann Arbor. Funded by the National Institute for Dental and Craniofacial Research (NIDCR), this week-long workshop provided an excellent opportunity to explore the role of oral health–related quality of life in research and clinical practice. More than 80 participants from as far away as Brazil and Great Britain, as well as 22 expert presenters from the University of Michigan, UCLA, and the University of North Carolina, collaborated in this workshop. The multidisciplinary perspective of the workshop is clearly reflected throughout the chapters in this book. Quality-of-life research is presented from various fields, including psychology, public health, and general health care. Such background considerations are supplemented by specific discussions of how a patient-centered approach can be applied to basic oral and craniofacial research, clinical dental practice, community dental health issues, and dental education. The book also addresses how oral health–related quality of life relates to treating and understanding different patient populations, such as children with special needs, medically compromised patients, patients with oral cancer, and patients with chronic facial pain. Also discussed are how factors such as race/ethnicity, gender, and age can affect oral health–related quality-of-life concerns and treatment strategies. Finally, the book offers an outlook on the role that oral health–related quality of life will play in future research and dental education.

It is our hope that this book, the first to be published on this topic, will provide all researchers, clinicians, and educators in the dental field with a basic understanding of the significance of oral health–related quality-of-life issues and will inspire and challenge them to embrace this concept in their professional lives.

Acknowledgments

This book owes its existence to a multitude of people. We especially would like to thank Dr Lisa Tedesco, the former associate dean of academic affairs at the University of Michigan School of Dentistry. She sent us to the 1996 conference on the measurement of oral health–related quality of life organized by Dr Gary Slade, with support from NIDCR, which inspired us to become involved in this topic. A wonderful role model, Dr Tedesco opened countless doors for us and was supportive of this project throughout.

We would like to thank NIDCR for funding the interdisciplinary workshop on oral health–related quality of life that took place in May 2000 at the University of Michigan in Ann Arbor. We especially want to thank Dr Patricia Bryant from NIDCR for her encouragement and constant support. We also very much appreciate Dr Bryant and Dr Dushanka Kleinman's willingness to share the NIDCR's perspective on the relevance of oral health–related quality of life with the workshop participants.

The May 2000 workshop, which provided the impetus for this book, could not have been conducted without the support and work of many persons. We want to thank Dr Bill Kotowicz, dean of the University of Michigan School of Dentistry, and Dr Martha Somerman, our department chair, for their support during the preparation and conduct of the workshop and their encouragement in all aspects of our work. Their support made this book possible. We also want to thank our wonderful collaborators from the various departments at the University of Michigan who helped us to prepare for and presented at the interdisciplinary workshop: Drs Toni Antonucci, Brian Burt, Bernardine Cimprich, Marcio da Fonseca, Steve Eklund, John (Jack) Gobetti, James Jackson, Charles Kowalski, Laurel Northouse, Chris Peterson, Penny Pierce, Jonathan Ship, Martha Somerman, Christian Stohler, George Taylor, and Angela Wandera. Despite their busy schedules, they all generously gave their time and expertise to make this workshop, and ultimately this book, happen. We also want to express our sincere and heartfelt gratitude to our grant consultants and outside expert presenters at the workshop, Drs Kathryn Atchison (UCLA) and Gary Slade (UNC). We thank them for their advice and mentoring before, during, and since the workshop.

Without the many staff members from the University of Michigan School of Dentistry neither the workshop nor this volume could have become reality. We especially want to thank Diane Lafferty, Hetty Pate, Beverly Sutton, and Barbara Wolfgang from the Department of Periodontics, Prevention, and Geriatrics for their help with the preparation and administration of the grant and the workshop. We also want to thank Amy Reyes and her wonderful staff at the continuing education office, who helped us at every stage of making the workshop a success. Finally, we would like to acknowledge the Center for Biorestoration of Oral Health at the University of Michigan for their commitment to oral health research.

A special thank you goes to all the workshop participants who came from far and near to bring life and diverse views to our discussions during the workshop, and who encouraged us to put this volume together. May this volume inspire them to continue to work on quality-of-life issues!

Completing this volume was interesting and rewarding because it was a true delight to work with everyone involved. We especially want to thank everyone from Quintessence Publishing Co. This book would not be in print without their vision of this topic as worthwhile for inclusion in their family of books, and it was the expertise and patience of the Quintessence staff that made the book the professional product it is.

We want to thank every single contributor to this book. Their collaboration made this book possible. Their chapters inspired us and will contribute to the introduction of quality-of-life considerations into oral health–related research, clinical practice, and education. It was an honor and a true pleasure to work with them. We thank them for being our colleagues and collaborators.

A heartfelt thank you to our spouses, Ronald and Linda, and our children, Ronald, Marita, and Sara, for their loving support. They improve the quality of our lives and helped to make this volume possible.

Contributors

Toni C. Antonucci, PhD, is a professor of psychology and a senior research scientist in the Survey Research Center of the Institute of Social Research at the University of Michigan. Dr Antonucci's research focuses on how social relations and other psychosocial factors influence quality of life and well-being, particularly for older adults.

Kathryn A. Atchison, DDS, MPH, is a professor, associate dean of research, and director of information technology at the UCLA School of Dentistry. She has substantial experience conducting and leading collaborative multidisciplinary, community-based research projects, has published extensively on outcomes assessment and quality-of-care issues, and developed the widely used Geriatric/General Oral Health Assessment Index (GOHAI).

Robert A. Bagramian, DDS, DrPH, is a professor in the Department of Periodontics, Prevention, and Geriatrics in the School of Dentistry at the University of Michigan. He has published extensively in the area of public health and epidemiology. Dr Bagramian has a strong commitment to educating dental students to provide dental care to underserved populations and increasing the quality of life of all members of our community.

Wenche S. Borgnakke, DDS, MPH, PhD, is a senior health sciences research associate in the Department of Cariology, Restorative Sciences, and Endodontics at the University of Michigan School of Dentistry. She is involved in clinical research on oral health and oral health care for special populations and is currently working with Dr George Taylor on studying the role of periodontitis in diabetes mellitus.

Patricia S. Bryant, PhD, is director of the Behavioral and Social Science Research Program in the Division of Population and Health Promotion Sciences at the National Institute for Dental and Craniofacial Research (NIDCR). She has a distinguished career in research administration and is familiar with the history, current status, and potential future developments of research on oral health–related quality of life.

Brian A. Burt, BDS, MPH, PhD, is a professor and director of the dental public health program in the Department of Epidemiology in the School of Public Health at the University of Michigan. He is also a project principal investigator in the Detroit Center for Research on Oral Health Disparities and editor of the journal *Community Dentistry and Oral Epidemiology*. His research has centered around the epidemiology of oral diseases and fluoride effects on caries and fluorosis.

Bernadine Cimprich, PhD, RN, FAAN, is an associate professor in the School of Nursing at the University of Michigan. She is also the co-director of the socio-behavioral research program and established and leads the interdisciplinary quality-of-life research program at the University of Michigan Comprehensive Cancer Center. She is a fellow in the American Academy of Nursing and is well-known for her research on quality of life in cancer patients.

Marcio A. da Fonseca, DDS, MS, is a clinical associate professor in the Department of Orthodontics and Pediatric Dentistry at the University of Michigan School of Dentistry. Dr da Fonseca heads the Pediatric Dentistry Service at the University of Michigan Medical Center, where children and adolescents with special health care needs are treated. He also provides consultative services for pediatric specialty clinics.

Stephen A. Eklund, DDS, DrPH, is a professor of dental public health in the School of Public Health and an adjunct professor in the Department of Cariology, Restorative Sciences, and Endodontics in the School of Dentistry at the University of Michigan. Dr Eklund has published extensively in the areas of community dentistry and public health as it relates to oral health.

Sara L. Filstrup, DDS, MS, is a pediatric dentist in private practice. Her master's thesis was about the effects of early childhood caries on children's oral health–related quality of life.

John P. Gobetti, DDS, MS, is a professor of dentistry in the Department of Oral Medicine/Pathology/Oncology in the School of Dentistry at the University of Michigan. His research centers on understanding the ways in which dental health care providers can contribute to improving patients' quality of life.

Guido Heydecke, DDS, Dr Med Dent, is a prosthodontist and a visiting professor on the faculty of dentistry at McGill University in Montreal, Canada. Dr Heydecke conducts clinical trials using patient-based outcome measures in an elderly population. His main interests are the impact of chronic conditions, partial and complete edentulism, and prosthodontic therapy on quality of life and satisfaction.

Marita Rohr Inglehart, Dr phil habil, is an associate professor in the Department of Periodontics, Prevention, and Geriatrics in the School of Dentistry and an adjunct associate professor in the Department of Psychology at the University of Michigan. Her research interests focus on understanding how psychosocial factors affect oral health, oral health behavior and care, and oral health–related outcomes.

Dushanka V. Kleinman, DDS, PhD, is the chief dental officer and a rear admiral of the US Public Health Service Commissioned Corps. She also has served as the deputy director of the National Institute of Dental and Craniofacial Research (NIDCR) since 1991. Dr Kleinman hopes to further facilitate the goal of improving science transfer to the public and throughout the profession.

Charles J. Kowalski, PhD, is a professor in the Department of Biologic Sciences at the University of Michigan School of Dentistry. His research focuses on the measurement and analysis of biologic as well as psychosocial factors in oral health.

Linda V. Nyquist, PhD, is a senior research associate for the social sciences in the Institute of Gerontology at the University of Michigan. Originally trained as a social psychologist, Dr Nyquist underwent postgraduate training in geriatrics and gerontology and has since been involved in research on older adults and their quality of life.

Amber G. Paterson, PhD, is a postdoctoral fellow in the behavioral medicine clinic at the University of Michigan Medical School and serves as the contact person for much of the clinic's psycho-oncology initiative at the University of Michigan Comprehensive Cancer Center. Dr Paterson oversees the implementation and data collection for a number of research projects aimed at screening, evaluating, and treating distress, as well as assessing its impact on quality of life in cancer patients and those at increased risk for cancer.

Christopher Peterson, PhD, is a professor of psychology at the University of Michigan. He has a long-standing interest in how cognitive personality traits relate to psychologic and physical well-being. His most recent project is to create a classification system for positive personality traits.

David P. Sarment, DDS, MS, is a clinical assistant professor in the Department of Periodontics, Prevention, and Geriatrics at the University of Michigan School of Dentistry. His research and clinical work focus on the use of dental implants to provide optimal care to all patients, especially older adults.

Jonathan A. Ship, DMD, is a professor in the Department of Oral Medicine and the director of the Bluestone Center for Clinical Research at the New York University College of Dentistry. His clinical research is in oral medicine, oral oncology, and geriatric oral health and is dedicated to understanding how to maintain oral health and function as people age in order to preserve their oral health–related quality of life.

Susan F. Silverton, MD, PhD, is the associate dean of academic affairs in the School of Dentistry at the University of Nevada in Las Vegas. Her research has centered on the inclusion of women's health and oral health issues in the dental school curriculum. She is leading the administrative and faculty teams in developing an integrated, competency-based predoctoral curriculum for the new School of Dentistry in Las Vegas.

Jeanne C. Sinkford, DDS, PhD, is the associate executive director of the American Dental Education Association and director of their Center for Equity and Diversity in Washington, DC. She has been responsible for the recruitment and retention of minority members in the dental profession with the long-term goal of improving the health and quality of life for all Americans, especially disenfranchised and underrepresented minority citizens. She also has worked to promote cultural competency in dental education.

Gary D. Slade, BDSc, DDPH, PhD, is an associate professor in the Department of Dental Ecology at the University of North Carolina. He is a co-author of the Oral Health Impact Profile (OHIP), which he has used in a range of clinical and population studies exploring determinants of oral health–related quality of life. He also convened and authored the proceedings of the first international conference on research methods in oral health–related quality of life in 1995. Dr Slade's published research in oral health–related quality of life includes several cross-cultural studies, one of which received the distinguished William J. Gies award.

Martha J. Somerman, DDS, PhD, is a professor of dentistry in the Department of Periodontics, Prevention, and Geriatrics and the associate dean for research at the University of Michigan School of Dentistry. Dr Somerman is a basic scientist and a clinical periodontist with extensive experience in dental education.

Christian S. Stohler, DMD, Dr Med Dent, is a William R. Mann professor and chair of the Department of Biologic and Materials Sciences in the School of Dentistry at the University of Michigan. His primary research interest is the pathogenesis of persistent pain.

George W. Taylor, DMD, MPH, DrPH, is an associate professor in the Department of Cariology, Restorative Sciences, and Endodontics at the University of Michigan School of Dentistry. His current research activities involve studying relationships between oral diseases and other systemic diseases, particularly the role of oral infections in diabetes mellitus and cardiovascular disease. He also conducts research on factors affecting the oral health status and dental care utilization of minority populations.

Lisa A. Tedesco, PhD, is a professor of dentistry in the Department of Periodontics, Prevention, and Geriatrics and vice president and secretary of the University of Michigan. As a behavioral science researcher and dental educator and a past president of the American Dental Education Association, she has focused on bringing a patient-centered approach to dental curricula.

Her research focuses on understanding how psychosocial factors influence oral health and oral health care.

Richard W. Valachovic, DMD, is the executive director of the American Dental Education Association. This position provides him with unique insights into dental education and its future.

Angela Wandera, BDS, MS, is the former predoctoral program director in pediatric dentistry at the University of Michigan. Her research interests and publications address infant oral health, early childhood caries, prevention, and caries risk assessment. She currently engages in private practice in the Minneapolis/St Paul area and serves as a part-time faculty member in the School of Dentistry at the University of Minnesota.

Marilyn W. Woolfolk, DDS, MPH, is the assistant dean for student services and an associate professor in the Department of Periodontics, Prevention, and Geriatrics at the University of Michigan School of Dentistry. She is actively involved in efforts to increase opportunities for underrepresented students to pursue careers in dentistry. Her clinical research focuses on understanding health behavior and oral health status discrepancies among different population groups.

CHAPTER 1

Oral Health–Related Quality of Life: An Introduction

Marita Rohr Inglehart, Dr phil habil

Robert A. Bagramian, DDS, DrPH

During the second half of the twentieth century, a "silent revolution" took place in highly industrialized societies such as the United States.[1,2] The emphasis shifted from materialistic values that focus on economic growth and security to postmaterialistic values that give priority to self-actualization and self-determination. For a patient with a materialistic value orientation, dental care concerns might extend only to the maintenance of physically healthy teeth and gums, whereas for a patient with a postmaterialistic value orientation, they also might include esthetic concerns and the impact of facial appearance on self-esteem and interactions with others. Consistent with these value changes in society at large and their impact on the health care field, in 1946 the World Health Organization (WHO) introduced a paradigm shift in the definition of health. In the preamble of its constitution, the WHO states that "Health is a state of complete physical, mental, and social well-being and not merely the absence of disease and infirmity."[3] For the field of dentistry, this new perspective on health suggested that the ultimate goal of dental care, namely good oral health, should no longer merely be seen as the absence of caries or periodontal disease; a patient's mental and social well-being should be considered as well. The concept of "oral health–related quality of life" (OHRQOL) captures the aim of this new perspective. This fact is perhaps most strikingly reflected in the first Surgeon General's Report on Oral Health[4] of the year 2000, which stressed the importance of understanding the significance of good oral health and quality of life (QOL) and the need to ensure access to care for everybody.

This volume on OHRQOL, a timely response to this new perspective, has two main goals: *(1)* to inform the reader about research on OHRQOL, and *(2)* to challenge clinicians as well as researchers to make OHRQOL the ultimate focus of all their work. To help the reader establish an understanding of OHRQOL issues, this volume includes basic background information about OHRQOL and provides descriptions of how psychologists, public health researchers, health care providers, and dental researchers are approaching QOL issues in their professional work. This book also presents overviews of OHRQOL's application to and relevance for specific patient populations, such as children and older adults, patients with chronic pain, and patients with special needs, and describes how clinical practice, dental research, and dental education can benefit from seeing a patient's QOL as the ultimate goal of any endeavor. The changes brought about by such a shift in perspective are evaluated at a societal level[1,2] as well as from the perspective of the health care field, particularly in the oral health care arena.[4]

What Is Oral Health–Related Quality of Life?

In 1997, Locker[5] outlined the shift from a disease-centered, biomedical approach to a patient-centered, biopsychosocial approach in health care.[6,7] He argued that it is useful to conceptualize disease and health not as endpoints of one single dimension, but rather as "independent dimensions of human experience." For example, despite having hypertension, an individual might perceive his or her own health as excellent. The disease might not affect the person's self-perceived health status in any way. In other situations, disease can be one of several factors that a person considers when assessing his or her health. Given the fact that disease and health are largely independent concepts, the next question then concerns the relationship between health and QOL. Locker[5] stated that while some measures of QOL include items that are indistinguishable from measures of health, QOL is much broader than health. Following the model of Wilson and Cleary,[8] Locker stated that QOL is determined both by characteristics of the person as well as by nonmedical factors. However, the concepts of health and QOL remain vague as a result of the ambiguity of the definitions of these terms that still exist in the literature.[5]

In this volume, chapters such as those by Kathryn Atchison (chapter 3) and Gary Slade (chapter 4) offer various definitions of oral health and QOL and describe similar concerns about the conceptual ambiguity of these terms. However, while different definitions might be useful in the context of a specific work, for pragmatic reasons it seems worthwhile to establish a working definition of OHRQOL as a starting point for this volume. It is suggested that health-related QOL be defined as a person's assessment of how the following types of factors affect his or her well-being: *(1)* functional factors; *(2)* psychologic factors (concerning the person's appearance and self-esteem); *(3)* social factors (such as interactions with others); and *(4)* the experience of pain/discomfort. When these considerations center around orofacial concerns, *oral* health–related QOL is assessed (Fig 1-1).

How Is Oral Health–Related Quality of Life Assessed?

This working definition has implications for the way in which OHRQOL and these four groups of factors can be measured and included in clinical practice and research. It seems important to point out that the four sets of factors and the resultant sense of OHRQOL are a function of the person (P), the situation (S), and the interaction between the person and the situation (P × S), as captured by the following short equation:

$$OHRQOL = f\ [P + S + (P \times S)]$$

A person's background and cultural upbringing; current and past experiences with oral disease or health care; current states of mind such as depression or happiness; as well as hopes for the future will determine their response to situations. An assessment of one's OHRQOL is likely to consider different situations that relate to the aforementioned four groups of factors (see Fig 1-1). For example, a patient's considerations might include the following: "When I go

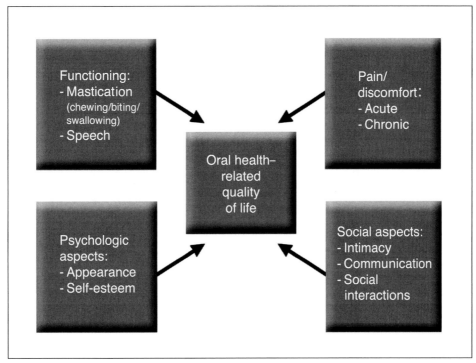

Fig 1-1 The main components of OHRQOL.

out for dinner, can I chew/bite all food served?" "Do I have pain/discomfort when I eat sweet, hot, or cold food?" "Do I like to smile in front of others?" or "Do I feel good about myself when I look in the mirror?" These questions illustrate that the assessment of an individual's OHRQOL may vary based on the context of the situation.

Importance of Oral Health–Related Quality of Life

As shown in the previous section, the concept of OHRQOL brings a new perspective to clinical care and research. It shifts the focus of clinicians and researchers from the oral cavity alone to the patient as a whole. In this way, the concept of OHRQOL can make an invaluable contribution to the clinical practice of dentistry, dental research, and dental education (Fig 1-2).

Clinical practice has a long tradition of being intimately, but implicitly, tied to the patient's QOL. Although modern dentistry might not explicitly consider it, QOL concerns have contributed to the development of dentistry more than any other factor. In the beginning, patients sought out dentists because of QOL concerns such as pain and discomfort. Even today, a high percentage of patients in the United States, particularly those from lower socioeconomic backgrounds, have unmet dental care wants and see a dentist primarily in emergency situations.[9] However, historical documents show that other QOL aspects, such as function and esthetics, have also played a role in patients' demand for dental care from the beginning. For example, edentulous patients' desire to have some form of dental prosthesis can be traced back at least as far as President Washington, who, having lost most of his teeth because of smallpox infection, had dentures made of various sub-

3

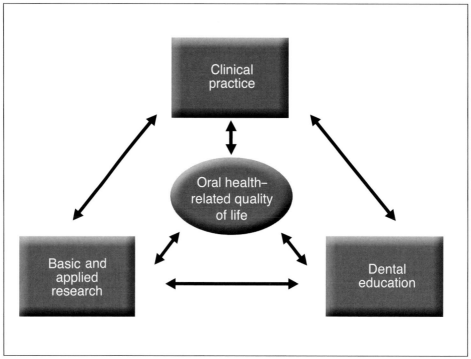

Fig 1-2 OHRQOL and dentistry.

stances. Even while he was the commander of the American forces during the Revolutionary War, he corresponded frequently with his dentist in Philadelphia about these false teeth.[10] Teeth were made out of wood or other substances, such as pigs' teeth, not only to allow some sort of functioning, but also to satisfy esthetic concerns. Furthermore, QOL concerns influence what dental treatments are performed and how they are carried out, which is why local anesthetics have been called dentistry's most important drugs.[11]

Experienced clinicians are well aware that they do not treat teeth and gums, but human beings. They know that QOL concerns motivate patients to engage in good oral health promotion, have regular checkups, and spend considerable amounts of money on esthetic dental services. The more aware clinicians are of this

fact, the more efficiently they will ultimately provide care, prevent oral disease, and restore their patients' oral health.

The role of OHRQOL concerns in dental research is equally important. However, it might be even more challenging to convince researchers of the significance of OHRQOL concerns for their professional work. Researchers might focus on such a narrow and specific research question that they lose sight of the fact that the findings of their research are ultimately only successfully implemented if patients and providers accept these innovations, and such acceptance is highly dependent on whether the innovations address QOL concerns.

OHRQOL concerns are central to each type of dental research: basic sciences research, clinical studies, and behavioral/community-oriented research (Fig 1-3). For example, basic research

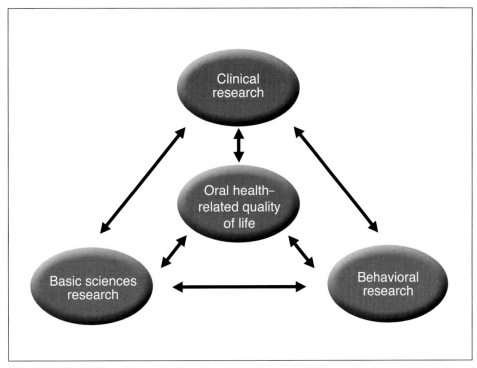

Fig 1-3 OHRQOL and dental research.

on chemotherapy in the treatment of patients with cancer might show its effectiveness at a cellular level, and clinical research might show its clinical effectiveness. Nevertheless, the patient might refuse the treatment and decide to have a shortened life expectancy with a higher QOL instead of a longer life expectancy that is accompanied by complicated and uncomfortable/painful treatment. Successful research is research that makes a contribution to patients' QOL, and, ultimately, QOL concerns should direct researchers both in the laboratory and in clinical settings as to which research questions to study and which solutions to explore. Researchers in the fields of community dentistry and behavioral science can assist in this effort by developing QOL measurement instruments[6] and outlining the role of QOL in oral health care and access to care (see chapter 7).

The concept of OHRQOL is also essential in dental education. In its 1995 report on the future of dental education, the Institute of Medicine not only pointed out that dental health needs to be seen as integrally connected with general health, but also stressed the significance of making dental education patient centered.[12] Regardless of whether a traditional or a problem-based educational approach is chosen, patient-centered education will benefit from considering improvement in a patient's QOL as the ultimate goal of every treatment. Informing dental educators about (1) OHRQOL, (2) how OHRQOL affects health care and oral health promotion, and (3) how OHRQOL can be integrated in a curriculum infusion approach in dental and dental hygiene curricula will help shape the future of dental education.

Conclusion

This volume on OHRQOL comes at a time when health is no longer seen as merely the absence of disease, but as a concept that focuses on the whole person. The study of QOL issues responds to this changed perspective on health by considering the impact of health on all aspects of the person's life and his or her resultant well-being. With this perspective, QOL concerns can play a role in all levels of health care. On a personal level, these concerns can influence the decision-making process for a patient and the treating physician, and on a social level, they can lead to an understanding of the needs of others. In addition, QOL concerns can be used for advocacy on a political level. For example, currently, decayed, missing, and filled teeth (DMFT) scores in children with early childhood caries are used as a common measure of dental health. However, politicians might get a better sense of the need for providing oral health care to underserved populations if they realize that these scores translate into impaired QOL for a child, ie, that a child with a high DMFT score may be malnourished because of an inability to eat certain kinds of food, and may not be able to sleep through the night or concentrate in school because of the associated pain. Thus QOL can become a tool to understand and shape not only the state of clinical practice, dental research, and dental education, but also that of the community at large.

References

1. Inglehart RF. The Silent Revolution. Princeton, NJ: Princeton University Press, 1977.
2. Inglehart RF. Culture Shift. Princeton, NJ: Princeton University Press, 1990.
3. World Health Organization. Constitution of the World Health Organization. Geneva: World Health Organization, 1948.
4. US Department of Health and Human Services. Oral Health in America: A Report of the Surgeon General—Executive Summary. US Department of Health and Human Services. Government Printing Office, 2000.
5. Locker D. Concepts of oral health, disease and quality of life. In: Slade GD (ed). Measuring Oral Health and Quality of Life. Chapel Hill: University of North Carolina–Dental Ecology, 1997:11–24.
6. Slade GD (ed). Measuring Oral Health and Quality of Life. Chapel Hill: University of North Carolina–Dental Ecology, 1997.
7. Engel GL. The need for a new medical model: A challenge for biomedicine. Science 1977;196:129–136.
8. Wilson I, Cleary P. Linking clinical variables with health-related quality of life: A conceptual model of patient-outcomes. JAMA 1995;273:59–65.
9. Mueller CD, Schur CL, Paramore LC. Access to dental care in the United States. J Am Dent Assoc 1998;129:429–437.
10. Nesbit J. Washington's letter to his dentist lets British chief wondering about tactics. Available at: http://www.umich.edu/~urecord9798/Feb18_98/wash.htm. Accessed October 19, 2001.
11. Malamed SF. Local anethetics: Dentistry's most important drugs. J Am Dent Assoc 1994;125:1571–1589.
12. Institute of Medicine. Dental Education at the Crossroads: Challenges and Changes. Washington, DC: National Academy Press, 1995.

Quality of Life and Basic Research in the Oral Health Sciences

Martha J. Somerman, DDS, PhD

Basic research has provided information critical for designing improved therapies for individuals, from preventive programs to diagnosis of diseases, to specific therapies, to evaluating the outcomes of treatment. Nevertheless, there remains a gap between the knowledge gained from patient-centered research and that obtained from basic research in the same area. All too often the rationale for using a specific therapy is not explained to the patient. At the instructive level, it is imperative that new technologies alone should not dictate the way the next generation of oral health care professionals is educated. Clinicians must take a broader, more patient-centered approach in establishing the best therapies for each patient. This must include an increased appreciation for varied responses by individuals to specific therapies, and also for different treatment plans based on individual needs.

This chapter provides a broad overview of oral health issues related to quality of life. It touches upon a few areas that require further research at the basic, translational, and clinical

level to improve the quality of life for individuals. The initial section is followed by a section on opportunities in research and in practice for improving oral health for patients. The third section describes attempts to regenerate orocraniofacial tissues. The last section deals with ways in which oral health care researchers and providers can improve treatment for individuals and thus enhance their patients' quality of life.

Oral Health Issues

There are substantial issues of concern for oral health care providers and researchers. The basic statistical facts listed in Box 2-1 clearly demonstrate that there is an urgent need to improve the orocraniofacial health of the community. These goals can be achieved through:

1. Basic science research focused on mechanistic aspects of disease

Box 2-1 Oral health and changing demographics*

One infant every hour is born with craniofacial birth defects (1:500 to 1:750 live births).
More than 20% of all preschool children (2 to 5 years of age) have dental caries.
More than 30% of all children (5 to 17 years of age) have dental caries.
Twenty million cases of orocraniofacial dental trauma are seen each year.
Four people per hour are diagnosed with head and neck cancer.
One person per hour dies of oropharyngeal cancer.
Twenty-five percent of all patients with cancer have oral complications after therapy.
Almost 5 million people have temporomandibular disease.
Almost 22% of all adults report some form of orofacial pain in the last 6 months.
More than 60% of adults present with some form of periodontal disease.
More than 18 million people suffer from diabetes mellitus types 1 and 2.
More than 22 million people suffer from arthritis and osteoporosis.
Tremendous health disparities exist relative to gender, age, socioeconomic status, and ethnicity.

*Data from the National Institute of Dental and Craniofacial Research.

2. Translational research, including studies targeted at improving methods for diagnosing disease, developing superior restorative materials, and improving the design of existing instrumentation
3. Health services and epidemiology research that includes defining the links between oral and systemic health and determining the association of genetic-environmental profiles with disease patterns
4. Educational programs (dental, dental hygiene, medical, nursing, and specialty programs)
5. Health care providers

Ongoing research in many of these areas will provide answers to some of these questions in this decade. Areas of ongoing research include:

1. Identifying the causes of temporomandibular joint dysfunction and orofacial pain, thereby developing improved therapies (see chapter 15)
2. Determining the link between oral bone loss and other mineralized tissue disorders, eg, osteopenia and osteoporosis (this includes such research questions as "Should oral therapies be different for such patients?" "Are they at an increased risk of developing periodontal dis-

ease?" and "Should implants be used more cautiously in this population?")[1,2]
3. Defining the relationship between changes in sex hormones and orocraniofacial health[3,4]
4. Establishing the relationship among oral infections, host-response to inflammation, and systemic health, including diabetes and cardiovascular disease[5–8]
5. Determining the genes related to increased susceptibility to oral disease[9–11]
6. Understanding the socioeconomic barriers to achieving optimal health[12,13]

Opportunities in Research and Practice

These are exciting times for private practitioners as well as for dental educators and researchers. With the sequencing of the human genome, improved technologies for diagnosing disease, and new information obtained through research efforts, dental health care providers are in a position to provide better care for all patients than ever before. At the clinical level, a comprehensive care program for all patients can and must be provided. Such a comprehensive care pro-

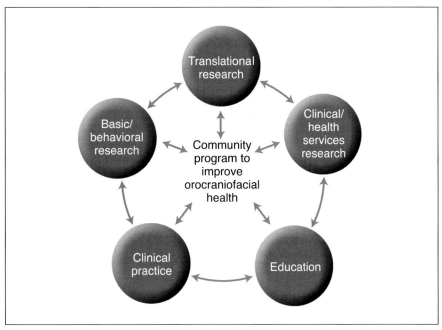

Fig 2-1 Model for community program to improve orocraniofacial health.

Health promotion, disease prevention, outcomes research
Prenatal care, birth defects, early childhood development
Early childhood dental caries research
Orocraniofacial dental trauma
Biomimetics, biomaterials, tissue engineering
Head and neck cancer (oropharyngeal, laryngeal, tonsillar)
Oral infections and systemic disease (diabetes, autoimmune disorders, viral infections, premature births, cardiovascular disease)
Chronic disabling diseases and disorders (temporomandibular disorders, osteoporosis, chronic facial pain, periodontal diseases, fibromyalgia, psycho-immunology)

*Data from the National Institute of Dental and Craniofacial Research.

gram should include obtaining detailed health histories, family profiles, and an indication of susceptibility to diseases. This will allow the treatment provider to design individualized treatment plans. Furthermore, there is a need for increased communication between oral health care providers in private practice and academicians in order to increase the understanding of disease processes. There are numerous areas in which there is a need to cross boundaries between basic and behavioral research, translational research, and clinical and health services research to define preventive strategies, diagnostic tools, treatment plans, and theories. The improvement of orocraniofacial health must be a community effort (Fig 2-1). Examples of areas that need the attention of all oral health care communities are listed in Box 2-2.

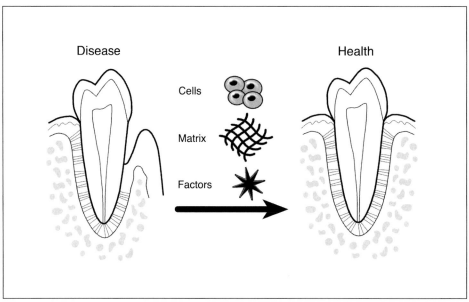

Fig 2-2 Elements required for regeneration of the periodontium.

Regenerating Orocraniofacial Tissues

In the areas of biomimetics, biomaterials, and tissue engineering, positive outcomes have been seen with several therapies currently used to regenerate or restore tissues lost to disease.[14–16] Nevertheless, existing therapies have limitations, including lack of predictable outcomes and limited success in conditions of severe disease, eg, Class III furcation involvement. Many factors need to be considered in designing therapies to achieve more predictable outcomes than those obtained with current methods.

Factors to consider in this area include the following:

1. What cells within the local environment are required for successful regeneration of periodontal tissues (Fig 2-2)?
2. What factors are needed to trigger cells within the local environment to function as cementoblasts, osteoblasts, or periodontal ligament cells (see Fig 2-2)? For example, is it sufficient to provide a specific factor that promotes cell proliferation, thus providing a critical cell population, or is a factor that promotes cell differentiation, such as certain bone morphogenetic proteins, a better choice? Alternatively, a slow delivery material that allows the release of a growth factor, followed by a differentiation factor, may be required.
3. What scaffold is required to provide the required release profile without secretion of toxic factors?
4. Is the newly formed tissue mechanically satisfactory?
5. Is the procedure costly?
6. Are there differences in responsiveness of individuals to this regenerative therapy? If yes, are alternative therapies available?
7. What impact do age, diet, and systemic health have on the therapy used?
8. What are the clinical and oral health–related outcomes such as esthetic aspects, discomfort, and predictability?
9. How safe is the procedure?
10. What is the time commitment for the patient and for the provider?
11. What percentage of patients are satisfied with the regenerative therapies they have received?

There are many unanswered questions in this area. Clinicians must provide input regarding patient satisfaction with existing therapies, predictability of procedures, and long-term outcomes. In addition, clinicians must describe the types of diseases that require regenerative therapy and the success of treatment of these diseases using the regenerative materials currently available. Basic researchers need to give input regarding the types of experimental systems available to address clinical issues. Finally, the clinical manifestation of the disease must be fully understood.

Future Directions

The oral health care community must work together to improve therapies for all patients (see Fig 2-1). Partnerships must be developed that allow the dissemination of information and the open discussion of issues related to oral health care. Currently, the translation of research findings to the clinical setting is slow. Increased communication between the clinician and the researcher, especially in the form of updates regarding areas of success and failure, would be beneficial to both groups. Ultimately, this will improve oral health and oral health–related quality of life of patient communities. One approach to achieving this goal may be to initiate study groups (which already exist independently in private practice and the research environment) that include individuals exclusively in private practice and those whose primary appointment is at a university. Improving oral health–related quality of life would be the unifying goal of this endeavor.

Acknowledgment

This chapter was supported by the National Institutes of Health (grant Nos. R01-DE09532 and R01-DE13047).

References

1. Grossi S, Jeffcoat MK, Genco RJ. Osteopenia, osteoporosis and oral disease. In: Rose L, Genco R, Cohen D, Mealey B (eds). Periodontal Medicine. Hamilton, Ontario: BC Decker, 1999:167–182.
2. Cooper LF. Systemic effectors of alveolar bone mass and implications in dental therapy. Periodontol 2000 2000;23:103–109.
3. Otomo-Corgel J, Steinberg BJ. Periodontal medicine and the female patient. In: Rose L, Genco R, Cohen D, Mealey B (eds). Periodontal Medicine. Hamilton, Ontario: BC Decker Inc, 1999:151–165.
4. Jeffcoat MK, Lewis CE, Reddy MS, Wang CY, Redford MA. Post-menopausal bone loss and its relationship to oral bone loss. Periodontol 2000 2000;23:94–102.
5. Lalla E, Lamster IB, Drury S, Fu C, Schmidt AM. Hyperglycemia, glycoxidation and receptor for advanced glycation endproducts: Potential mechanisms underlying diabetic complications, including diabetes-associated periodontitis. Periodontol 2000 2000;23:50–62.
6. Beck JD, Slade G, Offenbacher S. Oral disease, cardiovascular disease and systemic inflammation. Periodontol 2000 2000;23:110–120.
7. Kinane DF, Lowe GD. How periodontal disease may contribute to cardiovascular disease. Periodontol 2000 2000;23:121–126.
8. Williams RC, Offenbacher S. Periodontal medicine: The emergence of a new branch of periodontology. Periodontol 2000 2000;23:9–12.
9. Hodge P, Michalowicz B. Genetic predisposition to periodontitis in children and young adults. Periodontol 2000 2000;26:113–134.
10. Hart TC, Hart PS, Michalec MD, et al. Localisation of a gene for prepubertal periodontitis to chromosome 11q14 and identification of a cathepsin C gene mutation. J Med Genet 2000;37:95–101.
11. Hart TC, Marazita ML, Wright JT. The impact of molecular genetics on oral health paradigms. Crit Rev Oral Biol Med 2000;11:26–56.
12. Anderson RT, Sorlie P, Backlund E, Johnson N, Kaplan GA. Mortality effects of community socioeconomic status. Epidemiology 1997;8:42–47.
13. Ismail AI, Sohn W. The impact of universal access to dental care on disparities in caries experience in children. J Am Dent Assoc 2001;132:295–303.
14. Lynch S, Genco R, Marx R (eds). Tissue Engineering: Applications in Maxillofacial Surgery and Periodontics. Chicago: Quintessence, 1999.
15. Drisko CH. Nonsurgical periodontal therapy. Periodontol 2000 2000;25:77–88.
16. Wang HL, Greenwell H. Surgical periodontal therapy. Periodontol 2000 2000;25:89–99.

CHAPTER 3

Understanding the "Quality" in Quality Care and Quality of Life

Kathryn A. Atchison, DDS, MPH

Just as the use of the word *quality* by Ford Motor Company in their car marketing scheme suggests reliability, longevity, and performance, the use of the word *quality* in health care has become synonymous with expertise, successful treatment, and interest and concern in the patient's welfare. Increasingly, the provision of health care services is moving rapidly from a biomedical model, in which treatment of disease is the most appropriate goal, to embracing a holistic approach much like Engel's biopsychosocial model, in which the whole patient is treated.[1] This is readily seen by the expansion of health plans to include complementary and alternative health services, expansion of mental health benefits, and reimbursement for treatments such as breast reconstruction after cancer, which used to be seen as a purely cosmetic procedure. Oral health care is a full partner in this process. Indicators of this fact include that orthodontic services for severe malocclusion must be covered by Medicaid and that the federal Child Health Insurance Programs consider oral health benefits to be necessary because of the number of school days lost because of oral health problems. To understand how quality of life (QOL) and quality of clinical care may be related, it is useful to begin with a model that describes the fluidity of health.

Putting Health in the Context of Health Care

A recent study proposed that the number of missing teeth in rural Guatemala could stand as an indicator of the QOL of third-world villagers. This statement was based on the strong interrelationships among the retention of sound—or at least treatable—natural teeth, access to health care, poverty, lack of health education, malnutrition, and disease.[2] As Fig 3-1 suggests, a number of factors can contribute to the degradation of a person's health. These factors include an individual's level of stress, disease, behavior, lifestyle, poverty,

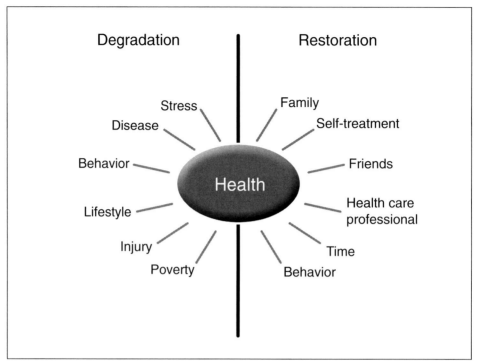

Fig 3-1 Descriptive model of the interrelationships among health factors.

and injury. Any of these may have an impact on a person's health and thus on the success of clinical care. People who smoke may have a slower and less successful recovery after periodontal surgery. Likewise, people living in poverty may have poorer nutrition, even associated vitamin deficiencies, and may report poorer health; thus an oral surgeon may note slower healing. Comprehensive clinical care must take into account such behavioral or nutritional deficiencies (and, if possible, compensate for them, perhaps by prescribing dietary supplements) to ensure quality care and thus improve the patient's QOL. Clinical research questions will be defined herein to distinguish components of the degraded health that are attributable to general factors such as nutrition or smoking from those that are attributable to oral disease or its treatment.

Once health is degraded, a number of factors far beyond the services provided by a health care professional may contribute to its restoration (see Fig 3-1). Recognizing the limitations of health care services helps one understand why QOL and quality of care are both necessary. Family and friends can be important determinants of whether a person will maintain good health. Research on the influence of social networks confirms the importance of having family and friends to improve physical and mental health.[3] Behavior is a factor that can have a positive or negative impact on health. For example, smoking is a behavior that many clinicians may consider negative when determining a treatment plan for oral conditions. However, on the positive side, a patient's decrease in alcohol or tobacco use can decrease his or her risk for oral cancer. Thus, behavior can be equally important to health care in predicting both the risk of disease as well as the likelihood of successful treatment.

Many disease processes are self-limiting. Time itself can be a healer, as indicated by the fact that a clinician can expect an injury to demonstrate more healing 1 month after surgery compared with 1 day after surgery. Cousins[4] notes that the primary role of the clinician is to assist the body in healing itself. Thus, understanding the effectiveness of QOL will require assessment of health over time. Additionally, improvements in health or the ability of the body to heal itself may be initiated by patients themselves through self-treatment, eg, taking nutritional supplements.

Understanding Health-Related Quality of Life As a Multidisciplinary Concept

The definition of health by the World Health Organization as "a state of complete physical, mental, and social well-being, and not merely the absence of disease or infirmity"[5] led to the development of a multidisciplinary approach to health. It distinguished wellness from lack of disability, disease, and illness. All of these components of health must be considered when clinicians develop treatment goals for their patients.

Quality of life recognizes the value of an individual's health in the broader psychologic and social aspects of his or her life. The clinician's diagnosis alone is not sufficient to understand a patient's health. The diagnosis of a single component of oral health is also not sufficient to justify a diagnosis of overall oral health. Good periodontal condition does not guarantee good oral health, which includes both a subjective and an objective dimension. For example, a patient might view severely stained teeth as a far greater problem for finding employment than an asymptomatic periodontal problem. This implies that while the clinician may objectively pronounce the patient's oral health to be adequate, the patient may subjectively rate his or her oral health as poor based on appearance.

The QOL construct considers patients' satisfaction with their present health state as well as their goals for the future. It considers the time and resources needed to improve health, as well as the dichotomy between quantity and quality of life. It asks the question, "Are all days equally valuable?" A patient may say, "I would rather have more days in which I am feeling no chronic pain and fewer days when I have chronic pain, even if it means I die several weeks earlier." In this case the physician should try to strategize treatment goals to maximize good days over days filled with pain. Such clinical decisions are made, for example, in cases of oral cancer when deciding whether to have resection of a mandible instead of radiation if clinician-projected survival rates are similar. Or, a surgeon may feel that the chances of successful healing are too slim in a heavy smoker to risk surgery and rule it out as an option if the patient is a smoker who values the comfort of tobacco over the possibility of a longer survival rate associated with pain and the absence of tobacco. Thus the person's values and priorities, the time required, and the resources needed are all elements that a clinician must consider when making treatment decisions.

Quality of life is a multidisciplinary concept that includes survival, or duration of life; the absence of impairment, disease, or symptoms; appropriate physical oral functioning; the absence of discomfort and pain; emotional functioning; social functioning associated with the performance of normal roles; perceptions of adequate oral health; satisfaction with oral health; and absence of social or cultural disadvantages related to oral health.[6] It is a value assigned by individuals, groups, or societies to the duration of survival, as modified by impairments, functional states, perceptions, and social opportunities and as influenced by disease, injury, treatment, or policy. Thus QOL reflects human experiences that will influence a person's well-being or satisfaction with life. It can incorporate the totality of the person's existence, including factors such as poverty, employment status, job satisfaction, or marital status. For example, a person who is poverty-stricken and has difficulty providing for the family may not be worried about improving his or her oral health by replacing missing teeth with a $2,100 fixed partial denture. There may be other factors that are more important to such an individual's QOL. An astute clinician will recognize this fact and adjust the treatment accordingly.

Incorporating Quality of Life into Clinical Research

Early measures of the success of a health care system were varied but narrow. For example, infant mortality, a critical index used internationally to assess the success of a country's health care system, only considered whether an infant lived or died. It failed to consider inequalities of socioeconomic status or level of parental health education. Although infant mortality is now reported by age group and ethnic status of the mother, which provide a somewhat improved basis for understanding the importance of other health factors, as an index, infant mortality still ignores the future health of the toddler.

Moreover, most early measures of success of a health care system focused on acute diseases and the early killers. Influenza was a noted killer of short duration, typically lasting less than 1 week. If influenza did not kill the patient, the patient would usually recover with no reduction in state of health. However, other common diseases are associated with a very different pathogenesis and prognosis. For example, heart disease, currently a common condition that kills both men and women, may be asymptomatic, last for years, and cause subtle or substantial problems, such as shortness of breath, for the remainder of the individual's life. These effects may impede the person's ability to continue normal activities like gardening, walking, or even climbing stairs. Thus chronic diseases, which have a significant impact on patients' QOL, must also be considered when measuring the success of health care systems.

As recognition of the importance of considering the patient as a whole when treating diseases and conditions increased, the field of health measurement changed accordingly. Today, clinical research is undertaken for three reasons:

1. To better understand disease, its course, and its impact on a patient's health and QOL
2. To predict high-risk or target patients for whom it is likely that treatment will be successful or cost effective
3. To measure improvement in health following treatment

Early clinical research on QOL related to oral health arose from the desire to correct misconceptions held by the broader health profession regarding oral disease, namely that it is not life threatening and does not extend beyond the oral cavity, and therefore has no impact on the patient as a whole. Thus research was designed to create a better understanding of oral disease and its impact on a patient's health and QOL. Later, as the health care industry became more committed to recognizing the time and growing resources associated with health care, the success or failure of treatment assumed greater importance, and measurement of oral health and QOL was used increasingly for outcomes assessment.

Interaction Among Components of Health-Related Quality of Life

The interactive model for health-related QOL presented in Fig 3-2 describes the ultimate goal of health care as preserving or improving QOL over the lifespan of an individual. The components of this model—impairments; physical, psychologic, and social functioning; health perceptions; and health care opportunities[7]—are integral to a clinical researcher's understanding of how a patient's disease, condition, or injury may affect QOL.

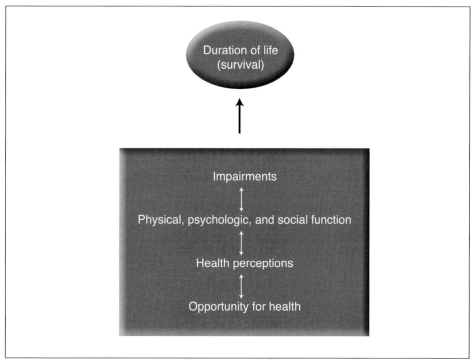

Fig 3-2 Model showing health-related quality of life constructs for a patient with a disease, condition, or injury.

As an illustration of this model, an older individual may notice that a denture is loose (disease or condition) and slips while she is eating or speaking (functional limitations). She perceives the problem as having a negative impact on her health (health perception), and because she has both a source of dental treatment and the financial means to afford care (opportunity for health), this patient makes an appointment to have new dentures made. The new dentures improve her QOL. In contrast, this patient's roommate is an older woman who suffers from mild dementia and denture problems (condition), and her denture problem goes undetected by herself and her nurse. As the problems with eating escalate, she retreats more and more from meals and becomes malnourished (impairment).

In recent years, clinical studies have assessed the impact of QOL associated with a number of oral diseases and their treatment: tooth removal,[8,9] skeletal disharmony,[10] craniofacial abnormalities, oral and head and neck cancers,[11] and treatment for mandibular fracture. Clinical research has also been conducted to assess the impact of elective treatments such as orthodontic and orthognathic surgery.[12] Clinical studies of oral health–related QOL may include some or all of the components of the model in Fig 3-2. While research based on a comprehensive model is ideal, research constraints may dictate that some factors be excluded. If a noncomprehensive model is used, discussion of results will likely point to limitations due to the missing components. Table 3-1 describes examples of clinical oral health studies measuring QOL and the components selected in these studies.[8,11–16] The table includes selected research that provides examples of individual components of the model.

Table 3-1 Clinical research to study the effectiveness of treatment and quality of life

Oral condition	Duration of life	Impairments	Construct — Physical, psychologic, and social function	Health perceptions	Opportunity for health	Treatment
Head and neck cancer[13]	% alive at year 1; status at 2 years; measurement times	Symptoms: Fatigue, pain, nausea, dyspnea, insomnia, vomiting, etc; previous malignancy	Physical, role, cognitive, emotional, and social function	Global health status	Perceived financial impact of disease	Chemotherapy, surgery, radiation
Orthognathic surgery[12]	Success 24 months after surgery	OHSQ* (pain, sensitivity); SIP† (ambulation, mobility, sleep, body care)	SIP† (physical, psychosocial, role); OHSQ* (oral functions)			Rigid and wire fixation
Oral and laryngeal cancer[11,14]		Symptoms: Fatigue, nausea, vomiting, pain	Physical, role, cognitive, emotional, and social function	Global Health-Related Quality of Life scale	Perceived financial impact	None
Oral quality of life[15]		Symptoms: Pain and discomfort	Physical function, oral anxiety, general emotional function, psychologic disability			Implants vs partial dentures
Third molar surgery[8]	1 week after surgery	Change in problems with eating, swallowing, speech, sensory loss		Enjoyment of food, expectations of appearance, willingness to repeat operation	Time off from work	Removal of third molars under general anesthesia
Orofacial pain[16]		Pain symptoms, temporomandibular pain, and neurologic signs	OHIP‡ (physical disability, functional limitations, social disability, handicap)			None

*OHSQ, Oral Health Status Questionnaire.
†SIP, Sickness Impact Profile.
‡OHIP, Oral Health Impact Profile.

Opportunity for Health

Broadly, opportunity for health—as it relates to QOL—incorporates aspects of how oral health (eg, poor oral esthetics or halitosis) may affect one's ability to engage in social interactions, find employment, make friends, or even engage a caregiver's interest. It also includes such components as the social or cultural impediments to receiving health care services faced by patients. Few clinical studies on oral health and QOL directly study the opportunity for health, but examples abound demonstrating how these aspects are considered anecdotally or as a corollary to the study. For example, there are many reports of patients feeling disadvantaged because of a health stigma. Researchers in the area of acquired immunodeficiency syndrome (AIDS) reported that because of the stigma associated with their condition, patients with AIDS did not disclose their health problem for fear of discrimination and rejection by health professionals.[17] Receipt of mental health benefits also has generated a negative societal reaction that stigmatizes individuals in the employment world and leads to a poor QOL.

To demonstrate the impact of the opportunity factor on QOL in a clinical study, Hammmerlid et al[13] compared responses given by dropouts with those given by full participants of a study of patients with head and neck cancer to identify possible biases in dropout rates. For the majority of items regarding the impact of head and neck cancer on social and physical health, there was an overall tendency toward lower mean scores in the patients who dropped out of the study. However, for the item on perceived financial impact of cancer, the mean score of the 35 individuals who completed the study was 5 (SD, 5) compared with a mean score of 29 for the 9 individuals who did not complete the study. This suggests that study dropouts may have been unduly affected by the high costs of treatment, which thus adversely affected their QOL.

Another intrinsic aspect of opportunity is resilience or the individual's capacity for health. Psychoneuroimmunology represents a basic research discipline that studies the association between the mind and the body, such as the person's ability to withstand stress and heal successfully. Some hypothesize that the mind can directly affect the basic physiology of the body, suggesting a biologic mechanism for the clinical study of QOL.

Health Perceptions

A person's health perceptions are among the major indicators that clinicians and clinical researchers use to understand an individual's rating of health. Measures of perceived health represent the individual's subjective view of his or her health and include the often-used perceptions of overall general health (and the patient's satisfaction with health), perceptions of esthetics or appearance, and even perceptions of mouth dryness. Such measurements are important because perceived need for health care has been found to be a driving force behind an individual seeking out oral health care services.[18]

The following issues contribute to a better understanding of the use and interpretation of health perceptions in clinical studies on QOL: (1) self-perceptions vs the clinician's ratings, (2) impact of culture on ratings, (3) predictors of health perceptions, and (4) usefulness of health perceptions as clinical outcome measures.

Self-perceptions vs the clinician's perception

Clinicians' ratings of health often do not correspond to patient self-ratings. Table 3-2 demonstrates differences among dentists and older adults in independent ratings of each subject's oral health using a single rating of oral health, with five response categories—excellent, very good, good, fair, and poor.[19] The clinicians rated 294 (38%) of the patients as being in excellent oral health compared with 142 subjects (18%) who rated themselves as being in excellent oral health. Overall, the clinicians rated the patients' health higher than the patients themselves did in 383 (49%) of the cases; 231 (30%) of the cases were rated identically by both patients and clinicians; in 162 (21%) of the cases, the clinicians' ratings were lower.

Table 3-2 Single-item self-rating of oral health by patients compared with rating of clinicians*†

Patient rating	No.	No. of patient ratings identical to clinician rating	No. of higher clinician ratings	No. of lower clinician ratings
Excellent	142 (18%)	84	0	58
Very good	228 (29%)	62	118	48
Good	244 (31%)	45	150	49
Fair	130 (17%)	33	90	7
Poor	32 (4%)	7	25	0
Total	776	231 (30%)	383 (49%)	162 (21%)

*Mantel test of linear association = 135.0, $P \le .001$.
†Data from Atchison et al.[19]

Who is the final arbiter in determining the appropriate rating of oral health, the clinician or the patient? When considering QOL, it must be the patient, because the QOL represents the individual's perception of health, and most oral health effects considered in QOL research involve problems recognized internally, rather than those readily detectable by the clinician. A comparison of regression predictors of a higher oral health rating in the study by Atchison and colleagues[19] demonstrates a fundamental lack of congruity between the oral health ratings given by clinicians and those given by the individuals themselves. Older adult patients' ratings of higher oral health were associated with having teeth; not having a high amount of caries; having few functional problems when eating or speaking; experiencing little pain and few other limitations such as worrying about oral health or social embarrassment; not perceiving a need for dental treatment; and having good esthetics. Thus the subjective factors were highly predictive of how the older adults perceived their oral health. However, clinicians, unaware of the patients' criteria, rated the subjects' oral health according to clinical markers of disease, proffering higher ratings to older adults having more teeth, not having a lot of mobile teeth, and not having dryness of the oral mucosa.[19] An interesting question for the future will be whether clinicians, once armed with knowledge of patient symptoms and problems associated with QOL, would provide ratings of the subjects' oral health that were more similar to those given by the subjects.

Impact of culture on ratings of oral health

The elements of culture that describe one's self or group membership—gender, racial and ethnic status, education level, marital or living status—are often found to have significant associations with health perceptions. Based on a conceptual model that states that immutable characteristics help to frame the manner in which one views disease as well as one's capacity to manage or prevent disease, Landrine and Klonoff[20] reported that college students of color attributed illness to supernatural causes to a greater extent than did Caucasian college students. Other researchers have also reported attribution of illness to moral or religious factors. Indeed, such cultural beliefs may strongly guide one's expectations for health and care-seeking behavior.

A number of studies have examined the influence of culture on health perceptions. While results are mixed, studies generally show that at least one aspect of culture is related to oral health perceptions. Women have been shown to report their oral health less positively than do men in a national survey conducted in the United Kingdom,[21] but other studies[22–24] have shown no difference. In a qualitative analysis, Hunter and Arbona[2] present possible explanations for the association between gender and oral health perceptions. They report, "Young [Guatemalan] females, with full parental approval and support, are far more likely to seek extractions and to be fitted for dental plates, whereas men stubbornly postpone extraction and never use prostheses." The ultimate goal of these actions, closely tied with perceptions of the value of oral health, is to demonstrate good appearance and financial attainment, as well as to avoid the additional pain that a deterioration of oral health may bring with it. "Extraction obviously avoids future pain, but plates are also meritorious in their own right because of links with courtship and marriage. A full set of prosthetic white teeth, preferably with gold edges, seems to be idealized preparation for marriage, providing that parents can make the financial sacrifice."[2]

A less positive perception of oral health is often reported by groups of ethnic and racial minorities. Matthias et al[22] reported higher self-ratings of appearance by white individuals. All three US sites of the International Collaborative Study for Oral Health Outcomes demonstrated lower oral health perceptions among minority participants (African American, Lakota, and Hispanic) compared with individuals from majority groups (Caucasian and Navajo).[24] Atchison and colleagues[25] compared predictors of physical outcomes and worry about oral health and social oral health, two subscales of the General Oral Health Assessment Index, and found that employment and income were associated with both scales for disadvantaged Hispanic individuals. For African American individuals, employment was associated with both subscales.

Positive perceptions are also reported by younger adults in some studies,[21,24] but not in others.[26,27]

Predictors of self-ratings of health

Recognizing that minority groups often have limited access to care and more missing teeth, one might attribute poor health ratings to higher levels of missing teeth and limited access to care. Use of multivariate models allows the parsing out of the portion of variance that is attributable to culture or sociodemographic factors rather than to a lack of access to care. The International Collaborative Study II includes multiple studies with similar comprehensive models to investigate predictors of health perceptions. In their New Zealand National Oral Health Survey, Chen and Hunter[23] combined two items of perceived oral well-being—self-rating of oral health and perceived appearance. Predictors of higher perceived oral well-being for children aged 12 to 13 years included larger family size, frequent brushing and flossing, and fewer decayed teeth. For adults (aged 35 to 44 years), predictors of higher perceived oral well-being included lower levels of education; a perception that their general health was good; a higher likelihood of residing in small urban areas; asymptomatic visits to the dentist; and fewer decayed, missing, or filled teeth. Ethnicity was not included in the New Zealand study. For the US sites, ethnic differences in oral health perceptions existed, even after controlling for age, gender, income, education, marital status, perceived general health, health beliefs, number of teeth, usual source of care, insurance status, oral symptoms, and oral health behaviors.[24]

To support the idea that culture, rather than clinical variables, may provide answers to how patients may rate their oral health, the following finding can be considered. At the Baltimore and Indian Health Service sites, for older adults only, either having no teeth at all or having the greatest number of teeth were related to positive perceptions of oral health.[24] Thus the participants who rated their oral health the lowest were those individuals who had already lost several teeth, were experiencing pain, and were undergoing multiple dental treatments to restore oral health. Therefore, while a clinician would view the possession of teeth as being preferable

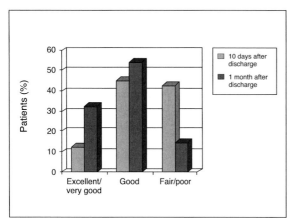

Fig 3-3 Comparison of self-rated general health status of patients treated for orofacial injuries 10 days and 1 month after discharge (N = 164).

to edentulism in all cases, for many people, the oral health problems associated with having natural teeth may overshadow the benefits. Thus, health perceptions may vary by ethnic group and may give great insights into the value priorities of an individual or population group.

Use of health perceptions in clinical studies of quality of life

The effectiveness of treatment in improving patients' QOL is being increasingly evaluated to guide both patients and clinicians regarding the most appropriate mechanisms of care. Like many measures of QOL, health perceptions can be generic, such as the single-item self-rating of oral health, or specific, such as perceived appearance. Atchison and colleagues (unpublished data, 2001) used the single-item oral health rating as an outcome measure to compare the effectiveness of treatment for mandibular fracture among a disadvantaged minority population in South Central Los Angeles, California. Subjects were interviewed on their oral and general health 10 days after treatment and 1 month after discharge. Figure 3-3 shows the improvement in rat-

ings as the subjects healed. Ratings of "excellent" or "very good" increased from 12% at 10 days after discharge to 32% at 1 month after discharge. At the other end of the scale, 10 days after discharge, more than 40% of the subjects reported they were in "fair" or "poor" health; this percentage decreased to 12% a month later. This is a brief, global perspective of patient improvement in oral health during treatment. Despite its lack of specificity, global self-ratings can provide a rapid, valid assessment of improvement to a busy clinician.

Physical, Psychologic, and Social Functioning

Functional health status is a critical dimension of QOL. Maintaining good function and preventing deterioration of function are primary goals when treating the chronically ill and the growing elderly population. In the oral health field, past studies have demonstrated many functional impacts associated with oral diseases and treatments, including loss of days of work or school associated with oral disease; problems with functioning among patients with complete dentures; and problems with eating, speaking, and swallowing associated with surgical treatment of oral cancer.

A number of instruments have been developed that measure the impact of oral diseases and conditions on functional status.[28–31] Other studies have adapted generic measures of health in assessing functional status and QOL.[11,32,33] Most studies of functional status are derived from a combination of literature reviews and interviews with patients and health professionals to determine the types of impact that may be associated with oral diseases and conditions. Themes common to most instruments have been items concerning patients' ability to eat, speak, swallow, and engage in social roles without noticeable psychologic limitations.

As previously mentioned, with the growing emphasis on assessing the quality of care, clinical outcomes research developed from a field focused on understanding the impact of disease

Table 3-3 Comparison of oral impacts reported by healthy older adults and patients with mandibular fracture

Item	Percent responding "always" or "often"	
	Healthy older adults (n = 1,755)	Patients with mandibular fracture (n = 164)
Limit kinds or amounts of food you eat	10	81
Trouble biting or chewing food such as firm meat or apples	13	81
Able to swallow comfortably	95	49
Teeth prevent you from speaking	3	66
Limit contact with people	1	32
Pleased and happy with appearance	72	43
Use medication to relieve pain or discomfort	3	59
Worried or concerned about the problems	10	62
Feel uncomfortable eating in front of people	4	38
Feel nervous or self-conscious	6	37
Teeth or gums are sensitive to hot, cold, or sweets	7	39

to one focused on measuring the effectiveness of treatment. Table 3-3 presents a comparison of responses to the 12 items included in the General Oral Health Assessment Index, which originally was developed to assess oral functioning and QOL for older populations,[25,28,34] and recently was used to estimate the physical and psychosocial impact associated with healing of mandibular fractures resulting from orofacial violence.[35] The table compares the responses given by healthy older adults with those given by patients with mandibular fractures 10 days after treatment. It is clear that the impact of the fractures on QOL is considerable. While fewer than 30% of healthy subjects reported any physical or psychosocial problems, most patients with mandibular fracture reported "always" or "often" having physical problems with eating, speaking, and swallowing. They also reported social problems with appearance and interaction with others and psychologic problems such as worry or embarrassment.

Social functioning defines a person's usual roles and demonstrates how health may place limitations on the individual. Social functioning activities include integration in the community, participation in religious activities, attendance at school or work, intimacy and sexual functioning, or, for an edentulous person in a nursing home, being comfortable eating or socializing with other people. It involves a combination of the quality of interaction with others, the quantity of connections with others, utilization of social interaction (spending time with others), importance of the social relationship, availability of social interactions (having people or animals there when needed), and satisfaction with social relationships.[36] As seen in Table 3-3, more than 30% of patients undergoing treatment for mandibular fracture limited their contact with people and felt uncomfortable eating with people, and 57% were not pleased with their appearance.

Psychologic functioning considers the affective and cognitive domain, in particular noting distress and well-being. Murray and colleagues[16] described the psychologic impact in patients referred to a craniofacial pain unit as substantial. Of these patients, 67% reported problems such as disturbed sleep, difficulty relaxing, depression and feeling upset, inability to concentrate, and embarrassment.

Table 3-4 Acute posttraumatic stress disorder (PTSD) symptoms associated with orofacial injury 1 month after injury (N = 172; $P < .001$)*

Symptoms	Mean score of individuals without PTSD[†] (SD)	Mean score of individuals with PTSD[‡] (SD)	t
Upsetting thoughts	1.78 (1.05)	2.90 (1.11)	6.30
Bad dreams	1.37 (0.74)	2.33 (1.17)	5.47
Reliving event	1.32 (0.67)	2.21 (1.07)	5.56
Emotionally upset	1.63 (0.98)	2.69 (0.94)	6.64
Physical reaction	1.39 (0.78)	2.10 (0.91)	5.18
Avoids thinking about event	1.58 (0.94)	2.63 (1.10)	6.38
Avoids reminders of event	1.82 (1.14)	2.90 (1.07)	5.99
Unable to remember event	1.43 (0.87)	2.15 (1.04)	4.77
Loss of interest in activities	1.59 (0.99)	2.83 (1.04)	7.39

*Abstracted from Glynn and colleagues[38] with permission. Note that all subjects did not respond to every item.
[†]n=120.
[‡]n=52.

When measuring psychologic functioning in clinical studies, it is critical to consider the time at which the measurement is taken, the health state of the subject, and the subject's stage of treatment. Disregarding such issues can result in measurement failure. For example, in one study,[35] psychologic health of patients undergoing treatment for mandibular fractures was assessed at the time of discharge from the hospital and 10 days after treatment. Using the five-item Mental Health Inventory,[37] which was validated on community populations, the data showed little improvement during this time and the clinicians were concerned that the instruments were not sensitive enough to detect improvement in health. However, a closer look at the data showed that patients still had wires fixed and were receiving pain medication when the second assessment was taken. Furthermore, patients reported substantial pain and could not return to their social roles.

Clinical studies must select measures consistent with the severity of the disease to ensure that measures will be valid in a new setting. For example, when considering a higher level of disability-associated psychologic functioning, namely acute posttraumatic stress disorder symptoms, Glynn and coworkers[38] reported that many patients who had suffered orofacial injury described having upsetting thoughts and bad dreams, and reliving the event that caused their fractures 1 month after the injury (Table 3-4). Patients were emotionally upset, had a physical reaction when they thought about the event, and even experienced a loss of interest in other activities.

Impairments

Impairment is the dimension that examines symptoms, complaints, and signs of clinically assessed disease. Pain is one of the most common oral health symptoms reported. As Murray and coworkers[16] demonstrate, patients with chronic pain commonly report other physical, social, and psychologic limitations. Often, a combination of patient- and clinician-assessed measures can evaluate the level of impairment. In a study of oral cancer and patients' QOL, Schliephake and colleagues[39] compared patient-assessed measures with clinician-assessed measures. They reported a significant, moderate correlation between the Functional Living Index, a self-administered questionnaire with physical, psychosocial, and social functioning components, and cancer. Further, they noted that patient reports of impairments (dysphagia, reflux of fluids, and sleep disorders) significantly affected the objective, clinician-assessed Karnowsky Index.

Duration of Life (Survival)

The survival, or duration of life, domain incorporates mortality, survival, and years of life lost. This domain has been analyzed at the levels of both patient survival as well as the survival of the tooth. As mentioned earlier, for patients with chronic diseases, particularly for those with cancer, studies may often consider whether a person will select a treatment intended to extend life or one that will promote QOL at the expense of duration of life. It asks the question, "Is all life equally valuable?" A number of clinical studies demonstrate uses of construct-specific QOL measures in oral health research. A few general questions should also be considered when selecting the research design and instruments to maximize the potential for a successful outcome (Box 3-1).

As previously described, the use of QOL measures has evolved from merely describing or measuring the impact of decrements of health to evaluating the relative success of various treatments. The intended use shapes the selection of a measure. A descriptive study is likely to be interested in the breadth of the measurement tool to capture previously unreported impacts on health. In contrast, a diagnostic study is intended to identify high-risk populations or individuals by differentiating dimensions associated with the disease or condition under study. Finally, a clinical outcome study

designed to compare treatments will often concentrate more narrowly on specific, preselected symptoms or functional limitations that are anticipated and measured with great sensitivity. Thus, for both diagnostic and outcome studies, a pretested and carefully validated measurement tool that will specifically examine the areas of interest to the clinician and patient should be used.

Generic measures provide the advantage of being readily available, containing a broad measure of health status encapsulated in one measure, and allowing the clinician to compare effects across conditions. In cases in which little information is known about the types of disease-specific limitations and symptoms, a generic measure might highlight an unexpected impact. Nonetheless, generic measures also offer disadvantages to the busy clinician. For example, a generic measure is often a lengthy instrument that may not be relevant to the disease under consideration, may be unable to detect disease-specific impacts, and is associated with a possible loss of sensitivity to critical changes in the condition.

A disease-specific instrument usually offers brevity and the ability to focus on the unique aspects of the disease being studied. Meanwhile, however, the clinician loses the ability to make comparisons across diseases. In the case of cancer, the field has addressed this problem by developing basic cancer measures with condition-specific addenda. This combined approach offers the advantages of the generic measure, which allows comparison of the many shared impacts and impairments across all forms of the disease, along with the ability to highlight the condition-specific impairments necessary to evaluate unique QOL effects.

In making the selection, it is important to determine whether a generic measure is valid for the specific disease. Ideally, one prefers a measure with proven validity and sensitivity for the condition. Atchison and colleagues[25] studied the distinction between oral and general health measures using the 12 items in the General Oral Health Assessment Index as well as the 9 physical and social functioning items and 5 items from the mental health survey portion of the SF-36, a 36-item QOL measure for general health. The factor analysis confirmed that the oral health items were distinct from the general health items. General physical/social items (eg, being prevented from working, inability to do the work, inability to bend and lift objects, and limitation of social activities) factored together with no cross-loading on the oral factors or mental health items. Thus, the SF-36, although well-validated and tested, would be less desirable if a sensitive oral health measure is necessary to assess the impact of an oral disease.

Hatch and colleagues[12] compared the effectiveness of rigid fixation with that of nonrigid wire fixation on treatment of orthognathic surgery. They used the Sickness Impact Profile (SIP), a comprehensive, generic measure of disease with 136 items, and the Oral Health Status Questionnaire (OHSQ), a specific measure of oral health and function designed for use with patients undergoing orthognathic surgery. They reported that neither instrument demonstrated significant differences in QOL from either treatment regimen. Patients undergoing surgery "exhibited progressive and statistically significant improvement in health-related QOL across a wide variety of functional domains, regardless of fixation method." By recognizing possible shortcomings associated with generic measures, they demonstrated that only 14 of 136 SIP items, coming from 8 different subscales, were endorsed most frequently (by more than 10% of people) on the SIP at baseline. Only 5 of them showed statistically different percentages endorsing those items 2 years later. Thus, the remainder of the 136 items were not relevant to the intended use, ie, detecting potentially meaningful differences between two treatment modalities in orthognathic surgery cases. Two SIP factors of potential interest to clinicians evaluating patients undergoing oral surgery, the communication subscale and eating subscale, showed no differences. Similar trends ie, decreased disability followed by a return to presurgical levels, were observed using the OHSQ.

Global measures are broad measures or indices of health that, unlike generic measures such as the SIP, involve little expansion of individual domains of health. The most frequently used global indicator is the single-item rating of health, which has been shown to be related to mortality and morbidity. While global measures have been found to have good predictability for some uses, they can be difficult to interpret because of their breadth. One potential complication involves the interpretation of summary scores for multi-scale constructs. In a study comparing QOL in patients with no treatment, implants, or removable partial dentures, Kuboki and coworkers[15] stated that there was no difference in the total scores among the three groups, although the implant and denture groups showed superior QOL in subscale scores. Allison and colleagues[11] concluded that there is much to learn about the interpretation of global health-related QOL instruments, particularly the unique aspects of patient differences. They stated that health-related QOL instruments "may demonstrate within-subject changes over time, but are less likely to show within-group changes over time because of the range of baseline values and the different ways in which individuals perceive change."

Proxy measures are used in studies in which the subject is unable to provide specific information about health, symptoms, or functional limitations. Questions of reliability and validity arise when considering proxy measures. For example, when Ogden and coworkers[40] compared the responses of patients and clinicians following third molar removal, they noted that clinicians overestimated the impact of pain and interference on patients' daily activities and underestimated the "importance of chewing, swallowing, and general enjoyment of food" in the postoperative stage. Thus, reliance on subjective indicators of disease, such as health perceptions, would be considered more risky than measures with more objectivity, such as measures of functional status. The latter would therefore be preferable when information is gathered by proxy.

Conclusion

The application of QOL evaluations to oral clinical studies is a rapidly developing area of research. Both generic and condition-specific instruments are being developed and tested. Results show that the clinical oral health status affects a person's overall QOL. Findings of early research indicate that QOL measures can be used to assess the outcome of treatment, and ongoing studies are evaluating whether QOL instruments can distinguish possible target groups in which clinical care would have a higher likelihood for treatment. In all cases, it is readily apparent that the information provided by QOL instruments is a valuable adjunct to clinical care, both in encouraging communication between the clinician and the patient and in informing the clinician about the aspects of care and health that are critical to the patient's overall QOL.

Acknowledgment

The data provided on orofacial injury patients was supported by the UCLA King/Drew Regional Research Center for Minority Oral Health (grant No. P50/DE-10598 from the National Institute of Dental and Craniofacial Research).

References

1. Engel GL. The need for a new medical model: A challenge for biomedicine. Science 1977;196:129–136.
2. Hunter JM, Arbona SI. The tooth as a marker of developing world quality of life: A field study in Guatemala. Soc Sci Med 1995;41:1217–1240.
3. Lubben JE. Assessing social networks among elderly populations. Fam Community Health 1988;11:42–52.
4. Cousins N. The holistic health explosion. Saturday Rev 1979;6(7):17–19.
5. World Health Organization. Constitution of the World Health Organization. Geneva: World Health Organization, 1948.
6. Gift HC, Atchison KA. Oral health, health, and health-related quality of life. Med Care 1995;3(11, suppl):NS57–NS77.
7. Patrick DL, Erickson P. Health Status and Health Policy. New York: Oxford University Press, 1993.
8. Savin J, Ogden GR. Third molar surgery: A preliminary report on aspects affecting quality of life in the early postoperative period. Br J Oral Maxillofac Surg 1997;35:246–253.
9. Shugars DA, Benson K, White RP Jr, Simpson KN, Bader JD. Developing a measure of patient perceptions of short-term outcomes of third molar surgery. J Oral Maxillofac Surg 1996;54:1402–1408.
10. Bennett ME, Phillips CL. Assessment of health-related quality of life for patients with severe skeletal disharmony: A review of the issues. Int J Adult Orthodon Orthognath Surg 1999;14:65–75.
11. Allison PJ, Locker D, Wood-Dauphinee S, Black M, Feine JS. Correlates of health-related quality of life in upper aerodigestive tract cancer patients. Qual Life Res 1998;7:713–722.
12. Hatch JP, Rugh JD, Clark GM, Keeling SD, Tiner BD, Bays RA. Health-related quality of life following orthognathic surgery. Int J Adult Orthodon Orthognath Surg 1998;13(1):67–77.
13. Hammerlid E, Bjordal K, Ahlner-Elmqvist M, Jannert M, Kaasa S, Sullivan M. Prospective, longitudinal quality-of-life study of patients with head and neck cancer: A feasibility study including the RORTC QLQ-C30. Otolaryngol Head Neck Surg 1997;116:666–673.
14. Allison PJ, Locker D, Feine JS. The relationship between dental status and health-related quality of life in upper aerodigestive tract cancer patients. Oral Oncol 1999;35:138–143.
15. Kuboki T, Okamoto S, Suzuki H, et al. Quality of life assessment of bone-anchored fixed partial denture patients with unilateral mandibular distal-extension edentulism. J Prosthet Dent 1999;82:182–187.
16. Murray H, Locker D, Mock D, Tenenbaum HC. Pain and the quality of life in patients referred to a craniofacial pain unit. J Orofac Pain 1996;10:316–323.

17. Marcus M, Freed JR, Coulter ID, et al. Perceived unmet need for oral treatment among a national population of HIV-positive medical patients: Social and clinical correlates. Am J Public Health 2000;90:1059–1063.

18. Dolan TA, Corey CR, Freeman HE. Older Americans' access to oral health care. J Dent Educ 1988;52:637–642.

19. Atchison KA, Matthias RE, Dolan TA, et al. Comparison of dentist and patient ratings of oral health in dentate elders. J Public Health Dent 1993;53:223–230.

20. Landrine H, Klonoff EA. Cultural diversity in causal attributions for illness: The role of the supernatural. J Behav Med 1994;17:181–193.

21. McGrath C, Bedi R, Gilthorpe MS. Oral health related quality of life: Views of the public in the United Kingdom. Community Dent Health 2000;17:3–7.

22. Matthias RE, Atchison KA, Lubben JE, De Jong F, Schweitzer SO. Factors affecting self-ratings of oral health. J Public Health Dent 1995;55:197–204.

23. Chen MS, Hunter P. Oral health and quality of life in New Zealand: A social perspective. Soc Sci Med 1996;43:1213–1222.

24. Atchison KA, Gift HC. Perceived oral health in a diverse sample. Adv Dent Res 1997;11:272–280.

25. Atchison KA, Der-Martirosian C, Gift HC. Components of self-reported oral health and general health in racial and ethnic groups. J Public Health Dent 1998;58:301–308.

26. Matthias RE, Atchison KA, Schweitzer SO, Lubben JE, Mayer-Oakes A, De Jong F. Comparisons between dentist ratings and self-ratings of dental appearance in an elderly population. Spec Care Dentist 1993;13:53–60.

27. Gift HC, Atchison KA, Drury TF. Perceptions of the natural dentition in the context of multiple variables. J Dent Res 1998;77:1529–1538.

28. Atchison KA, Dolan TA. Development of the Geriatric Oral Health Assessment Index. J Dent Educ 1990;54:680–687.

29. Slade GD, Spencer AJ. Development and evaluation of the Oral Health Impact Profile. Community Dent Health 1994;11:3–11.

30. Gooch BF, Dolan TA, Bourque LB. Correlates of self-reported dental health status upon enrollment in the Rand Health Insurance Experiment. J Dent Educ 1989;53:629–637.

31. Kressin NR, Atchison KA, Miller DR. Comparing the impact of oral disease in two populations of older adults: Application of the Geriatric Oral Health Assessment Index. J Public Health Dent 1997;57:224–232.

32. Reisine ST. The effects of pain and oral health on the quality of life. Community Dent Health 1988;5:63–68.

33. Reisine ST, Fertig J, Weber J, Leder S. Impact of dental conditions on patients' quality of life. Community Dent Oral Epidemiol 1989;17:7–10.

34. Atchison KA. The General Oral Health Assessment Index (The Geriatric Oral Health Assessment Index). In: Slade GD (ed). Measuring Oral Health and Quality of Life. Chapel Hill: University of North Carolina, Department of Dental Ecology, 1997:71–80.

35. Atchison K, Shetty V, Belin T. Predictors of physical and psychosocial outcomes for orofacial injury patients [abstract 3088]. J Dent Res 1999;78(special issue):491.

36. Thoits PA. Conceptual, methodological, and theoretical problems in studying social support as a buffer against life stress. J Health Soc Behav 1982;23:145–159.

37. Berwick DM, Murphy JM, Goldman PA, Ware JE Jr, Barsky AJ, Weinstein MC. Performance of a five-item mental health screening test. Med Care 1991;29:169–176.

38. Glynn SM, Asarnow JR, Asarnow R, et al. Orofacial injury and the development of acute PTSD. Int J Oral Biol 1999;24:25–29.

39. Schliephake H, Rüffert K, Schneller T. Prospective study of the quality of life of cancer patients after intraoral tumor surgery. J Oral Maxillofac Surg 1996;54:664–670.

40. Ogden GR, Bissias E, Ruta DA, Ogston S. Quality of life following third molar removal: A patient versus professional perspective. Br Dent J 1998;185:407–410.

CHAPTER 4

Assessment of Oral Health–Related Quality of Life

Gary D. Slade, BDSc, DDPH, PhD

At the start of the twenty-first century, the relevance of health-related quality of life (QOL) has undergone a quantum shift. Where it was once regarded as a secondary outcome, occasionally useful to complement biologic and clinical markers of disease, QOL issues are now at the forefront of public health policy. The first goal of the US Department of Health and Human Services' initiative "Healthy People 2010" "is to help individuals of all ages increase life expectancy *and* improve their quality of life."[1] Moreover, Donna E. Shalala, Secretary of the US Department of Health and Human Services, in her foreword to the Surgeon General's report on oral health, left no doubt about the relevance of QOL to *oral* health: "oral health problems can lead to needless pain and suffering, causing devastating complications to an individual's well-being, with financial and social costs that significantly diminish quality of life and burden American society."[2]

The priority accorded to oral health–related quality of life (OHRQOL) demands that we have a solid, scientific basis for assessing it. This is not to deny the "political currency" that can be earned by asserting that good teeth are important for our well-being. Undoubtedly, many policy makers and politicians have a basic understanding (perhaps from personal experience) of the suffering that can be caused by oral pain and the beauty of a healthy smile. While these perceptions lie at the core of OHRQOL issues, researchers, clinicians, and public health practitioners have a responsibility to document and evaluate OHRQOL using rigorous, reliable, and valid assessment tools.

The main emphasis in this chapter is on quantitative assessment methods used in studies of populations and groups of patients. Hence, several important aspects of assessment will not be covered, such as qualitative research methods, assessment of OHRQOL in the treatment of individual patients, and generic QOL measures used in medicine and other health care disciplines. This review does not examine clinical indices, measures of patient satisfaction with treatment, or quality assurance measures used to monitor health care delivery.

Historical Perspective

The prominence of OHRQOL in public policy, as expressed by the US Surgeon General, is a relatively recent phenomenon.[2] Only four decades earlier, researchers dismissed most oral diseases as conditions that are essentially personal experiences that constitute little more than an inconvenient interruption—certainly nothing that could be related to general health status. For example, in a study of lay perceptions about oral disease, Gerson[3] found a general belief that oral conditions should not constitute a justification for exemption from work. Because the conditions were rarely associated with the classic "sick role," oral disease was not viewed as illness.[3] Dunnell and Cartwright[4] argued that frequent complaints such as headaches, rashes, burns, and trouble with teeth were seen as "trivial" problems, and not recognized or accepted as ill health. Indeed, persons with such conditions were found to report better health status than persons with none. Based on a sociologic analysis of data from the first International Collaborative Study of Dental Manpower Systems, Davis[5] suggested that, aside from pain or rare life-threatening neoplasms, oral disease is associated only with esthetics or perceptions of self-esteem, rather than effects on social roles.

The circumstances that have catapulted OHRQOL into prominence can be traced to important philosophic changes in the perception of health, beginning in 1948 with the World Health Organization's definition of health as a "complete state of physical, mental, and social well-being, and not just the absence of infirmity." Equally important were pressures within the United States and other Western countries to provide evidence that escalating expenditures on health care were improving the health of the population, which could not be demonstrated using insensitive health statistics such as mortality and clinical markers of morbidity.[6]

As the demand grew for measures of health status (in contrast to clinical measures of disease status), researchers began to develop standardized questionnaires that could be used in clinical settings or larger population surveys. Several textbooks now summarize the large number of generic and disease-specific instruments that exist for that purpose.[7-11] QOL measures are used in randomized clinical trials,[12] technology assessments in health care,[13] and evaluation of health care delivery systems.[14] Furthermore, QOL outcomes are now required as evidence of drug efficacy by some regulatory agencies.[15,16] Approaches for applying QOL to clinical care have also been developed.[17]

The same factors motivating the development of measures of health status prompted calls for new measures that could adequately reflect the impact of oral conditions on individuals' personal and social well-being.[18] By the early 1980s, evidence emerged of the impact of oral disorders within populations, refuting earlier claims by Davis[5] and others that oral conditions were merely a private experience. Most significant was Reisine's documentation[19] of the societal impact of oral conditions. Using data from the US National Health Interview Survey, she reported that 8.87 million dental conditions occurred in the US population in 1981, resulting in 17.7 million days of restricted activity, 6.73 million days of bed disability, and 7.05 million days of work loss.[19] Another key development that precipitated much of the methodological work in developing standardized questionnaires for oral health was the landmark discussion by Locker[20] of the theoretic framework for measuring oral health. During the 1980s and 1990s, more than a dozen researchers working in different settings around the globe launched methodological studies that led to the development of standardized OHRQOL questionnaires. By 1996, when the first international conference on methodological research in this area was held, no fewer than 11 standardized questionnaires had been developed and undergone testing for reliability and validity.[21] These questionnaires are summarized later in this chapter.

Table 4-1 Concepts and domains of health-related quality of life*

Domain	Characteristics
Opportunity	Social or cultural handicap, individual resilience
Health perceptions	Satisfaction with health, general health perceptions
Functional status: Social	Limitations in usual roles, integration, contact, intimacy
Functional status: Psychologic	Affective states, cognitive capacity
Functional status: Physical	Activity restrictions, fitness
Impairment	Complaints, signs, self-reported disease, physiologic measures, diagnoses
Death and duration of life	Mortality, survival, longevity

*Data from Patrick and Erickson.[22]

What is Oral Health–Related Quality of Life?

While the term "health-related QOL" has no strict definition, there is consensus that it is a multidimensional construct capturing people's perceptions about factors that are important in their everyday lives. For example, "Healthy People 2010" refers to "a personal sense of physical and mental health and the ability to react to factors in the physical and social environment."[1] The Surgeon General's Report on Oral Health notes that OHRQOL derives from a multidimensional construct that reflects (among other things) people's comfort when eating, sleeping, and engaging in social interaction; their self-esteem; and their satisfaction with respect to oral health.[2]

Patrick and Erickson[22] identified and provided more formal definitions of the multiple dimensions representing health-related QOL (Table 4-1). Interestingly, this list includes traditional clinical measures (eg, diagnoses) and epidemiologic indices (eg, mortality) that were specifically rejected by the sociomedical indicators movement, which sought to redress an over-reliance on traditional medical measures.[6] Hence, most efforts at assessing health-related QOL focus on the first six concepts listed in Table 4-1.

Not surprisingly, these broadly defined concepts have generated various approaches to the assessment of OHRQOL. The remainder of this chapter provides an overview of three categories of OHRQOL measures: societal indicators, global self-ratings of OHRQOL, and multiple-item questionnaires of OHRQOL.

Assessment of the Societal Impact of Oral Conditions

When assessing the societal impact of oral conditions, large population surveys inquire about days of restricted activity, work loss, and school absenteeism due to oral conditions. These surveys typically yield rates of impact that are negligible for individuals, but substantial when expressed in terms of the population's burden of illness in a given year. In part, this is because of the high prevalence of oral conditions, the ability of many such conditions to cause disabling pain in the head and neck region, and the tendency for many oral diseases to persist and recur. For example, Reisine's pioneering study[19] regarding societal impact of oral disease in the US population revealed that oral conditions caused more days of work loss than stroke, and, in younger adults, as much work loss as all neoplasms combined.

Subsequent studies have clarified the nature of this societal impact. Gift's analysis[23] of the 1989 US National Health Interview Survey revealed more days of restricted activity due to oral disease or dental visits among women com-

Table 4-2 **Restricted activity days per 100 children because of dental problems or visits based on income***

Annual household income	No. of restricted days per 100 children
< $10,000	14.2
$10,000 – < $20,000	10.7
$20,000 – < $35,000	1.0
> $35,000	1.1

*Data from General Accounting Office.[24]

pared with men, adults compared with children, and disadvantaged compared with more affluent socioeconomic groups. Data from the 1994 National Health Interview Survey revealed marked socioeconomic disparities in disability days among children (Table 4-2).[24]

While societal measures are useful for demonstrating public health significance of oral diseases, there are obvious limitations in using measures such as work loss to assess OHRQOL. For example, even quite severe levels of discomfort or distress can occur without causing work loss. Furthermore, many individuals are not in the workforce. Even for those in the workforce, the need to take time off work is influenced by the structure, organization, and delivery of dental services. In baseline interviews conducted in a longitudinal study of work loss due to dental conditions, Reisine[25] found that 95% of work-loss episodes in the baseline study occurred because of dental visits for preventive or curative treatment. Finally, from a statistical perspective, societal indicators such as work loss are simply too infrequent to be sensitive markers of impact in epidemiologic studies or clinical trials.[26]

Notwithstanding these limitations, societal indicators continue to be valuable markers of the population's oral health. This is particularly important in public health, where it is essential to document the burden of illness using mea-

sures that are meaningful to policy makers. In this regard, oral health clearly is important in relation to other leading causes of morbidity. Based on studies of societal impact, Gift[23] concluded: "While an average of 1.5 hours of work lost per person per year was of little consequence for the individual, it represented a substantial societal impact."

Assessment of Individuals' OHRQOL Using Global Self-Ratings

An intuitively appealing method to assess OHRQOL is to ask respondents a global question about their self-rated oral health. For example, subjects are asked "How would you rate the health of your teeth, gums, and mouth?" with responses provided on a five-point ordinal scale ranging from "Excellent" to "Very poor." While the exact words used to phrase a single, global question and the response categories provided are very important, a general assumption made in this assessment method is that respondents will interpret, for themselves, the dimensions of QOL that are important to them; make judgments about the impact of oral status on those dimensions; and assimilate their judgments into a single rating. Undoubtedly this

Table 4-3 Global self-rating of oral health among dentate adults in the United States*

Condition of natural teeth (scale score)†	Persons (%)
Excellent (1)	11.2
Very good (2)	18.2
Good (3)	34.8
Fair (4)	23.7
Poor (5)	12.1

*Data from Gift et al.[27]
†Mean scale score = 3.07 (SE = 0.03).

process will vary from individual to individual. For example, some persons may regard their oral health to be excellent as long as they have not experienced recent dental pain, whereas others may feel that their oral health is "fair" because they have lost several teeth.

The potential for different individuals to use different yardsticks in evaluating their oral health is not seen as a limitation, but rather as a strength of the method, because it permits respondents to integrate multidimensional experiences and decide for themselves which experiences are most salient. Another feature of single, global assessments is that they offer positive response categories (eg, "excellent") and hence are not limited to measuring only adverse impacts of oral health. Finally, global self-ratings require just a single question with a simple response format. It is therefore feasible to include them in large interviews or questionnaires that explore numerous research questions, as often occurs in national health surveys.

A single global self-rating of oral health was used in the third National Health and Nutrition Examination Survey of the US adult population.[27] In this cross-sectional study of a representative sample of the US population comprising 7,336 dentate adults older than 18 years, respondents were asked: "How would you describe the condition of your natural teeth?" The five response categories provided ranged from

"excellent" to "poor." Approximately equal percentages of respondents rated their oral health at the extreme ends of this scale (Table 4-3).

When responses were coded from 1 to 5, as indicated in Table 4-3, the mean value was 3.07, which Gift and colleagues[27] described as somewhere between "good" and "fair." However, it would be a mistake to interpret this as an average rating of the nation's oral health, because there is no physical scale that can be anchored to the response categories. For example, there is no particular basis to believe that the difference between "excellent" and "very good" is equivalent to the difference between "good" and "fair," despite the fact that the numerical differences between the scores assigned to these particular ratings by the researchers are identical.

One approach to this psychometric problem is to offer respondents a numerical scale, such as a visual analog scale (VAS) that is used frequently in pain research. For example, with anchors set at 0 and 100, respondents place a mark at any point on the line that best represents their perceived health status. In principle, a VAS response could be used as the response format for the same global self-rating question used in National Health and Nutrition Examination Survey III. However, it would be illusory to believe that this improves the metric qualities of the response scale, because there is no reason to believe that different respondents would use

Table 4-4 Global self-ratings of oral health in seven study locations*

| | Persons reporting poor or very poor oral health (%) | | |
| | Children | Adults | |
Study site	12–13 y	35–44 y	65–74 y
Yamanashi, Japan	17	39	—
Indian Health Service—Lakota	10	40	39
Indian Health Service—Navajo	6	13	24
Baltimore, Maryland	6	8	9
New Zealand	4	7	4
Lodz, Poland	4	33	61
Erfurt, Germany	1	17	15

*Data from Chen et al.[28]

identical subconscious yardsticks when deciding on where to mark the VAS. For example, even if a VAS was anchored at "very poor" and "excellent," one individual may conceive of a midpoint on the scale as corresponding with "good" OHRQOL, while another respondent may place "fair" at the middle of that scale. Hence, the creation of a numeric response (using a unit of measure such as millimeters, for example) cannot transform an inherently abstract judgment about global OHRQOL into a true metric index.

Instead, the usefulness of an average score is to examine factors associated with perceived oral health. For example, an average score that is lower for Caucasian respondents compared with respondents from other racial/ethnic groups would indicate that Caucasions tended to respond with more favorable reports of oral health status than people in other racial/ethnic groups. In their multivariate analysis, Gift and colleagues[27] found that the factors associated with self-rated oral health were missing teeth, decayed teeth, loss of periodontal attachment, perceived treatment need, race/ethnicity, and education.

The ease of administering single-item questions makes them ideal candidates for large-scale health surveys, including surveys conducted at multiple sites in several countries. The second International Collaborative Study interviewed and examined children and adults in seven study locations. This cross-sectional study selected age groups in Erfurt (Germany), Lodz (Poland), Yamanashi (Japan), New Zealand, and three sites in the US, namely Baltimore and two Indian Health Service sites (Navajo and Lakota). The interview asked children aged 12 to 13 years, and adults aged 35 to 44 and 65 to 74 years: "How would you describe the health of your teeth and gums? Is it excellent, very good, good, fair, poor, or very poor?" However, in this study, attention was focused on the proportion of subjects who reported poor or very poor oral health, hence ignoring the ordinal scale of six possible responses. In all age groups, there was striking variation in the frequency of poor or very poor oral health (Table 4-4). There was a predominant trend within countries for adults to report more poor oral health than did children. However, in New Zealand, generally low levels of poor oral health were reported in all age groups, and the prevalence was only 4% in both children and older adults.

Assessment of Individuals' OHRQOL Using Multiple-Item Questionnaires

The other method commonly used to evaluate multiple dimensions of OHRQOL is to ask subjects numerous specific questions. For example, some questions focus on function, some are concerned with pain and discomfort, and others evaluate self-image and social interaction. This approach attempts to delineate the specific experiences that encompass the researcher's definition of OHRQOL. Furthermore, multiple-item questionnaires typically capture more statistical variation than do single-item questions. This is simply because of the basic principle of measurement that an additional item in a questionnaire will yield additional information. This principle holds provided that the additional question is not redundant and that it meets some basic psychometric requirements of measurement. Hence, the motivation to develop multiple-item questionnaires often is both philosophic (researchers focusing on specific dimension of OHRQOL using a predetermined set of questions and response categories) and methodological (researchers attempting to capture maximum variation in OHRQOL).

Given that definitions of OHRQOL are vague, it is not surprising that there is great heterogeneity in the focus, length, and format of the 10 multiple-item questionnaires developed to evaluate OHRQOL to date. Table 4-5 summarizes the properties of the 10 instruments presented at the First International Conference on Measuring Oral Health.[21] As indicated in Table 4-5, some questionnaires capture content areas limited to just a few dimensions (eg, pain, worry, and conversation, as measured using the RAND Dental Health Index). Other questionnaires capture half a dozen or more dimensions ranging from chewing to social relations. Questionnaires range in length from 3 to 56 items. The format of questions and responses vary from simple, fact-based questions with yes/no responses (eg, "Are there any types of foods you have difficulties chewing?") to four-part questions that inquire about the frequency, severity, and importance of a specific problem (eg, Oral Impacts on Daily Performances). While most questionnaires are limited to the negative impacts of oral diseases, two questionnaires ask if oral conditions have had either an adverse or beneficial impact on the respondent's well-being (ie, Oral Health Quality of Life Inventory and Dental Impact Profile).

The information in Table 4-5 is a descriptive summary of questionnaires that have undergone testing to evaluate their measurement properties, particularly their reliability, validity, and precision. However, psychometric properties are important methodological characteristics that need to be considered in addition to the content area and format of a questionnaire. Also not shown in Table 4-5 is the fact that several questionnaires have been translated into languages other than English. Each of these instruments is described in detail in the proceedings of the first international conference on measuring oral health.[21]

A common feature of the OHRQOL questionnaires presented in Table 4-5 is that they can be analyzed as responses to individual questions and summarized as numeric scores. For several of the questionnaires, subscales can be computed. For example, the Oral Health Impact Profile (OHIP) has seven subscales, each measuring a hypothesized unique dimension of OHRQOL (eg, functional limitation). In some instances, these summary scores do not have a true metric. For example, the General Oral Health Assessment Index (GOHAI) assigns a value of 0 through 5 to responses of "never" to "always," respectively, to each of the 12 items queried. In those instances, the interpretation of the summary scores needs to be tempered by the same measurement issues that limit the interpretation of global self-ratings, namely that the mean values are valid only for comparing and ranking levels of OHRQOL among subgroups. However, in some instances, summary scores are computed as the number of items endorsed at a particular threshold. In these instances, the values have literal meaning. For example, an alterna-

Table 4-5 Oral health–related quality-of-life questionnaires

Measure	Dimensions measured	No. of questions	Example of question	Response format
Sociodental Scale[29]	Chewing, talking, smiling, laughing, pain, appearance	14	Are there any types of foods you have difficulties chewing?	Yes/no
RAND Dental Health Index[30]	Pain, worry, conversation	3	How much pain have your gums and teeth caused you?	4 categories: "not at all" to "a great deal"
General Oral Health Assessment Index[31]	Chewing, eating, social contacts, appearance, pain, worry, self-consciousness	12	How often did you limit the kinds or amounts of food you eat because of problems with your teeth or dentures?	6 categories: "always" to "never"
Dental Impact Profile[32]	Appearance, eating, speech, confidence, happiness, social life, relationships	25	Do you think your teeth or dentures have a good effect (positive), a bad effect (negative), or no effect on your feeling comfortable?	3 categories: good effect, bad effect, no effect
Oral Health Impact Profile[33]	Function, pain, physical disability, psychologic disability, social disability, handicap	49	Have you had difficulty chewing foods because of problems with your teeth, mouth, or dentures?	5 categories: "very often" to "never"
Subjective Oral Health Status Indicators[34]	Chewing, speaking, symptoms, eating, communication, social relations	42	During the last year, how often have [dental problems] caused you to have difficulty sleeping?	Various, depending on question format
Oral Health Quality of Life Inventory[35]	Oral health, nutrition, self-rated oral health, overall quality of life	56	Two-part questions: (A) How important is it for you to speak clearly? (B) How happy are you with your ability to speak clearly?	Part A: 4 categories (not at all important to very important) Part B: 4 categories (unhappy to happy)
Dental Impact on Daily Living[36]	Comfort, appearance, pain, daily activities, eating	36	How satisfied have you been, on the whole, with your teeth in the last 3 months?	Various, depending on question format
Oral Health–Related Quality of Life[37]	Daily activities, social activities, conversation	3	Have problems with your teeth or gums affected your daily activities such as work or hobbies?	6 categories: "all of the time" to "none of the time"
Oral Impacts on Daily Performances[38]	Performance in eating, speaking, oral hygiene, sleeping, appearance, emotion	9	Four-part questions: (A) In the past 6 months, have [dental problems] caused you any difficulty in eating and enjoying food? (B) Have you had this difficulty on a regular/periodic basis or for a period/spell? (C) During the last 6 months, how often have you had this difficulty? (D) Using a scale from 0 to 5, which number reflects what impact the difficulty in eating and enjoying food had on your daily life?	Various, depending on question format

tive method of summarizing the 49-item OHIP is to report the number of items answered with "occasionally," "fairly often," or "very often." In such instances, the mean value has intuitive meaning, unlike the abstract concept of "between good and fair," and hence may be more interpretable for users of the data.

Findings from Cross-Sectional Population Studies

An important factor to consider when evaluating measures of OHRQOL is the track record of their use: the populations in which they have been used, the research questions addressed, and the study designs employed. A common feature of both global self-rating measures and multiple-item questionnaires is their predominant use in cross-sectional studies of community-dwelling adults, frequently older adults. As noted already, single-item global self-ratings are necessarily short, and hence they are more likely to be used in larger population surveys. In contrast, most of the multiple-item questionnaires have been used in epidemiologic studies that addressed specific research questions using smaller sample sizes. However, lengthy questionnaires have been used in large-scale studies, including a study of 2,338 older adults in Australia, Canada, and the United States that used the 49-item OHIP questionnaire.[39] The 1998 Adult Dental Health Survey of the United Kingdom assessed OHRQOL using the (relatively) short, 14-item version of the OHIP.[40]

Cross-sectional studies of OHRQOL typically have focused on factors associated with poor OHRQOL. Although most of these studies used different questionnaires, and hence overall prevalence of OHRQOL cannot be compared, it is striking that many researchers have reported a similar array of factors associated with poor OHRQOL. As indicated in Table 4-6, the following factors have consistently been associated

with poorer OHRQOL: fewer teeth, more diseased teeth, other untreated dental disease, unmet treatment needs, episodic dental visits to treat dental problems, and lower socioeconomic status. In the United States, nonwhite respondents generally have poorer OHRQOL compared with white respondents.

The relevance of Table 4-6 for this discussion is the general consistency of findings with all methods of OHRQOL assessment, ranging from single-item global ratings to lengthy, multidimensional questionnaires that have complex response formats. Furthermore, many of these correlates of poor OHRQOL are the same factors associated with societal indicators reviewed previously. At one level, this pattern of consistency should not be surprising, given that clinical oral disease and lack of timely treatment of disease is likely the most immediate factor causing poor OHRQOL. Similarly, in most of the countries studied, the incidence of oral disease and certainly access to dental care are strongly associated with socioeconomic status.

At a pragmatic level, the consistent findings seen in Table 4-6 broadly endorse the validity of the various OHRQOL measures used. This is not to deny that different measures vary in scope and measurement properties. For example, Kressin and colleagues[37] noted that the Oral Health–Related Quality of Life Index evaluates impacts on daily activities, social activities, and conversation, but reveals fewer adverse effects than an instrument such as the GOHAI, which examines specific oral symptoms. Hence, the Oral Health–Related Quality of Life Index is subject to a lower "floor" effect, in which respondents endorse no adverse effects, than the more detailed and specific GOHAI. While the broad similarity of findings reported in Table 4-6 suggests that no single questionnaire is inferior (or superior) for detecting factors associated with OHRQOL, numerous additional characteristics of assessment instruments must be considered before selecting a specific questionnaire to address a specific research question.

Table 4-6 Factors associated with OHRQOL in cross-sectional population studies

Study	Questionnaire	Population	Groups identified with poorer OHRQOL
Cushing and Sheiham[41]	Sociodental Scale	UK workers	< Functioning teeth; > decayed teeth
Gooch et al[42]	RAND Dental Health Index	US insured adults 18–61 y	> Decayed teeth, > periodontal disease; nonwhites; < education; < income
Atchison and Dolan[31]	General Oral Health Assessment Index	US Medicare recipients > 65 y	< Teeth; perceived need for dental care; wearing removable denture
Locker and Miller[34]	Subjective Oral Health	Canadians > 18 y	Edentulous; < teeth
Locker and Slade[43]	Oral Health Impact Profile	Canadian adults > 50 y	< Teeth; < general health; < age; > life stress; < household income; no dental insurance
Slade and Spencer[33]	Oral Health Impact Profile	Australian adults > 60 y	Edentulous; problem motivated dental visits; last dental visit > 1 y
Hunt et al[44]	Oral Health Impact Profile	North Carolina adults > 65 y	< Teeth; > periodontal disease; blacks; episodic dental visits
Leao and Sheiham[36]	Dental Impact on Daily Living	Brazilians 35–44 y	< Teeth; > decayed teeth; > gingival bleeding; > calculus; > periodontal probing depths; < social class
Coates et al[45]	Oral Health Impact Profile	Australian dental patients	HIV-infected individuals
Kressin[46]	Oral Health–Related Quality of Life Index	US men > 47 y	Problem-based dental visits
Gift et al[47]	Global self-rating	US adults > 18 y	< Education; nonwhite; last dental visit > 2 y
Gilbert et al[48]	Subjective Oral Health Status Indicators	Florida adults > 45 y at high risk of dental disease	> Root fragments; > caries; > mobile teeth; > missing teeth; > symptoms
Chen et al[28]	Global self-rating	Seven countries in Second International Collaborative Study; children, adults, and elderly	12–13 y: Poorer general health, < tooth brushing, > decayed, missing, and filled teeth; 35–44 y: Poorer general health, < preventive dental visits, > decayed, missing, and filled teeth, > periodontal disease; 65–74 y: Poorer general health, income (variable effects), < preventive dental care, > tooth brushing
Atchison et al[49]	General Oral Health Assessment Index	California minority groups seeking care at low-cost clinics	Unemployed; < income

Assessment of OHRQOL Changes Using Longitudinal Studies

Many OHRQOL measures have been used in cross-sectional study designs; however, only a few have been used to assess change in OHRQOL using longitudinal study designs such as clinical trials. In principle, longitudinal study designs represent a scientific way to quantify change in health status, and hence provide better evidence about causes of disease and effects of treatment than do cross-sectional studies. One of the features of longitudinal studies that makes them superior to cross-sectional studies is the ability to properly establish a temporal sequence of events between a putative cause and subsequent effect. Hence, it should be possible to measure OHRQOL before a specific event occurs (eg, treatment) and then measure OHRQOL again after that event to determine if there has been a change. With sufficient numbers of subjects and other study design features that permit comparisons between groups experiencing different events, it becomes possible to attribute a cause-and-effect relationship between the event and OHRQOL.

There are important theoretic and methodological obstacles to assessing change in OHRQOL that can complicate this idealized model of scientific inquiry. Allison and colleagues[50] have drawn attention to biases that can be introduced when researchers assume that the frame of reference used by study subjects to evaluate their own OHRQOL changes during the conduct of a longitudinal study. This concern underlies an ongoing controversy about the most appropriate way to quantify change in subjective measures such as OHRQOL that necessarily rely on a respondent's judgments, which may be influenced by temporal factors. Locker[51] provides a detailed analysis of this controversy and examples of four methods that have been proposed to measure change in health status.

1. Before-and-after comparison of (unmatched) group summary scores. This handles pre-event and postevent scores as independent samples, and hence does not characterize within-subject change.

2. Computation of change scores by subtracting pre-event scores from postevent scores. This identifies individuals whose OHRQOL improves or deteriorates, outcomes that may cancel one another using the first method; however, it relies on an assumption that individuals use consistent points of reference to evaluate their OHRQOL over time.

3. Making retrospective judgments about global change in OHRQOL by asking subjects at some defined period after an event to rate whether their OHRQOL has improved, stayed the same, or worsened. This is an intuitively appealing method of capturing change that removes the statistical uncertainties about consistency in reference point by placing the onus on the respondents to judge both their current OHRQOL and the earlier OHRQOL, and then decide whether there has been a net change.

4. Retrospective judgments about extent of change in OHRQOL using scales. Statistically, this is an extension of the previous method, which calls on respondents to rate the extent of change on a numeric scale.

Locker[20] analyzed these methodological alternatives using data from a longitudinal study of older adults in Ontario, Canada. At baseline and again 3 years later, subjects in that study completed a multiquestion measure of OHRQOL and the Subjective Oral Health Status Indicators (see Table 4-5). At the follow-up assessment, they also answered global questions about change in oral health during the preceding 3 years. When baseline and follow-up responses were compared as independent samples (method No. 1 described earlier), there was no change: 24.7% of the respondents reported fair/poor oral health at baseline compared with 24.0% at follow-up. However, when using a computation of change scores (method No. 2) it was clear that OHRQOL had worsened for some individuals (for example,

20.3% had more pain) and had improved for some individuals (24.1% had less pain). When asked to make a retrospective judgment about global change (method No. 3), 21% reported a deterioration, 11% reported an improvement, and the remaining 68% reported no change. Although the associations between retrospective judgments and computed change scores were statistically significant, Locker[51] concluded that the measurement of change in OHRQOL is controversial and complex, and no approach is universally accepted.

Further methodological complexities in longitudinal studies of OHRQOL have been studied for two of the multiple-item questionnaires presented in Table 4-5. In a randomized trial of a community health promotion program among elderly dentate adults in California, change in OHRQOL was quantified using the 12-item GOHAI as well as global self-ratings of oral health.[52] Both instruments were administered at baseline as well as annually thereafter for 3 years. At each interval or follow-up, computed changes in global self-ratings revealed that most people underwent some change. At the end of the 3-year period, OHRQOL had declined in 37.3% of the subjects, improved in 24.0%, and remained stable in only 38.7%. The pattern of change was further evaluated by characterizing subjects' OHRQOL as stable, steady improvement, steady decline, or fluctuation (some improvements, some declines) during the three annual intervals. By comparing these transitions to computed changes in GOHAI scores, there was a tendency for GOHAI scores to improve among those respondents who had a steady improvement in global self-rating, but to deteriorate among those who had a steady decline in global self-rating. However, the differences were not statistically significant. In comparing their results to the Canadian study of Locker,[51] Dolan and colleagues[52] concluded that retrospective judgments about global change may be less sensitive than computed change in OHRQOL.

Another multiple-item questionnaire from Table 4-5 that has been subjected to methodological evaluation for use in longitudinal studies is the 49-item OHIP. Using data from an observational cohort study of elderly dentate Australians, Slade[53] compared baseline responses to the OHIP with responses at a 2-year follow-up.[53] Net change was computed using the conventional approach of subtracting baseline impact scores from follow-up scores. The analysis demonstrated a statistical problem termed *regression to the mean*, which can distort results when evaluating changes between groups with different baseline scores. Hence, two additional methods of computing change were evaluated. The increment score identified people who experienced any amount of worsening in impacts, as evidenced by one or more OHIP items reported at follow-up that were not reported at baseline. Conversely, a decrement identified people who experienced any amount of improvement in impacts as evidenced by one or more OHIP items at baseline that were not reported at follow-up. A decrement was quantified for an individual regardless of whether or not an increment had occurred (and vice versa). Hence, more people experienced an increment in OHIP scores (17.5%) than had a positive net change score (14.7%) and more people experienced a decrement (17.5%) than had a negative net change score (12.2%).

As expected, increments were more likely among three hypothesized high-risk groups—people who experienced concurrent tooth loss, people who usually visited the dentist because they had problems, and people who reported financial hardship—indicating that they experienced deterioration in OHRQOL. Surprisingly, the same high-risk groups also experienced a higher rate of decrements in impact (indicating that they experienced improvement in OHRQOL). Slade[53] argued that this apparent paradox may reflect a real phenomenon in which some events can simultaneously improve one aspect of OHRQOL for an individual, while causing a deterioration in another aspect of OHRQOL for the same individual. For example, a person experiencing tooth loss may have a reduction in pain (producing a decrement in the OHIP), but an increase in chewing problems

Table 4-7 Evaluation of OHRQOL in clinical trials

Study	Population	Intervention	Outcome
Fiske and Watson[54]	UK patients with disabilities (n = 100)	General dental care	74% improved to optimal QOL
Dao et al[55]	Canadian patients with temporomandibular disorders (n = 63)	Splint vs 2 placebo (randomized clinical trial)	Improvements in quality of life VAS for all treatment groups
Schliephake et al[56]	German patients with oral cancer (n = 85)	Surgery	Improvements in 22-item VAS
Allen et al[57]	UK edentulous patients (nonrandomized trial)	Conventional vs implant-retained full dentures	Greatest improvement in OHIP scores in implant group
Awad et al[58]	Canadian edentulous patients (randomized trial)	Conventional vs implant-retained full dentures	Significant improvement in OHIP scores for implant but not conventional group

(causing an increment in the OHIP). He concluded that categoric enumeration of change (as represented by increment and decrement scores) can identify people who experience both improvement and deterioration in OHRQOL—a phenomenon that can be overlooked using conventional net change scores, in which increments and decrements cancel one another.[53]

Findings from Clinical Studies of OHRQOL

The preceding methodological analyses highlight complexities that affect measurement of change in OHRQOL. The extent to which the potential methodological traps affect interpretation of results from longitudinal studies of OHRQOL depends on additional features of the study. These features are the research question, the study design, the type of interventions or intervening events that subjects experience, and the method of evaluation. Clinical studies represent a specific category of longitudinal studies in which these factors need to be considered in addition to the methodological complexities reviewed in the previous section. Table 4-7 illustrates some of these issues by summarizing five clinical studies that have used OHRQOL as a primary outcome measure. Fiske and Watson[54] compared pretreatment with posttreatment OHRQOL among handicapped persons with extensive untreated dental needs. All of these patients underwent general dental care that included restorations, extractions, and provision of prostheses as needed. Measurements of OHRQOL were made using the Sociodental Scale (see Table 4-5), which revealed a striking posttreatment improvement. Nearly 75% of subjects experienced improvements to the level of optimal OHRQOL using this instrument. Despite the weakness of the study design (in particular, a lack of a concurrent control group) and the potential problems of computing change scores, the sheer magnitude of change represents an unambiguous improvement that is undoubtedly meaningful for the subjects concerned.

Dao and colleagues[55] conducted a more elaborate study by randomly assigning subjects to three concurrent treatment groups; the patients did not know which type of treatment was provided to them. At baseline and at seven follow-up visits, OHRQOL was evaluated using global ratings recorded on a VAS. Simple plots of the mean and standard deviation of VAS scores revealed virtually identical baseline OHRQOL levels among the three treatment groups—a phenomenon that is expected under random assignment. While mean values showed improvements in OHRQOL over time, the striking finding was that all three treatment groups continued to have virtually identical scores. In both these studies, more elaborate methodological approaches for assessing change hardly seem warranted: one study found an unambiguous improvement after treatment[54] and another study found an equally unambiguous equivalence in treatment effects.[55]

Less equivocal interpretations can be made of the other three studies, and hence it becomes important to consider not only the method of assessing change, but also other study design features. In a study of rehabilitation after surgery for head and neck cancer, Schliephake and colleagues[56] evaluated OHRQOL with a 22-item questionnaire that used a 154-mm VAS response format. They reported a statistically significant increase of approximately 20 mm in mean VAS scores over a 12-month follow-up period for the 85 patients treated. Yet the interpretation of this net change is difficult because of the theoretic and methodological issues noted earlier. Specifically, changes in group means frequently mask individual change, and a 20-mm net change is difficult to interpret in clinical terms.

Allen and colleagues[57] conducted a clinical trial that compared patients receiving conventional dentures with patients receiving implant-retained dentures. All patients had initially sought implant-retained dentures, but the final decision to provide implants was based on presenting clinical status, and hence subjects were not assigned at random to treatment groups. Change in OHRQOL was assessed by computing net change in individuals' OHIP scores. The results revealed a much greater reduction in oral health impacts for subjects receiving implant-retained dentures (nine fewer impacts) compared with subjects receiving conventional dentures (five fewer impacts). In the absence of other information, this result alone could be criticized on various methodological grounds, including the lack of randomization and possible regression-to-the-mean effects. However, the

study included a third treatment group consisting of people who had not sought implants, but instead obtained routine replacement dentures. Following treatment, these patients also experienced a reduction of approximately four fewer impacts, despite starting with approximately half the level of impact as the two groups seeking implants. This magnitude of change in a qualitatively different third group helps bolster the finding that the magnitude of change in the implant recipients was clearly in excess of change in comparable, albeit nonrandomized subjects. It was certainly much greater than any possible effects caused by nonrandomization or regression to the mean.

Finally, Awad and colleagues[58] addressed a similar research question concerning efficacy of implant-retained dentures. In this instance, subjects were assigned at random to receive implant-retained dentures or conventional dentures. In a 2-month follow-up survey, subjects who received implant-retained dentures had a reduction in impacts that was four times greater than that of the control group, which received conventional dentures. This randomized study design provides more powerful evidence than the nonrandomized study design used by Allen and colleagues.[57] However, more importantly, both studies provide consistent evidence that the same treatments provide large improvements in OHRQOL as assessed with the same questionnaire. An additional striking finding reported by Awad and colleagues[58] was that the large difference between groups detected with this measure of OHRQOL was not observed using a physiologic measure of chewing effectiveness.

Summary

This review highlights several features of quantitative OHRQOL assessment and attempts to make the following major points:

1. For public health purposes, oral health can be quantified at the macro level using societal measures of oral conditions, which demon-

strate that oral disease creates a substantial burden of illness, particularly among disadvantaged groups.

2. Single-item global ratings represent the simplest method of assessing OHRQOL; they lend themselves for use in large studies (including national health surveys) and the results are readily understood.

3. Multiple-item questionnaires explore specific dimensions of OHRQOL in greater detail and generally offer greater statistical precision for identifying group differences in OHRQOL.

4. Numerous multiple-item OHRQOL questionnaires with adequate psychometric properties have been developed and used in cross-sectional studies. These questionnaires range in the scope, length, and complexity of questions and responses, and most have been applied using cross-sectional study designs in several research settings. Hence, there is a diverse menu of questionnaires available to researchers for cross-sectional assessment of OHRQOL.

5. While the same questionnaires can be used in longitudinal studies, such study designs pose significantly greater methodological challenges for assessing change in OHRQOL.

6. These challenges have led some researchers to reject the approach of computing change using OHRQOL questionnaires administered at two (or more) time points. Instead, they advocate assessing change retrospectively by asking subjects to report changes in OHRQOL, if any, during a defined period. This controversy continues, and no single approach is universally accepted.

7. Clinical studies are a category of longitudinal studies in which additional methodological issues may affect the interpretation of results from OHRQOL assessments. In some instances, the effect (or lack of effect) of treatment is clear, therefore the methodological issues cited earlier are not critical. In most instances, results are less profound, in which case additional study groups or additional clinical trials may be necessary to clarify whether treatment effects exceed methodological uncertainties in assessing change in OHRQOL.

Directions for Future Research

Following are the most notable deficiencies in the methods currently used to assess OHRQOL and recommendations for future research:

1. There is a need for questionnaires to measure QOL in additional population groups, particularly children and/or their caregivers who have been excluded from all but one study reviewed herein.

2. While some questionnaires focus on adverse impacts of OHRQOL, additional methods are needed to capture positive dimensions of health. This is particularly important for tracking improvements among people who are initially symptom-free.

3. Previous studies have concentrated on a limited set of factors that are associated with OHRQOL. There is a need to identify additional determinants of OHRQOL, including psychologic and social variables and those describing organization of health care systems.

4. There are only a few studies of the impact of specific treatments on QOL. Additional research is needed to evaluate the treatment of existing disease, the prevention of disease, and the enhancement of health.

5. Clinical decision-making calls for integration of additional health outcomes in addition to OHRQOL including clinical indices, patient satisfaction, longevity, and costs. Yet OHRQOL has been evaluated as a primary outcome in most studies, and methods have not been developed to permit clinicians to systematically incorporate OHRQOL with other relevant patient-based outcomes.

Acknowledgment

This chapter was supported by the National Institute of Dental Research (grant No. R29-DE12366).

References

1. US Department of Health and Human Services. Healthy People 2010. US Department of Health and Human Services. Government Printing Office, 2000:8.

2. US Department of Health and Human Services. Oral Health in America: A Report of the Surgeon General. NIH publication 00-4713. Rockville, MD: US Department of Health and Human Services, National Institute of Dental and Craniofacial Research, National Institutes of Health, 2000:7.

3. Gerson LW. Expectations of 'sick role' exemptions for dental problems. Can Dent Assoc J 1972;10:370–372.

4. Dunnell K, Cartwright A. Medicine takers, prescribers and hoarders. London: Routledge and Kegan, 1972.

5. Davis P. Compliance structures and the delivery of health care: The case of dentistry. Soc Sci Med 1976;10:329–335.

6. Elinson J. Toward sociomedical health indicators. Social Indicators Res 1974;1:59–71.

7. Bowling A. Measuring Health: A Review of Quality of Life Measurement Scales. Buckingham, UK: Open University Press, 1991.

8. Bowling A. Measuring Disease. Buckingham, UK: Open University Press, 1995.

9. Kane RA, Kane RL. Assessing the Elderly. Lexington, MA: Lexington Books, 1994.

10. Streiner DL, Norman GR. Health Measurement Scales. Oxford, UK: Oxford University Press, 1989.

11. McDowell I, Newell C. Measuring Health: A Guide to Rating Scales and Questionnaires. New York: Oxford University Press, 1987.

12. Spilker B. Quality of Life Assessment in Clinical Trials. New York: Raven Press, 1993.

13. Mosteller F, Falotico-Taylor J. Quality of Life and Technology Assessment. Washington, DC: National Academy Press, 1989.

14. Newman L (ed). Medical Outcomes and Guidelines Sourcebook. New York: Faulkner and Gray, 1999.

15. Johnson JR, Temple R. Food and Drug Administration requirements for approval of new anticancer drugs. Cancer Treat Rep 1985;69:1155–1157.

16. Osoba D. The quality of life committee of the clinical trials group of the National Cancer Institute of Canada: Organization and functions. Qual Life Res 1992;1:211–215.

17. Wilson IB, Cleary PD. Linking clinical variables with health-related quality of life. JAMA 1995;273:59–65.

18. Cohen L, Jago J. Toward the formulation of sociodental indicators. Int J Health Serv 1976;6:681–687.

19. Reisine ST. Dental health and public policy: The social impact of dental disease. Am J Public Health 1985;75:27–30.

20. Locker D. Measuring oral health: A conceptual framework. Community Dental Health 1988;5:5–13.

21. Slade GD (ed). Measuring Oral Health and Quality of Life. Chapel Hill: University of North Carolina–Dental Ecology, 1997.

22. Patrick DL, Erickson P. Health Status and Health Policy. Quality of Life in Health Care Evaluation and Resource Allocation. New York: Oxford University Press, 1993.

23. Gift HC. Research directions in oral health promotion for older adults. J Dent Educ 1992;56:626–631.

24. General Accounting Office. Dental Disease Is a Chronic Problem Among Low-Income Populations. General Accounting Office publication GAO/HEHS-00-72. Government Printing Office, 2000.

25. Reisine ST. The economic, social and psychological impact of oral health conditions, diseases and treatments. In: Cohen LK, Bryant PS (eds). Social Sciences and Dentistry. Chicago: Quintessence, 1984:387–427.

26. Reisine ST, Fertig J, Weber J, Leder S. Impact of dental conditions on patients' quality of life. Community Dent Oral Epidemiol 1989;17:7–10.

27. Gift HC, Atchison KA, Drury TF. Perceptions of the natural dentition in the context of multiple variables. J Dent Res 1998;77:1529–1538.

28. Chen M, Andersen RM, Barmes DE, Leclercq MH, Lyttle CS. Comparing Oral Health Care Systems: A Second International Collaborative Study. Geneva: World Health Organization, 1997.

29. Cushing AM, Sheiham A, Maizels J. Developing sociodental indicators: The social impact of dental disease. Community Dent Health 1986;3:3–17.

30. Dolan TA, Gooch BF. Associations of self-reported dental health and general health measures in the Rand Health Insurance Experiment. Community Dent Oral Epidemiol 1991;19:1–8.

31. Atchison KA, Dolan TA. Development of the Geriatric Oral Health Assessment Index. J Dent Educ 1990;54:680–687.

32. Strauss RP, Hunt RJ. Understanding the value of teeth to older adults: Influences on quality of life. J Am Dent Assoc 1993;124:105–110.

33. Slade GD, Spencer AJ. Development and evaluation of the oral health impact profile. Community Dent Health 1994;11:3–11.

34. Locker D, Miller Y. Evaluation of subjective oral health status indicators. J Public Health Dent 1994;54:167–176.

35. Cornell JE, Saunders MJ, Paunovich ED, Frisch MD. Effects on well-being and quality of life. In: Slade GD (ed). Measuring Oral Health and Quality of Life. Chapel Hill: University of North Carolina–Dental Ecology, 1997.

36. Leao AT, Sheiham A. The development of a sociodental measure of dental impacts on daily living. Community Dent Health 1996;13:22–26.

37. Kressin N, Spiro III A, Bossé R, Garcia R, Kazis L. Assessing oral health-related quality of life: Findings from the Normative Aging Study. Med Care 1996;34: 416–427.

38. Adulyanon S, Vourapukjaru J, Sheiham A. Oral impacts affecting daily performance in a low dental disease Thai population. Community Dent Oral Epidemiol 1996;24:385–389.

39. Slade GD, Spencer AJ, Locker D, Hunt RJ, Strauss RP, Beck JD. Variations in the social impact of oral conditions among older adults in South Australia, Ontario and North Carolina. J Dent Res 1996;75:1439–1450.

40. Walker A, Cooper I (eds). Adult Dental Health Survey: Oral Health in the United Kingdom 1998. London: The Stationery Office, 2000.

41. Cushing AM, Sheiham A. Assessing periodontal treatment needs and periodontal status in a study of adults in North-West England. Community Dent Health 1985;2:187–194.

42. Gooch BF, Dolan TA, Bourque LB. Correlates of self-reported dental health status upon enrollment in the RAND Health Insurance Experiment. J Dent Educ 1989;53:629–637.

43. Locker D, Slade GD. Association between clinical and subjective indicators of oral health status in an older adult population. Gerodontology 1994;11:108–114.

44. Hunt RJ, Slade GD, Strauss RP. Differences between racial groups in the impact of oral disorders among older adults in North Carolina. J Public Health Dent 1995;55:205–209.

45. Coates AJ, Moore KR, Richards LC. Removable prosthodontics: A survey of practices and attitudes among South Australian dentists. Austr Dent J 1996; 41:151–158.

46. Kressin NR. Associations among different assessments of oral health outcomes. J Dent Educ 1996;60: 501–507.

47. Gift HC, Drury TF, Nowjack-Raymer RE, Selwitz RH. The state of the nation's oral health: Mid-decade assessment of Healthy People 2000. J Public Health Dent 1996;56:84–91.

48. Gilbert GH, Duncan RP, Kulley AM. Validity of self-reported tooth counts during a telephone screening interview. J Public Health Dent 1997;57:176–180.

49. Atchison KA, Der-Martirosian C, Gift HC. Components of self-reported oral health and general health in racial and ethnic groups. J Public Health Dent 1998;58: 301–308.

50. Allison PJ, Locker D, Feine JS. Quality of life: A dynamic construct. Social Sci Med 1997;45:221–230.

51. Locker D. Issues in measuring change in self-perceived oral health status. Community Dent Oral Epidemiol 1998;26:41–47.

52. Dolan TA, Peek CW, Stuck AE, Beck JC. Three-year changes in global oral health rating by elderly dentate adults. Community Dent Oral Epidemiol 1998;26: 62–69.

53. Slade GD. Assessing change in quality of life using the Oral Health Impact Profile. Community Dent Oral Epidemiol 1998;26:52–61.

54. Fiske J, Watson RM. The benefit of dental care to an elderly population assessed using sociodental measure of oral handicap. Br Dent J 1990;168:153–156.

55. Dao TTT, Lavigne GJ, Charbonneau A, Feine JS, Lund JP. The efficacy of oral splints in the treatment of myofascial pain of the jaw muscles: A controlled clinical trial. Pain 1994;56:85–94.

56. Schliephake H, Rüffert K, Schneller T. Prospective study of the quality of life of cancer patients after intraoral tumor surgery. J Oral Maxillofac Surg 1996;54: 664–670.

57. Allen PF, McMillan AS, Walshaw D. A patient-based assessment of implant-stabilized and conventional complete dentures. J Prosthet Dent 2001;85:141–147.

58. Awad MA, Locker D, Korner-Bitensky N, Feine JS. Measuring the effect of intra-oral implant rehabilitation on health-related quality of life in a randomized controlled clinical trial. J Dent Res 2000;79:1659–1663.

Health-Related Quality of Life: Conceptual Issues and Research Applications

Bernadine Cimprich, PhD, RN, FAAN
Amber G. Paterson, PhD

In the United States, efforts to evaluate an individual's quality of life (QOL) did not appear in the literature until the 1970s.[1,2] Before that time, the concept of QOL had been applied only to whole societies or populations.[3] More recently, scientific emphasis has focused on understanding how disease and its treatment may affect not only the quantity, but also the quality of an individual's survival.[4-6] Thus the concept of health-related quality of life (HRQOL) has evolved over the past 10 years, with a significant increase in the amount of related research activity across many different populations.[4,5,7-9] This chapter aims to provide a basic understanding of the current concepts, controversies, and challenges of HRQOL research. First, issues associated with current approaches to studying HRQOL will be identified, then the application of QOL concepts will be illustrated, using findings from an interdisciplinary research project with cancer survivors. The focus throughout the chapter will be on current theories and definitions of HRQOL and on the implications for its measurement.

Significance of QOL Evaluation in Research on Chronic Illness

The recent recognition of the importance of QOL outcomes in relation to chronic disease and treatment is largely the function of three factors, namely *(1)* an increased demand for data-based evaluations of the quality of extended survival,[6-10] *(2)* an emphasis on evaluations of the cost-effectiveness of treatment regimens that include adjustments for QOL outcomes,[7,11,12] and *(3)* a need for improved understanding and identification of short- and long-term health outcomes and related patient service needs.[13]

In the past decade, improvements in diagnostic and treatment modalities have resulted in longer survival times for many individuals with chronic illnesses. Despite the acknowledged beneficial effects of such treatments on length of extended survival, these also often carry with them the potential for negative long-term detrimental effects on physical and psychologic well-being. For example, survival time has been significantly lengthened by new cancer diagnostic and treatment modalities. At the same time, these new cancer therapies often have associated toxicities, raising concerns among providers, patients, and their families about the long-term psychosocial and functional effects of such treatments. Therefore, to better understand the burden of disease and short-term and long-term effects of many current treatments on patients' functioning, data-based evaluations of the quality of extended survival have become important considerations for clinical trials that evaluate the effectiveness of new therapies.[14]

The recent emphasis on the economics of health care and the need to evaluate the cost-effectiveness of treatment with adjustments for QOL outcomes has led to the development of new methodologies for evaluating treatment outcomes. For example, equations that calculate QOL-adjusted years[11] (QALYs) or quality-adjusted time without symptoms and toxicity[15] (Q-TWST) reflect QOL as well as morbidity, mortality, and cost considerations. It is now common for evaluations of treatment cost-effectiveness to include adjustments for QOL outcomes.

Finally, there is a need to improve the understanding of how complex medical treatments in individuals with chronic illness influence long-term functional and psychosocial outcomes.[13,16] As a result, a need exists for evidence-based evaluations of the short- and long-term QOL outcomes and related service needs of patients, survivors, and their families. Such information will permit the development of tailored cost-effective interventions that minimize the negative effects of treatment, facilitate recovery, and improve HRQOL outcomes.

As a result of these three driving forces, research on HRQOL no longer resides at the margins of medical research, but instead plays an essential role in clinical trials designed to assess the effectiveness of new therapies.[13,14]

Defining HRQOL

The concept of HRQOL is multifaceted and complex; therefore defining it is a challenge. Current definitions of HRQOL have been derived from the World Health Organization's designation of health as a state of complete physical, mental, and social well-being and not merely the absence of disease and infirmity.[17] Current definitions of HRQOL vary greatly. Some define it as a personal statement of the positive or negative attributes that characterize life[18,19]; others describe it as a perception of disease impact that is both subjective and culturally bound.[13] Still others define it as a multidimensional construct encompassing perceptions of both positive and negative aspects of physical, emotional, social, and cognitive functions; somatic discomfort; and other symptoms produced by a disease or its treatment.[5] Although there are currently at least 15 different definitions of HRQOL, a consensus has not been reached on a single one.

Despite this complexity, certain areas of conceptual agreement exist, each of which carries implications for measuring HRQOL.[9,10,13] First, it is generally recognized that QOL is a subjective experience, a perception of one's life circumstances.[4,5] Initial attempts at estimating HRQOL often relied on the evaluations and judgments of health care providers. However, research showed that provider ratings of patient HRQOL are not consistent with ratings given by either patients or their family members.[4] As a result, it is now recognized that provider ratings are insufficient to determine patient HRQOL. Subjective, self-report measures therefore are needed to capture individuals' perceptions of HRQOL.

A second area of conceptual agreement is that HRQOL includes both affective and cognitive components.[20] These two components are complementary. While the affective component reflects "happiness" (the perceived pleasantness or unpleasantness of a situation), the cognitive component reflects appraisals, thoughts, and perceived satisfaction with the situation.[1,2] This perspective also has implications for measurement. Whereas affect is thought to be more variable and related to mood states, cognitive appraisals are considered to be more stable and related to personal resources.[2,9] Researchers and clinicians interested in measuring individuals' HRQOL, therefore, need to evaluate instruments for affective and cognitive content to determine whether both components of the QOL experience are included and to ensure a more comprehensive assessment of HRQOL outcomes.

Appraisals of HRQOL are also generally considered to include both positive and negative aspects of an experience.[18,19] That is, both positive and negative thoughts, feelings, and experiences are included in personal ratings of HRQOL. This perspective represents a shift from earlier medical models of HRQOL that tended to emphasize deficits. Recent research indicates that patients are continually engaged in weighing the positive and negative aspects of their illness experiences in their overall ratings of HRQOL.[10,16] Therefore, HRQOL instruments need to include assessments of potential positive as well as negative outcomes of illness and treatment. In addition, particularly in longitudinal research, it is important to recognize that an individual's overall rating is a composite of changes in positive and negative aspects of HRQOL that may have differential effects on overall ratings over time; therefore, overall HRQOL ratings need to be considered in the context of such positive and negative health outcomes.

Another aspect of QOL on which there has been consensus is its multidimensional nature.[4,5,7] It is now generally understood that HRQOL encompasses multiple, overlapping, and related domains of functioning. Although these dimensions are often distinguishable, they are not necessarily discrete or mutually exclusive. Dimensions of HRQOL that are commonly included in current definitions are physical, emotional, psychologic, social, functional, and, more recently, spiritual domains of well-being. It is important for clinicians and researchers to use instruments that appropriately assess the relevant multidimensional aspects of HRQOL for specific populations and disease conditions.[8,11]

Finally, it is generally acknowledged that QOL is a dynamic concept. Recent research has revealed that an individual's perceptions of HRQOL change over time.[21] Previous health experiences may have altered individuals' expectations and standards of functional well-being. In response to such experiences, individuals adapt and often change their standards for evaluating their QOL. Thus, knowing an individual's rating of QOL at one time may not accurately predict the same individual's rating at another time, raising the issue of how to quantify changing perceptions of QOL adequately. To better capture shifting standards, assessments of HRQOL should be made on a continuum of low to high, better or worse, poor to excellent—ie, in relative terms, comparing historical life circumstances with current states of well-being.

One area that has not received much consideration in the definition and measurement of HRQOL is the influence of culture.[9,13] Quality of life is considered a subjective experience, and along with subjectivity comes the influence of culture. Evidence shows that culture influences a person's definitions of health and illness, appraisals, coping attempts, and behavioral expressions. In addition, formal definitions of HRQOL are influenced by researchers' cultural backgrounds, which may or may not match those of their respondents (study participants). Most of the research to date has focused on direct application of current models to minority populations without considering possible influences of culture on perceptions of HRQOL.[22] The following questions are yet to be answered: To what extent has the dominant Eurocentric culture influenced the current understanding and measurement of HRQOL or patient responses? Are different definitions and questionnaires required for each culture? Or, do enough commonalities exist between cultures and definitions of HRQOL that standard areas of agreement can be captured? Given these unanswered questions, it is prudent to be cognizant of the potential influence of culture when measuring HRQOL outcomes.

Theoretic Perspectives

A number of theoretic perspectives have influenced research and interpretations of HRQOL. Prominent models have been derived from theories focusing on uncertainty in illness,[23] stress and coping,[24,25] patients' search for meaning,[9,26–28] and general health policy.[9,29]

Padilla and colleagues[23] propose that perceptions of HRQOL are derived from the process of dealing with uncertainty in illness, which includes appraisal of threats and opportunities, and the effectiveness of coping strategies. This process continues through all phases of illness: diagnosis, treatment, recovery, recurrence, remission, and palliative care. Similarly, the stress and coping model suggests that HRQOL outcomes are mediated by the appraisal of illness, which is influenced by personal, social, and illness-related factors.[24,25] Some theorists propose that HRQOL may be determined by the meaning that people attach to their experiences with disease and illness,[26,28] that is, by placing an event or illness in its physical, psychologic, social, and spiritual contexts.[27] According to this view, it is thought that HRQOL outcomes are influenced by one's ability to make sense of events and to construct meanings for experiences within a larger context. Construction of meaning is an intrinsically personal, subjective process. Therefore qualitative methods, such as in-depth interviews or open-ended questions, may be most effective for capturing the richness of patients' experiences and their effects on HRQOL outcomes.

A relevant theoretic issue in this discussion is the idea of internalized standards of QOL, which refers to the subjective, evolving nature of individuals' perceptions of their own well-being. According to this view, the diagnosis of an illness can change the internal QOL standards of an individual.[30] As a person adjusts to a disease or a condition, internal standards of QOL also are adjusted. For example, as one adapts to limitations imposed by illness, internal standards are changed to reflect the new level of functioning.[23] Following this idea, "discrepancy" theories focus on the perceived gaps between health expecta-

tions and actual outcomes to explain successful or unsuccessful coping and perceptions of good or poor QOL.[31] This perspective presents unique challenges for assessing change in HRQOL over time because conventional quantitative methods often cannot capture shifting internal standards and relativity of judgments.

Finally, another prominent theoretic approach is based on health economics. The general health policy model[9,29] weighs the relative importance of HRQOL against life duration. This approach is often used in research that assesses the cost-effectiveness of medical treatments.

Research Application of HRQOL Concepts

The issues surrounding theoretic definitions and measurement of HRQOL suggest the need for both quantitative and qualitative approaches to ensure more comprehensive assessment. The use of multiple methods is more likely to capture the dynamic and subjective nature of HRQOL. At the same time, use of such methods often requires collaboration between researchers with expertise in quantitative and qualitative methodologies.

Cimprich and colleagues[32] describe an interdisciplinary, collaborative study design using both quantitative and qualitative assessments of HRQOL in long-term survivors of breast cancer. The objective of this multimethod research project was to generate in-depth data about the positive and negative aspects of HRQOL for breast cancer survivors and to examine the relationship between survivors' HRQOL and their service needs. The study sample consisted of women who had been diagnosed with breast cancer at least 5 years previously, had completed all treatment, and had no evidence of disease. Their HRQOL was assessed using mailed survey questionnaires to obtain quantitative data and follow-up interviews to obtain in-depth qualitative data.

The theoretic model used for this study was developed by Ferrell and colleagues,[16] who studied HRQOL in long-term survivors of cancer. This model is consistent with the prevailing consensus on the subjective, multidimensional nature of QOL and includes four major domains of HRQOL: physical, psychologic, social, and spiritual well-being. These domains are distinct but overlapping components of global QOL. Also, this model allows the inclusion of both positive and negative changes that may occur as a result of diagnosis and treatment for breast cancer. Thus, the model addresses many of the issues related to the definition of HRQOL, and encompasses the areas of consensus.

An instrument developed by Ferrell and colleagues[33] based on this model was used to assess each of these domains. The physical well-being domain includes symptoms and late side effects associated with diagnosis and treatment, such as functional ability, pain, and fatigue. Psychologic well-being encompasses emotional and cognitive sequelae, such as life enjoyment and satisfaction, as well as fears associated with the cancer diagnosis. Social well-being taps long-term effects of a diagnosis of breast cancer on interpersonal and family relationships and roles. Finally, the spiritual domain, often overlooked in studies of HRQOL, assesses changes in spiritual life, the search for meaning and purpose, and the extent to which positive life changes have occurred as a result of the cancer experience. To better capture possible shifts in internal standards, participants are asked to rate each item on a 10-point scale, anchored by polar opposite phrases that denote relative change (eg, better or worse).

To complement the information obtained from the mailed questionnaire, a qualitative component was included in the study design. Specifically, face-to-face, semistructured interviews were conducted with a subsample of participants to obtain more in-depth information about the participants' personal experience with breast cancer. This allowed the respondents to elaborate on the meaning of their quantitative ratings on a spectrum of HRQOL variables. These data were helpful to the researchers in interpreting the resulting data. It is thought that combining results from quantitative (questionnaire) and qualitative (interview) analyses will help to strengthen the validity of the findings.

As part of the interdisciplinary research project, the same combination of quantitative and qualitative methods was used to assess HRQOL in other populations of patients with cancer, including adult survivors of leukemia and lymphoma, survivors of childhood cancer, and their families.[26,34] This provides an opportunity to examine HRQOL outcomes across cancer survivor populations, taking into consideration the effects of possible influencing factors, including support systems and varying disease sites and treatment modalities. Because the studies examined survivors in every stage of life, comparative analyses will be possible, including examination of commonalities and differences in HRQOL outcomes across survivor populations.

Considerations and Directions for Future Research

The study of HRQOL is a relatively new field of research within the health sciences. Although a great deal of innovation and numerous advances have occurred in this area, particularly in the past 10 years, our understanding of many of the basic issues, such as the definition and measurement of HRQOL, remains limited. In addition, there are the following significant issues still to be considered.

First, little attention has been given to the potential impact of culture on basic perceptions of QOL. In developing theories and measures of QOL, it is important to consider the impact of ethnicity, race, and gender on perceptions and assessments of HRQOL.

Second, QOL is an innately personal assessment, the full nature of which may not be revealed through traditional quantitative methods. To increase understanding of HRQOL, more consideration should be given to the meanings people construct from their experiences. Qualitative methods provide a means to capture the full nature of individuals' experiences. In addition, more research is needed to compare qualitative and quantitative methods of assessing HRQOL.

Finally, longitudinal assessments of HRQOL rarely have been conducted. Greater understanding is needed regarding how HRQOL changes as an individual proceeds through stages of health, illness, treatment, and recovery. To achieve this, HRQOL must be assessed longitudinally, beginning with pretreatment baseline measurements. In addition, prospective studies of healthy people that capture normal changes in HRQOL over time are needed to distinguish illness-related changes from those that reflect normal aging and stage-of-life transitions. To accomplish this, more sensitive instruments that can provide finer discrimination in minor health changes are needed to allow longitudinal assessments of HRQOL in individuals as they move across the health-illness continuum.

Summary

Although there currently is heightened emphasis on HRQOL outcomes, research in this area is still in its formative stages. The concept of HRQOL is multifaceted and complex, and there is continuing debate about both theoretic definitions and measurement approaches. There is consensus regarding the subjective, multidimensional, and dynamic nature of HRQOL. Such consensus has direct implications for assessment across clinical populations and settings, specifically, the use of self-ratings, multidimensional measures, and longitudinal assessments. The influence of culture on perceptions of HRQOL and the use of quantitative and qualitative approaches to measurement must be further analyzed to ensure more comprehensive and valid assessments.

References

1. Campbell A. Subjective measures of well-being. Am Psychol 1976;31:117–124.
2. Andrews FM, McKennell AC. Measures of self-reported well-being: Their affective, cognitive, and other components. Soc Indicators Res 1980;8:127–155.
3. Tate DG, Dijkers M, Johnson-Greene L. Outcome measures in quality of life. Top Stroke Rehabil 1996;2:1–17.
4. Aaronson N, Meyerowitz BE, Bard M, et al. Quality of life research in oncology. Cancer 1991;67(suppl 3):839–843.
5. Osoba D. Lessons learned from measuring health-related quality of life in oncology. J Clin Oncol 1994;12:608–616.
6. Schipper H. Quality of life: Principles of the clinical paradigm. J Psychosoc Oncol 1990;8:171–185.
7. Cella DF, Tulsky DS, Gray G, et al. The Functional Assessment of Cancer Therapy Scale: Development and validation of the general measure. J Clin Oncol 1993;11:570–579.
8. Gift HC, Atchinson KA. Oral health, health, and health-related quality of life. Med Care 1995;33:NS57–NS77.
9. King CR, Haberman M, Berry DL, et al. Quality of life and the cancer experience: The state-of-the-knowledge. Oncol Nurs Forum 1997;24:27–41.
10. Mast ME. Definition and measurement of quality of life in oncology nursing research: Review and theoretical implications. Oncol Nurs Forum 1995;22:957–964.
11. Barr RD, Feeny D, Furlong W, Weitzman S, Torrance GW. A preference-based approach to health-related quality of life for children with cancer. Int J Pediatr Hematol Oncol 1995;2:305–315.
12. Hayman J, Weeks J, Mauch P. Economic analyses in health care: An introduction to the methodology with an emphasis on radiation therapy. Int J Radiat Oncol Biol Phys 1996;35:827–841.
13. Bloom JR. Quality of life after cancer. Cancer 1991;67(suppl 3):855–859.
14. Ganz PA, Moinpour CM, Cella DF, Fetting JH. Quality of life assessment in cancer clinical trials: A status report. J Natl Cancer Inst 1992;84(13):994–995.
15. Goldhirsch A, Gelber RD, Simes J, Glasziou P, Coates AS. Costs and benefits of adjuvant therapy in breast cancer: A quality-adjusted survival analysis. J Clin Oncol 1989;7:36–44.

16. Ferrell BR, Dow KH, Leigh S, Ly J, Gulasekaram P. Quality of life in long-term cancer survivors. Oncol Nurs Forum 1995;22:918–922.

17. World Health Organization. WHO Chronicle. Geneva, Switzerland: World Health Organization, 1947.

18. Aaronson NK. Quality of life research in cancer clinical trials: A need for common rules and language. Oncology 1990;2:59–66.

19. Grant MM, Padilla GV, Ferrell BR, Rhiner M. Assessment of quality of life with a single instrument. Semin Oncol Nurs 1990;6:260–270.

20. de Haes CJM, de Ruiter JH, Temperlaar R, Pennink JW. The distinction between affect and cognition in the quality of life of cancer patients: Sensitivity and stability. Qual Life Res 1992;1:315–322.

21. de Haes J, Van Knippenberg F. The quality of life of cancer patients: A review of the literature. Soc Sci Med 1985;20:809–817.

22. Pasick RJ. Socioeconomic and cultural factors in the development and use of theory. In: Glanz K, Lewis FM, Rimer BK (eds). Health Behavior and Health Education, ed 2. San Francisco: Jossey-Bass, 1997:425–440.

23. Padilla GV, Mischel MH, Grant MM. Nursing research into quality of life. Qual Life Res 1992;1:155–165.

24. Northouse LL, Caffey M, Deichelbohrer L, et al. The quality of life of African American women with breast cancer. Res Nurs Health 1999;22:449–460.

25. Scott DW, Oberst MT, Dropkin MJ. A stress-coping model. Adv Nurs Sci 1980;3:9–23.

26. Chesler M, Zebrack B, Orbuch T, Parry C. Mothers of childhood cancer survivors: Their worries and concerns. J Psychosoc Oncol (in press).

27. Cunningham AJ. Information and health in the many levels of man: Toward a more comprehensive theory of health and disease. Advances 1986;3:32–45.

28. Zebrack B. Cancer survivor identity and quality of life. Cancer Practice 2000;8:238–242.

29. Kaplan RM, Anderson JP. A general health policy model: An integrated approach. In: Spilker B (ed). Quality of Life Assessment in Clinical Trials. New York: Raven, 1990:131–149.

30. Breetvelt IS, Van Dam FS. Underreporting by cancer patients: The case of response shift. Soc Sci Med 1991; 32:981–987.

31. Linder-Petz S. Social psychological determinants of patient satisfaction: A test of five hypotheses. Soc Sci Med 1982;16:583–589.

32. Cimprich B, Ronis DL, Martinez G. Age at diagnosis and quality of life in breast cancer survivors. Cancer Pract 2002;10:85–93.

33. Ferrell BR, Dow KH, Grant M. Measurement of the quality of life in cancer survivors. Qual Life Res 1995; 4:523–531.

34. Zebrack B, Chesler M. Health-related worries, self-image, and life outlook of long-term survivors of childhood cancer. Health Soc Work 2001;26:209–288.

Quality of Life As a Psychologist Views It

Christopher Peterson, PhD

This chapter provides a broad overview of how psychologists approach quality-of-life (QOL) issues and an introduction to "explanatory style" (also sometimes referred to as "attributional style") and how this personality variable relates to QOL and physical well-being. Explanatory style research is by no means the sole approach to studying QOL issues. However, it serves as a representative strategy to outline the rationale underlying a psychologic study of QOL issues. For several decades, explanatory style has been used successfully to study topics ranging from popular songs to the performance of the stock market. Although to date few studies have been conducted focusing on its relationship with oral health, explanatory style has been shown to be related to overall physical health; therefore, one could reasonably assume that it also could be applied to more specific areas of health, including oral health. Indeed, in an explanatory style study using a simple self-report measure, Jackson and colleagues[1] showed a link between explanatory style and the number of caries lesions present in patients' mouths. It is the hope of the author that this chapter, which reveals possible avenues for future research on this relationship, will inspire further studies of this nature.

Despite the multidisciplinary nature of QOL issues, one might assume that psychologists understand these issues better than researchers from any other field. Psychology is, after all, the scientific study of the individual, and it is the individual who leads the life of quality. However, a closer look at the psychologic literature on QOL will reveal that psychologists have not grappled as fully with the topic as one might expect. It seems clear that a psychologic perspective has the potential to shed much light on QOL. The title of this chapter harks back to perhaps the most famous article ever written in psychology, "Psychology as the behaviorist views it," in which John Watson[2] defined the behaviorist agenda that shaped psychology for much of the twentieth century and, not incidentally, shifted attention away from QOL issues.

Psychology and QOL

How do psychologists approach QOL? One might expect psychologists to be proficient at explaining this concept; however, this is not the case. There have been several barriers to this endeavor, which can be explained by two historical biases. Although these biases may characterize other disciplines as well, psychologists in particular are acutely aware of them. The first bias, particularly within the field of clinical psychology, has been the predominant focus on the disease model. Psychologists have paid attention only to problems that demand solutions. When things are going well, no interventions are deemed necessary: "If it isn't broken, don't fix it." This might explain why psychologists know much more about psychologic disorders than they do about psychologic health (ie, doing well and leading a good life). This bias is changing; psychologists are finally beginning to look beyond the presence or absence of illness in an attempt to characterize what makes life worth living.[3] However, the historical bias imposed by the disease model might still get in the way of understanding the concept of QOL, leading psychologists to "pathologize" wellness. Therefore, a maxim directing the new research could be: "If it isn't broken, don't break it."

A second historical bias is the quiescence model. The two dominant psychologic theories of the twentieth century—Sigmund Freud's psychoanalysis and John Watson's behaviorism—both share a common assumption about human nature. They argue that humans are in the business of satisfying needs—discharging their instincts in ways allowed by society or reducing their drives via reinforcement. Human nature therefore entails the seeking of quiescence, collapsing in a pool of brief satiation until instincts or drives again rear their head and demand attention. To be sure, people have important needs to be met, and much of twentieth-century psychology articulated the hows and whys of these needs. However, there is more to QOL than is captured by this vision of human nature. In fact, the quiescence model does not even address QOL. It looks at human needs as basic and primal, and argues that the means of satisfying them are therefore ultimately and arbitrarily interchangeable. Authenticity, genuineness, fulfillment, and actualization—notions virtually demanded by a focus on QOL—are neglected.

The field of psychology underwent significant changes during the last decade of the twentieth century, at least in the United States. The economic prosperity and freedom from war experienced by this nation during that time period allowed the field to break free from the disease and quiescence models. The "business-as-usual" psychology had failed to deliver on its promise to create a psychologic utopia. Even with the vast resources available in the United States, more people than ever before are depressed.[4] Poverty and prejudice persist. The new breed of psychologists believes that the field of psychology, as well as people in general, have been asking the wrong questions and thus seeking the wrong goals. A positive QOL entails more than just the elimination of what is wrong. The current notions in psychology outlined in the following sections appear to seek answers to the same question: "What constitutes a 'good life' other than the absence of pathology and illness?"

Wellness

Contemporary psychologists are fond of the notion of wellness or psychologic well-being. They define wellness as more than the absence of illness. To characterize wellness in more positive terms, it might be defined as "striving and thriving." Carol Ryff,[5–7] a well-known proponent of psychologic well-being research, specifies the critical components of wellness as self-acceptance, positive relations with others, autonomy, environmental mastery, finding purpose in life, and personal growth. Although some researchers might disagree with these specific components, psychologists do agree that attention to wellness opens the door to better QOL.[8–10]

Answers to the questions of where and how does one strive and thrive can be found in Freud's writings. He argued that there are two important domains of life: work and love. In short, his approach indicates that humans should approach work in a caring way and approach love with effort and industriousness. Therefore, if humans can strive and thrive at work and love, then they are leading a good life. Contemporary research on this subject cites the similar concepts of agency and communion.[11] According to this viewpoint, people have two inherent motives: having an impact on the world (agency) and building bonds with other people (communion).

Subjective Well-Being

Subjective well-being comprises contentment, satisfaction, happiness, hope, and good feelings about one's past life, one's present life, and one's presumed future life. QOL can be approached from the outside, in the enumeration of one's possessions, friends, and the like. However, it also must be approached from the inside. People's beliefs about the quality of their own lives are important. Previous generations of psychologists either distrusted self-reports (eg, Freud) or regarded them as irrelevant (eg, Watson), but contemporary psychologists take subjective well-being very seriously.

Studies by Myers[12] and Myers and Diener[13] have summarized various psychologists' approaches to subjective well-being. One component of subjective well-being is the presence of positive affect, that is, a person's good feelings. A second component is the absence of negative affect, or not feeling bad. These two characteristics are independent of each other. There are people who only have positive affect and no negative affect; there are individuals with only negative affect; and there are persons who have neither positive affect nor negative affect. This last state is termed *anhedonia*. There are also people with a lot of positive affect and a lot of negative affect; they are commonly described as labile, emotional, unstable, or borderline. However, one could argue that they are just living life fully and richly, if not always happily. In any case, it is clear that QOL research must study both good and bad feelings to understand subjective well-being.

A third component of subjective well-being is satisfaction with life. In contrast to positive or negative affect, satisfaction is a summary judgment of how well one has done in the past and how well one expects to do in the future. Psychologists do not wish to focus only on momentary affect in understanding subjective well-being. For example, a person might have just received a parking ticket, and is therefore unhappy (momentary affect). However, this same person has a car that runs well enough to get him or her places, so this person might still be generally satisfied with life.

In fact, most people are reasonably happy and satisfied. This statement may be a generalization, but it is also accurate. Subjective well-being does not vary appreciably across the life span.[12] A person is not happiest when in college or when retired; rather, overall satisfaction with life is remarkably stable over a person's lifetime. Another generalization is that women report more joy and more misery than do men.[12] That is, women are both happier and sadder than are men. However, on average, women and men are equally happy and equally satisfied; therefore subjective well-being does not vary according to gender.[12] It has also been shown that life satisfaction in the United States does not vary by ethnicity.[12] Nor does happiness vary with income after the basic necessities of life are provided.[12] People who live in the deepest poverty are more unhappy than are those above the poverty line, but beyond this point more money does not bring more happiness: A 20% salary raise will not make a person happier in the long run.

Another important point is that while severe health problems take a toll on all the components of subjective well-being, minor health problems do not—a finding that should be interesting to all health professionals, particularly QOL researchers.[12] Clearly, one criterion of a good measurement instrument is that it has to be sensitive to change. If researchers undertake some sort of intervention and try to track its impact, the measure they use has to be sensitive. However, if they measure the effect of an intervention on general well-being in people with relatively minor, circumscribed health problems, they will not find any discernible change, regardless of the effectiveness of the intervention—or the measure. Another lesson for researchers working with patient populations is that because minor health problems do not affect general well-being, people with minor problems may not enter the health care system. If it takes a serious malady to make a person unhappy, and if one needs to be unhappy to seek help, it follows that the health care system is underutilized, especially for prevention.

Research also has produced "positive findings" about subjective well-being. These are findings that reflect differences among people in the criteria of happiness and satisfaction. For instance, results show that happiness varies according to the era in which the person lives (eg, people living in the 1950s have been shown to be happier than those living at the present time).[12]

Happiness also varies across cultures. These findings are important for all researchers and practitioners who work with diverse populations. People from collectivist cultures, such as Asian cultures, report less happiness than do people from more individualistic cultures, eg, mainstream United States and Western European cultures.[12] This difference may arise from the fact that subjective well-being is typically defined and measured with an emphasis on an individual's subjective feelings and beliefs. People who base their sense of personal well-being on the well-being of the group may find it more difficult to feel good than do those who base their sense of well-being on their own individual situation. In the United States, four traits characterize people with high subjective well-being: high self-esteem, personal control, optimism, and extraversion. The first three traits are presumably malleable, whereas extraversion is one of those characteristics that is largely genetically determined.

Another finding is that married people are happier than unmarried people, and that marriage is better for men than it is for women.[12] Research also shows that religious people are happier than nonreligious people.[12] This could be a

relevant finding for health care providers. Although they should not try to convert patients, health professionals could encourage their patients to talk about their beliefs, tap into them, and build on them.

Flow

Another contemporary idea relevant to QOL is the notion of flow, introduced and studied by psychologist Mihaly Csikszentmihalyi.[14] Flow is defined in contrast with happiness. Happiness is the explicit experience of positive feelings and/or the absence of negative feelings (ie, not feeling displeasure). Flow is what occurs when one is actively engaged with ongoing tasks and is unaware of any feelings or the passage of time, focusing only on the task at hand. One feels "in control" of what one is doing without focusing directly on this perception.

Flow may not be equivalent to the whole of good QOL, but it is an important component. According to Csikszentmihalyi,[14] flow occurs when one's skills are met by the demands of one's tasks and vice versa. Therefore, the conditions for flow themselves are constantly in flux. They change as a person's abilities change and as the task demands change. This concept is easily seen in the phenomenon of video game crazes. A person may enjoy playing a certain video game and find it nearly impossible to stop playing it. However, once the person has mastered the game, he or she will become bored and move on to another activity. The fact that flow follows this principle may be adaptive in that it prevents a person from stagnating, allowing them to achieve new and higher levels of success, whether it is in work, extracurricular activities, or interpersonal relationships.

It is important to keep in mind that individuals cannot report being in flow while in the state itself. Flow can only be noted after the fact. Therefore, when researching QOL it is important to keep in mind that in some cases directly asking people if they are having a good-quality experience is ineffective—this may be a judgment that can only be made in retrospect.

Hedonic Psychology

Another contemporary psychologic concept is that of hedonic psychology—that is, a psychology of emotional life.[15] For 50 years after Watson[2] described behaviorism, psychology was largely the study of behavior, that is, overt, observable actions. In the 1960s, behaviorism gave way to what is now called the *cognitive revolution*, the study of the contents and processes of thought.[16] Cognitive psychologists have used the computer as their dominant metaphor, and information-processing models of human nature have been exceedingly popular.[17] However, the cognitive revolution was also referred to as *cold cognition* because it lacked a study of emotion and motivation.

Human functioning is commonly divided into the three broad categories of doing, thinking, and feeling. Hedonic psychology therefore completes the picture begun by behaviorism and cognitive psychology. Although some psychologists have studied emotions in the past, it is only recently that psychologists have begun self-consciously labeling such research on emotions *hedonic psychology*.

Fredrickson,[18] one of the leading figures in this new hedonic psychology, has primarily focused on positive emotions. In the past, psychologists who did study emotions usually looked at such negative emotions as anger, fear, and anxiety, while neglecting positive emotions such as curiosity, joy, contentment, and love. Fredrickson has argued that positive emotions are not simply obverses or converses of negative emotions.

One possible contrast between positive and negative emotions pertaining to QOL points to the fact that negative emotions tend to limit a person. A person is afraid when threatened, and thus focuses on the threat and musters all of his or her resources to respond to it. This person's behavioral repertoire is narrowed to two options, namely fight or flight. Fredrickson[18] has argued that positive emotions, in contrast, broaden a person. They open the person up, allowing the person to notice more things, become more creative, and expand his or her be-

havioral repertoire. Fredrickson[18] has provided laboratory evidence of her theory. People experiencing positive emotions are better problem solvers and are more flexible in their thinking compared with those who are not. Therefore, QOL cannot simply be understood by examining the absence of negative emotions.

Positive Psychology

The field of positive psychology envisions an approach that focuses on strength as well as weakness, is interested in building the best things in life as well as repairing the worst, and is as concerned with fulfilling the lives of normal people as with healing the wounds of the distressed.[19] Positive psychology is therefore very relevant to understanding QOL.

The past concern of psychology with human problems will not be abandoned anytime in the near future because there always will be problems that demand psychologic solutions; however, psychologists interested in promoting human potential must ask questions different from those asked by their predecessors, who assumed a disease model of human nature.

Positive psychology is distinguished from the humanistic psychology of the 1960s and 1970s and the positive thinking movement by its reliance on empirical research to understand the human condition. Humanists were skeptical about the scientific method and what it could yield, and yet were unable to offer an alternative. In contrast, positive psychologists see both strength and weakness as authentic and amenable to scientific understanding.

Explanatory Style and Health

Psychologists have only recently started to study psychologic health, rather than focusing solely on disorders. They have entered this field of research with little education or expertise in this field. Moreover, measuring psychologic disease and disorder has proved to be difficult; measuring good health may prove to be even more challenging. Nevertheless, following are some of the insights gained by psychologists on measurement in particular and health psychology in general, including specific research findings on explanatory style and health.

Health Psychology

The French philosopher René Descartes (1596–1650) stated his thesis of mind-body dualism so persuasively that in the ensuing centuries minds and bodies became the subjects of completely different disciplines. The vocabulary developed for talking about minds became altogether different than that constructed for discussing bodies. Regardless of the fact that Descartes' original reasons for this division were political rather than scientific, health psychologists have found it difficult to rejoin the two concepts, and are unable to explain how minds and bodies influence one another without introducing awkward neologisms like psychoneuroimmunology.

Psychologists who are interested in measuring physical well-being must inevitably conclude that there is not just one method of measuring it. Multimethod assessments have long been useful in general psychology, and are just as useful a strategy in the more specific field of health psychology. Psychologists need to ask individuals how they feel, which is often described as a *patient-based approach*. Patients also need to be asked to describe symptoms such as aches, pains, and runny noses. Finally, the knowledge gained from years of medical technology cannot be dismissed; psychologists must assess the presence of germs and their effects on the immune system whenever relevant.

Psychologists frequently encounter a distinction between hard and soft data. *Hard data* usually refers to biologic test results, whereas *soft data* usually refers to information gathered by talking to a person. While test results are almost always preferred, this distinction does not necessarily translate into good data versus bad data. There are clearly bad hard data. For example, a patient's survival time after being diagnosed with cancer is an objective, hard measure. In recent times, certain forms of cancer are associated with increased survival time; however, this data may be misleading. Some of the breakthroughs of medical science involve early diagnosis. Although patients stay alive longer after diagnosis, it does not necessarily mean that they live longer; rather, it may indicate that the diagnosis occurred earlier. This is an example of hard data that may be deceiving. In some cases, even the simple decision regarding whether someone is alive or dead may be difficult because the criteria for death can vary by state. Some states recognize cessation of cardiac activity as death, whereas others believe it to be cessation of brain activity.

In contrast, there are soft data that are very valuable. An often-reported finding is that of self-reported predictors of longevity.[20] In several interviews, people are asked about some of these well-known predictors, such as smoking, drinking alcohol, and exercise. In addition, the answers to the question "On a five-point scale, how would you say your health is?" were found to predict longevity above and beyond the hard measures. It has been argued that subjective reports are just a marker for a hard predictor that was not assessed. However, taken at face value, it can be concluded that psychologic factors (ie, soft data) have an association with longevity that cannot be explained by hard data.

The different measures of health are often asymmetric and disconnected; therefore, it is important to measure well-being using different methods. The following two well-known examples illustrate the asymmetries: *(1)* It has been reported in the public health literature that women live longer, but have more illnesses than do men. Depending on the criteria used, the answer to the question of whether men or women are healthier varies. *(2)* Former basketball player Earvin "Magic" Johnson was diagnosed several years ago as HIV-positive, but is still living life more fully than many people who are virus-free. Whether he is healthy or ill is difficult to determine.

A psychologist's approach to well-being is to discover the antecedents of well-being. Typically, these antecedents are drawn from behavioral, cognitive, emotional, social, and community domains. A psychologist's work goes beyond merely demonstrating a correlation between a behavior and a consequence for well-being. These links, however interesting, are only a starting point for the real work: explaining how and why the link occurs. For example, it has been reported that optimistic people remain healthy decades longer than do pessimistic people.[21] However, there is no adequate explanation for this finding. Although psychologists know little about the interactions of the mind and body, they do know that these interactions are not always simple.

Interestingly, most common illnesses, especially in developed countries, can be said to result not from faulty immune systems but lifestyle. If one wishes to use the findings from health psychology to improve health, then one must change behavior. Psychologists are in an excellent position to make contributions toward this end. Psychologists occasionally need to move from specifying the mechanisms underlying good health to intervening to boost well-being. The most efficient intervention is primary prevention. Health psychologists may also treat those who are ill. For example, in a randomized clinical trial, Spiegel and colleagues[22] demonstrated that group therapy added meaningful years to the lives of patients with breast cancer. Although their results were remarkable, the mechanisms underlying this phenomenon are still unclear.

Explanatory Style

When bad events occur, people usually ask why it happened. Indeed, it might even be argued that asking and answering questions is the essence of the human condition. How such questions are answered has various repercussions, including psychologic cascades that result in health and illness.

Research on causal explanations and the explanatory style of a person show that the explanations for bad events entertained by people have three common properties: (1) A cause can be stable, ie, something that endures, or it can be

unstable and transient. (2) A cause can be global or circumscribed. This refers to the number of events and domains of life that are touched by the causal explanation. (3) The cause can be internal or external. This dimension focuses on whether an event is caused by an action or property of the person or some external factor.

By this characterization, it can be seen that using stable, global, and internal explanations for bad events entails turning events into catastrophes. This way of habitually explaining bad events is called a pessimistic, depressive, helpless, or hopeless explanatory style.[23] Conversely, individuals who habitually explain bad events with transient, circumscribed, and external causes have an optimistic, hopeful, or efficacious explanatory style.

Explanatory style arises out of the personal control tradition in psychology.[24] Personal control is the belief that one can behave in ways that maximize good outcomes and minimize bad outcomes. Explanatory style is an important influence on these beliefs about control. Catastrophic causes cannot be controlled by the person. In contrast, if the causes attributed to an event are circumscribed, one can be hopeful about the future and control what happens. An individual's belief in personal control may or may not be accurate. Research has shown that personal control can be self-fulfilling. People who believe they have control engage the world in a vigorous fashion and are better problem solvers; personal control is therefore a powerful psychologic variable. Box 6-1 illustrates this tradition by listing cognates of personal control, well-investigated psychologic constructs pertaining to perceptions of control.

There are two ways to measure explanatory style. The first is with a questionnaire in which the respondents imagine bad events such as "You cannot get the work done that others expect of you" and then write down what they believe would be the major cause of this event if it were to happen. The respondents rate this cause along seven-point scales corresponding to the three parameters of causal explanations explained earlier. The ratings are combined to yield an overall estimate of the optimism or pessimism of a respondent's explanatory style.[25]

The second assessment technique, termed *content analysis of verbatim explanation* (CAVE), adds great flexibility to research on explanatory style.[26] People make causal explanations all the time, and these explanations can be seen in their written or spoken communications. Using CAVE, these causal explanations are identified, rated, and explanatory style scores created.

Various studies on the concept of explanatory style have provided a detailed picture of individuals with a pessimistic explanatory style (ie, those who explain bad events with stable, global, and internal causes).[27,28] Such people tend to be depressed and anxious. Analyses of personality traits using this style can be useful to researchers and practitioners in the field of oral health because of the range of dental fears and responses to dental treatment. For example, attention to patients' explanatory styles might alert a clinician to fearful patients even before they sit in the dental chair. A pessimistic explanatory style is also associated with post-traumatic stress disorder. Persons with a pessimistic explanatory style are more apt to fare poorly in the wake of a traumatic event. Generally speaking, people with a pessimistic explanatory style cope poorly with various events. In contrast, those with an optimistic explanatory style sustain good cheer and morale and succeed in various domains: school, work, and athletics. For example, optimistic military leaders perform better than do pessimistic ones.

In a study published in 1988, Zullow and colleagues[29] analyzed the nomination acceptance speeches of US presidential candidates from 1900 through 1984. Using the CAVE technique, the candidates were designated as optimistic or pessimistic, efficacious or helpless. The more optimistic of the two candidates won 18 of the 22 elections held in this period. In another interesting study of explanatory style (unpublished data, 2000) the contents of annual reports to stockholders of Fortune 500 companies were analyzed. Although these reports vary greatly in content, most contain causal explanations for bad events that can be scored as relatively optimistic or pessimistic. After taking into account all the appropriate financial variables, companies with optimistic reports showed greater jumps in stock prices the following year than did those with pessimistic reports. The difference was substantially statistically significant; a 30% annual increase was seen in the return on investment if one took into account the optimism vs pessimism of the reports.

Morbidity and Mortality

Research has shown that compared with individuals with an optimistic explanatory style, those who have a pessimistic explanatory style are more likely to fall ill, stay ill, and die young. Evidence of this relationship between explanatory style and different indices of morbidity and mortality was shown in various studies.[30-32]

The links between explanatory style and physical well-being appear to be many and varied. Immunologic mechanisms may play a part in the explanatory style of people; pessimistic individuals show a less robust response of the immune system to an antigen challenge. Other biologic mechanisms such as testosterone and cortisol levels may also contribute. In addition, cognitive mechanisms have been recognized. For example, research shows that pessimistic college students see the world as filled with obstacles,[33] whereas optimistic students, when confronted with similar events, see them as challenges. Whether the students adopted a pessimistic or optimistic perspective predicted whether they would fall ill.

Explanatory style is closely linked to depression and anxiety, which are known risk factors for various conditions. Therefore emotional mechanisms also are involved in linking explanatory style and well-being. However, the most important mechanism might be behavioral, ie, habitual lifestyles. Pessimistic people do not live healthy lifestyles—they may not exercise, they may smoke, they may abuse alcohol, and they may not get adequate sleep. Pessimists do not believe there is any good reason to live healthily. Rather, a healthy lifestyle is a long-term investment made by those who are optimistic.

There may be social mechanisms linking explanatory style and well-being. Optimistic people are more likely to be socially engaged and have a network of friendships, and these optimistic persons are healthier. Cultural mechanisms may also be involved. Historian Leonard Sagan[34] has argued that increases in average life expectancy in the Western world did not coincide with breakthroughs in medicine or public health, but rather with changes in the cultural conception of the self. Once the self begins to be viewed as an agent, as apart from the world, and having an impact on the world, one sees huge jumps in life expectancy.

Explanatory style may also be influenced by genetics. However, there is no reason to think there is a gene that predisposes people to optimism. Rather, optimism is probably grounded in skills and abilities that are genetically determined. This means that if a person is coordinated, attractive, and intelligent, then this person is going to be more successful in life. These successes in turn are going to breed optimism.

The media frequently provide causal attributional lessons. Different television networks can cover the same story in different ways—some might underscore the horror and the chaos in the world, in effect telling people they are nothing more than potential victims. It is obvious that media coverage of trauma and failure will take a toll and affect attributional explanations made by the general public. These in turn will affect the physical well-being of the viewers.

Research shows that cognitive therapy can change someone from a pessimist to an optimist.[35] Research also shows that children can be taught different ways of construing failures and successes early in life so that they are more likely to be optimistic.[36] A study originally undertaken as a means of preventing depression in adolescents also showed that children in the intervention group did not get sick as often as did children in the control group.[37]

Conclusions

Research on explanatory style can be applied to oral health–related QOL in various ways. Dental experts should ask patients about their ownership of oral health. Who is responsible for their oral health? What determines whether one has good or bad teeth, good or bad gums? Does oral health just happen to a person or is it attributed to the clinician? External attributions may be an indication of future problems in compliance with home-care instructions and subsequent oral health.

However, it is also crucial to keep in mind that structural factors also determine QOL and well-being. A researcher cannot go to poor inner city neighborhoods where there are not enough clinicians for low-income individuals and tell people to take ownership of their health. The quality-of-life action is between the individual and what the real world affords.

References

1. Jackson B, Sellers RM, Peterson C. Pessimistic explanatory style moderates the effect of stress on physical illness. Pers Individ Dif 2002;32:567–573.
2. Watson JB. Psychology as the behaviorist views it. Psychol Rev 1913;20:158–177.
3. Seligman MEP, Csikszentmihalyi M. Positive psychology: An introduction. Am Psychol 2000;55:5–14.
4. Seligman MEP. Why is there so much depression today? The waxing of the individual and the waning of the commons. In: Ingram R (ed). Contemporary Psychological Approaches to Depression. New York: Plenum, 1990.
5. Ryff CD. Happiness is everything, or is it? Explorations of the meaning of psychologic well-being. J Pers Soc Psychol 1989;57:1069–1081.
6. Ryff CD. Psychologic well-being in adult life. Curr Dir Psychol Sci 1995;4:99–104.
7. Ryff CD, Singer B. The contours of positive mental health. Psychol Inquiry 1998;9:1–28.
8. Jahoda M. Current Concepts of Positive Mental Health. New York: Basic Books, 1958.
9. Maslow AH. Motivation and Personality, ed 2. New York: Harper & Row, 1970.
10. Peterson C, Seligman MEP. The VIA classification of strengths and virtues. Available at: http://psych.upenn.edu/seligman/taxonomy.htm. Accessed February 18, 2001.
11. Helgeson VS. Relation of agency and communion to well-being: Evidence and potential explanations. Psychol Bull 1994;116:412–428.
12. Myers DG. The Pursuit of Happiness. New York: Avon Books, 1993.
13. Myers DG, Diener E. Who is happy? Psychol Sci 1995;6:10–19.
14. Csikszentmihalyi M. Flow: The Psychology of Optimal Experience. New York: Harper & Row, 1990.
15. Kahneman D, Diener E, Schwarz N (eds). Well-Being: The Foundations of Hedonic Psychology. New York: Russell Sage, 1999.
16. Neisser U. Cognitive Psychology. Englewood Cliffs, NJ: Prentice-Hall, 1967.
17. Gardner H. The Mind's New Science: A History of the Cognitive Revolution. New York: Basic Books, 1985.
18. Fredrickson BL. What good are positive emotions? Rev Gen Psychol 1998;2:300–319.
19. Seligman MEP. Authentic Happiness. New York: Free Press (in press).
20. Kaplan GA, Camacho T. Perceived health and mortality: A nine-year follow-up of the human population laboratory cohort. Am J Epidemiol 1983;11:292–304.
21. Peterson C, Seligman MEP, Vaillant GE. Pessimistic explanatory style is a risk factor for physical illness: A thirty-five year longitudinal study. J Pers Soc Psychol 1988;55:23–27.
22. Spiegel D, Bloom JR, Kraemer H, Gottheil E. Effect of psychosocial treatment on survival of patients with metastatic breast cancer. Lancet 1989;109:888–891.
23. Peterson C, Seligman MEP. Causal explanations as a risk factor for depression: Theory and evidence. Psychol Rev 1984;91:347–374.
24. Peterson C. Personal control and well-being. In: Kahneman D, Diener E, Schwarz N (eds). Well-Being: The Foundations of Hedonic Psychology. New York: Russell Sage, 1999:288–301.
25. Peterson C, Semmel A, von Baeyer C, Abramson LY, Metalsky GI, Seligman MEP. The attributional style questionnaire. Cogn Ther Res 1982;6:287–299.
26. Peterson C, Schulman P, Castellon C, Seligman MEP. CAVE: Content analysis of verbatim explanations. In: Smith CP (ed). Motivation and Personality: Handbook of Thematic Content Analysis. New York: Cambridge Univ Press, 1992:383–392.
27. Buchanan GA, Seligman MEP (eds). Explanatory Style. Hillsdale, NJ: Erlbaum, 1995.
28. Peterson C, Maier SF, Seligman MEP. Learned Helplessness: A Theory for the Age of Personal Control. New York: Oxford Univ Press, 1993.
29. Zullow H, Oettingen G, Peterson C, Seligman MEP. Explanatory style and pessimism in the historical record: CAVing LBJ, presidential candidates, and East versus West Berlin. Am Psychol 1988;43:673–682.
30. Peterson C, Bossio LM. Health and Optimism. New York: Free Press, 1991.
31. Peterson C, Bossio LM. Healthy attitudes: Optimism, hope, and control. In: Goleman D, Gurin J (eds). Mind/Body Medicine: How to Use your Mind for Better Health. Yonkers, NY: Consumer Reports Books, 1993:351–366.
32. Peterson C, Bossio LM. Optimism and physical well-being. In: Chang EC (ed). Optimism and Pessimism: Implications for Theory, Research, and Practice. Washington, DC: American Psychologic Association, 2001:127–145.
33. Dykema K, Bergbower K, Peterson C. Pessimistic explanatory style, stress, and illness. J Soc Clin Psychol 1995;14:357–371.
34. Sagan LA. The Health of Nations: True Causes of Sickness and Well-Being. New York: Basic Books, 1987.
35. Seligman MEP, Castellon C, Cacciola J, et al. Explanatory style change during cognitive therapy for unipolar depression. J Abnormal Psychol 1988;97:13–18.
36. Gillham JE, Reivich KJ, Jaycox LH, Seligman MEP. Prevention of depressive symptoms in schoolchildren: Two-year follow-up. Psychol Sci 1995;6:343–351.
37. Buchanan GM, Gardenswartz CAR, Seligman MEP. Physical health following a cognitive-behavioral intervention: Prevention and treatment. Available at: http://journals.apa.org/prevention/volume2/. Accessed December 21, 1999.

Tooth Loss, Dental Caries, and Quality of Life: A Public Health Perspective

Stephen A. Eklund, DDS, DrPH

Brian A. Burt, BDS, MPH, PhD

Quality of life (QOL) is fundamental to the concept of public health; however, the connection is implicit rather than explicit. Data on QOL measures still are not commonly collected by public health practitioners for research or program administration. Moreover, there are few direct measures of QOL related to oral health at the population level, despite the well-recognized fact that when oral health is good, QOL is good. Indeed, the philosophy encompassed by this self-evident truth provides the rationale for most dental care. The research presented in this chapter shows that the oral health of the American public continues to improve. Based on the assumption that public health and QOL are inextricably woven together, the QOL of the American public must also be improving. Additional data show that the relationship between QOL and oral health can be subtle, and may pose some difficulty in making decisions about the allocation of resources.

The link between QOL and public health has been implicitly recognized for many years. This is evident from the well-known definition of health given by the World Health Organization (WHO) in 1946. In the postwar optimism of its institutional youth, WHO defined health as "a state of complete physical, mental, and social well-being, and not merely the absence of disease."[1] While this definition is more idealistic than practical, it does include QOL within the broader definition of health. This WHO definition shows that more than 50 years ago people were well aware of the importance of well-being not just in physical terms, but also in its mental, social, and, by implication, spiritual dimensions. These concepts of QOL dimensions have existed for a long time, even if not explicitly quantified and measured.

What Is QOL?

It is not easy to define QOL, especially oral health–related QOL. Although one may intuitively know what it means, its abstract nature makes a clear definition elusive.[2] It is multi-dimensional, involving both clinical measures as well as subjective responses to those measures. Pain and discomfort from oral diseases, or their sequelae, can be more intrusive and preoccupying than pain elsewhere in the body because the oral cavity is central to so many everyday functions. Freedom from oral pain and discomfort is likely to be associated with a nutritionally adequate and satisfying diet; choosing foods primarily because they do not provoke oral discomfort is incompatible with good nutrition. Moreover, because of the central role played by the mouth in interpersonal relationships, an individual's positive or negative self-image and all of the ramifications associated with that self-image are also inextricably bound with oral health.

What Is Public Health?

Public health is also hard to define clearly. An early definition that became broadly adopted says that "public health is the science and art of preventing disease, prolonging life, promoting physical health and efficiency through organized community efforts."[3] Clearly, at least three aspects of that definition can be included in QOL: preventing disease, prolonging life, and promoting physical health. "Organized community efforts" is the key phrase that distinguishes public health from other individual forms of health care. It implies that the primary focus in public health is on populations, on the functioning of people in groups, rather than on the individual patient (although such care is not excluded from public health considerations). This approach raises some interesting issues in the analysis of whether certain interventions or specific treatment procedures make sense at the community level. This approach involves cost-benefit/cost-effectiveness analyses, which use economic assessment techniques to judge whether a procedure that improves the QOL for one person needs to be balanced by the cost to the community. The results of these analyses can raise difficult but important trade-off questions.

This issue is discussed in more detail later in the chapter.

An influential report from the Institute of Medicine in the late 1980s defined public health's mission as "fulfilling society's interest in assuring conditions in which people can be healthy."[4] This elegant mission statement may not go far enough for some who would like to see a more active government role in health care. This statement of the public health mission, however, is well-crafted and acceptable to virtually all segments of our diverse society. In the same report, the Institute of Medicine described the three primary core functions of public health to be assessment, policy development, and assurance.[4] The Institute saw these functions as the responsibility of public health authorities at all levels of government, and it argued that these three functions must be fulfilled if public health were to function properly.

Assessment means that government has a responsibility to have in place some mechanism(s) to determine the state of the human condition and to monitor trends in disease and its treatment and prevention. This function relates to the collection of data (vital statistics, surveillance, surveys of needs, disease registries, special studies as needed) necessary for setting policies.

Policy development, the second core function of public health, should be based on data, but it must also encompass social, political, economic, and cultural dimensions. There is a great deal of flexibility as to how policy may be instituted, even when working with the same set of assessment data. Public health policies and programs in the United States are too often perceived as being nothing more than government-funded care programs for the poor; this, however, is just one policy pathway. The real policy decisions come from society as a whole, from what it wants or what it sees as the right way to discharge policy responsibilities. Looking around the world, one can see many different ways that governments choose to deal with public health activities. Some countries use private-sector programs, some implement government-funded programs, and others use a mix of both.

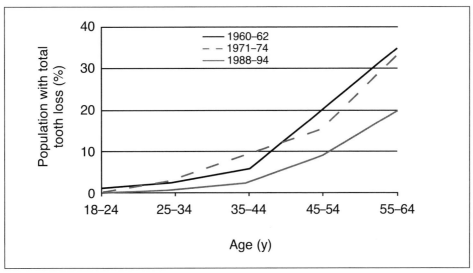

Fig 7-1 Edentulism, by age, in the United States in three national surveys. Data from US Public Health Service[5,6] and US Department of Health and Human Services.[7]

The third core function in public health is assurance. This means that public health agencies have the responsibility to ensure that services necessary to meet agreed-upon goals are provided. These services may come from the public or private sectors, whichever is most appropriate for the community, but the ultimate authority for assuring that care services are available rests with the public health agencies.

Fewer decayed teeth, less malocclusion, and reduced periodontitis and gingivitis will result in a better QOL than their alternative outcomes. When the water in a community is fluoridated, for example, it is fully assumed that QOL will improve consequently. In fact, the outcomes of such a program are frequently expressed to the lay community in QOL terms (eg, better smiles), although dentists may measure success in other terms (eg, scores of decayed, missing, and filled [DMF] teeth, which provides an index of cumulative caries experience). As the following data show, oral health has improved in the United States in the recent decades, resulting in an improved QOL.

Improved Oral Health in Adults

Total tooth loss (edentulism) is the ultimate dental failure. Although population-wide reductions in edentulism are taking place, it can take a few years to become evident because people who had lost all their teeth 30 years ago continue to affect the prevalence figures. Figure 7-1 shows that between 1960 to 1962, when the first national data were collected, and 1971 to 1974, not much seemed to have changed.[5] However, in the third National Health and Nutrition Examination Survey (NHANES III) of 1988 to 1994, clear-cut and substantial changes became evident.[6,7] Although these data do not directly measure incidence, one can infer that the incidence of edentulism is diminishing. It is likely that a great proportion of this change is attributable to a major shift in expectations that has occurred since widespread fluoride exposure became the norm. Today people do not expect to lose teeth as they grow older.

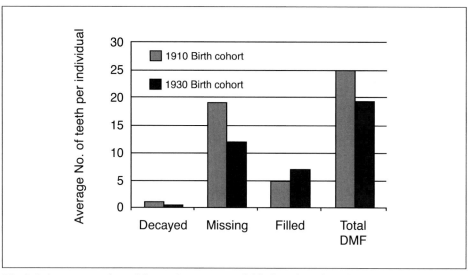

Fig 7-2 Average number of decayed, missing, and filled teeth and total DMF per individual in two cohorts of 60-year-old Americans, one cohort born in 1910, the second in 1930. Data from US Public Health Service.[5,6]

It is often instructive to compare oral health data from people in different birth cohorts. Figure 7-2 shows the average number of teeth affected by caries per individual for people born in 1910 and for those born in 1930. Both sets of data reflect oral conditions when the cohort was 60 years old, so the data from the 1910 cohort dates from 1970 and that from the 1930 birth cohort dates from 1990.[5,6] The figure shows the number of decayed, missing, and filled teeth separately as well as the total DMF score. The most apparent finding is the high numbers of missing teeth; the average 60-year-old in 1970 had approximately 18 missing teeth. Much of this tooth loss, although recorded in 1970, had happened in the 1920s and 1930s, when there existed only a rudimentary understanding of oral diseases and limited treatment options; dental caries and periodontal diseases therefore had resulted in tooth extractions. Examined together, the data from the different birth cohorts show the profound changes that occurred in the 20-year period between the births of the two groups, most notably in the area of tooth loss.

Figure 7-3 shows total tooth loss in these two cohorts. More than one third of the 60-year-olds in 1970 had no teeth at all. For the 1930 birth cohort, the prevalence of edentulism was 20% at age 60 years.[5,6] It is crucial to note that the patterns seen today and in succeeding birth cohorts are very much affected by what these people experienced when they were younger as well as the circumstances under which they grew up. The clinical outcomes are a combined effect of disease levels, peoples' expectations of the health care system, and what this health care system was able to offer. As mentioned earlier, all of this occurred at a time when diseases were poorly understood and treatment options were limited.

Figure 7-4 shows DMF scores for 40-year-old individuals born in 1920, 1930, and 1950.[5,6,8] There is little difference between the 1920 and 1930 cohorts, although a large number of teeth are affected. Substantial changes are evident in the 1950 birth cohort. In particular, the mean number of missing teeth dropped dramatically in individuals born in 1950, and it is also clear that

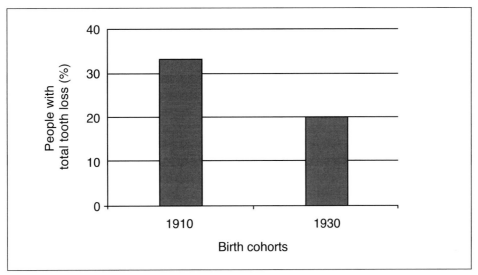

Fig 7-3 Edentulism in two cohorts of 60-year-old Americans, one cohort born in 1910, the second in 1930. Data from US Public Health Service.[5,6]

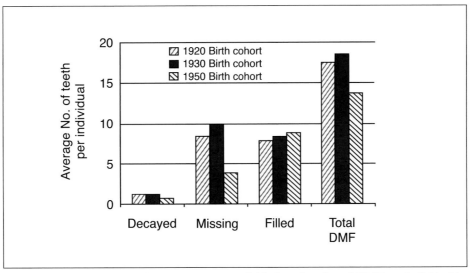

Fig 7-4 Average number of decayed, missing, and filled teeth and total DMF per individual in three cohorts of 40-year-old Americans, one cohort born in 1920, the second in 1930, and the third in 1950. Data from US Public Health Service.[5,6,8]

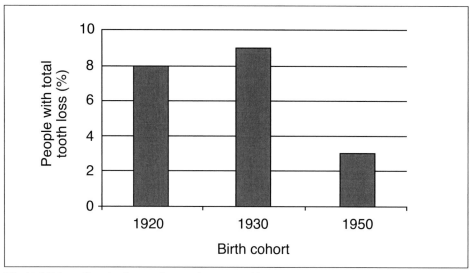

Fig 7-5 Edentulism in three cohorts of 40-year-old Americans, one cohort born in 1920, the second in 1930, and the third in 1950. Data from US Public Health Service.[5,6,8]

fewer teeth in general were affected by caries. The effect of the modern caries prevention approach can be seen in this cohort. When the total tooth loss among persons born in 1920, 1930, and 1950 is analyzed, again profound changes can be seen (Fig 7-5).[5,6,8] Nearly 10% of individuals in the 1920 and 1930 cohorts were edentulous by age 40. In the 1950 birth cohort, this figure was down to 3%, and almost certainly would be even lower today.

These data show that the challenge in dealing with oral health–related QOL issues relates mostly to disease and treatment experience early in life. The data show that these experiences have changed substantially in recent decades. In particular, it is interesting to note how these changes affect children.

Changes in Oral Health Among Children

Improvements in oral health are much more apparent in comparisons of child cohorts than in similar comparisons among adults. Figure 7-6

shows a tenfold improvement in tooth retention among children in the mid-1980s compared with children in the early 1970s.[9–11] Permanent tooth loss due to dental caries in US children is becoming an increasingly rare phenomenon. In fact, extrapolating from the most recent national surveys,[10,11] the average clinician performs approximately one extraction in a given year, excluding the extraction of third molars or that of premolars for orthodontic treatment. Figure 7-7 shows the reduction in DMF scores among children over a generation.[6,9–11] Many of these extraordinary changes can be attributed to widespread fluoride exposure. These changes include fewer teeth affected by caries, a slower progression of caries in the affected teeth, and fewer extracted teeth as a result of a general understanding among both dental practitioners and the public that tooth extraction often is not the best treatment option.

A cohort of adolescents aged 16 years was studied using a similar approach to that used for adults. Data for the 1930 birth cohort were taken from samples from Grand Rapids and Muskegon, MI, which were examined for community water fluoridation beginning in 1945–46.[12] Figure 7-8

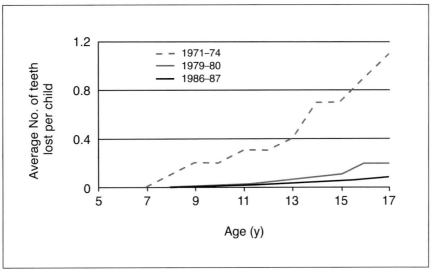

Fig 7-6 Loss of permanent teeth among US children aged 5 to 17 years in three national surveys. Data from US Public Health Service.[9–11]

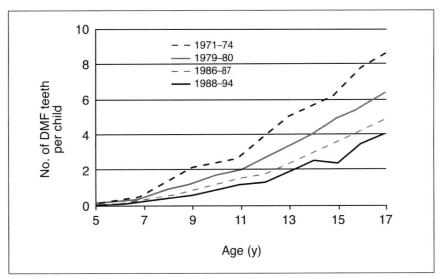

Fig 7-7 DMF scores among US children aged 5 to 17 years, in four national surveys. Data from US Public Health Service.[6,9–11]

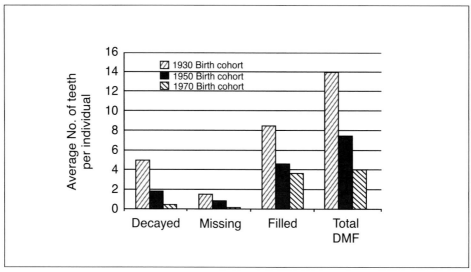

Fig 7-8 Average number of decayed, missing, and filled teeth and total DMF per individual in three cohorts of 16-year-old Americans. Data from US Public Health Service[11,12] and Dean et al.[13]

compares data from the 1930, 1950, and 1970 birth cohorts at age 16 years. The 1930 birth cohort showed an average of almost two missing teeth per child by age 16 years. In the 1950 cohort, the total number of teeth affected at age 16 years was cut approximately in half. Profound changes can also be seen in the 1970 birth cohort.[11–13]

Traditional Measures of Oral Health: Do They Still Work?

Health care professionals implicitly assume that what they do in health care, and certainly in public health, serves to improve QOL. There are certain outcomes that one would intuitively believe to lead to a better QOL. An example would be the retention of a complete dentition throughout life, or at least the minimization of tooth loss during a lifetime. However, like any firm cause-effect statement on health, this one is also unlikely to be universally true. There are some people who have suffered grievously from caries-induced toothaches, and whose lifetime dental

history is made up of constant pain from diseased teeth and oral infections. These patients can reasonably say that they would feel better and therefore have improved QOL if these teeth were not there. However, this degree of ravaged dentition from caries is becoming rare, and will become even rarer in the future. For the most part, our intuitive belief that greater tooth retention equals superior QOL is likely to be justified. At the same time, there are other measures that traditionally have been assumed to lead to a better QOL but need to be re-evaluated because of changing disease patterns.

Volume of Dental Visits

One measure requiring re-evaluation is the volume of annual dental visits. This indicator has historically been used to measure the performance of a dental care system, with a higher volume of visits assumed to reflect better QOL. The proportion of the population that makes an annual dental visit has been used as a standard National Health Interview Survey measure by the National Center for Health Statistics for several decades now. It is generally accepted that an in-

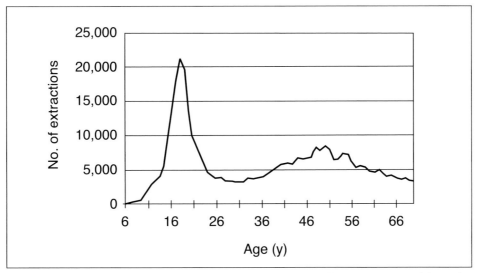

Fig 7-9 Total number of permanent tooth extractions by age for persons insured by Delta Dental Plan of Michigan, 1997.[14]

creasing percentage is a sign of improvement in people's health-related behavior. It is even currently the sole dental measure in the Healthplan Employer Data and Information Set (HEDIS). These measures are provided by the National Commission on Quality Assurance (NCQA) for rating managed care plans. The intent is to provide consumers with information to use when choosing health care plans. The NCQA is implicitly saying that an annual dental visit is a measure of better quality care provided by the managed care plan, which translates into better QOL.

However, whether the volume of annual dental visits is an accurate measure of oral health is questionable. In these days of increasingly polarized oral disease patterns, clinicians are realizing that patients with little disease activity and few risk factors for disease do not need to come in for a recall visit every 12 months. Although it is not yet a widespread pattern, some patients are being scheduled for recall at intervals longer than 12 months. Therefore, a higher frequency of recall may begin to indicate more disease activity rather than a healthier patient population, rendering inaccurate a measure that historically reflected better oral health.

Third Molar Extractions

The dental care patterns among the insured adolescent population of the United States suggest that many clinicians view the retention of third molars negatively, regardless of the presence of symptoms. As a consequence, extraction of third molars is considered an indicator of a healthier population that will consequently enjoy a better QOL. This is another issue that must be revisited.

Figure 7-9 shows 1997 data from Delta Dental Plan of Michigan.[14] The data are simple and descriptive, showing the number of permanent tooth extractions performed on patients aged 6 to 71 years that were paid for by an insurance carrier. There is an obvious spike in the curve around ages 18 to 25 years, which is the peak time for extracting third molars. Figure 7-10 illustrates the third molar issue more clearly by showing 1997 insurance claims data for tooth extractions by tooth type.[14] It is apparent that extractions of third molars (tooth numbers 1, 16, 17, and 32) dominate. In this sample of two million people of all ages, only slightly less than 50% of all extractions were performed on third molars.[14]

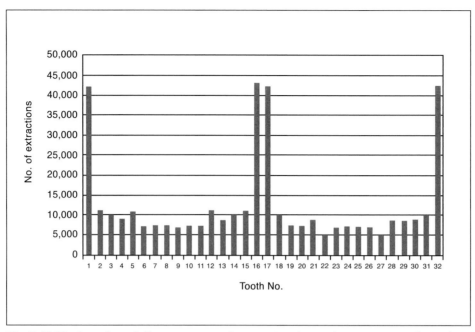

Fig 7-10 Total number of all permanent tooth extractions by tooth type (FDI tooth numbering system), for persons insured by Delta Dental Plan of Michigan, 1997.[14]

It is obvious from the data that, in spite of the fact that tooth loss due to caries in young people has decreased, third molar extractions continue to be prevalent. Additional analyses of data from approximately 200,000 young people aged 16 to 21 years would suggest that all of these teeth are not diseased, nor are they all causing symptoms.[14] If all these teeth were causing symptoms, one would expect a random distribution of the extractions by day of week and month of year. However, the analyses show that Friday is the most preferred day of the week for third molar extractions.[14] This has the look of careful planning, so that the young patient has the weekend to recover from this sometimes traumatic procedure before going back to school on Monday. When the months of the year were considered, the absence of a random pattern was again obvious. The preferred times of year for third molar extractions are July, August, and December.[14]

These data show that a large number of third molars are systematically extracted from young

people, and that it is most likely that these extractions are planned well in advance rather than as a response to acute symptoms.[15] Therefore, these extractions may not have a significant impact on oral health. In addition, Figs 7-11 and 7-12 show the percentage of all third molar extractions that are reimbursed as full or partial bony extractions versus simple erupted or soft tissue extractions. The full bony extractions presumably carry a higher fee, which is paid for by the insurance carrier, not the patient. It is apparent that even over the small increase in patient age from 15 to 20 years, the proportion of maxillary third molars that are full bony extractions drops sharply. At age 20 years, the proportion of simpler extractions reaches 50%, and it increases rapidly from there with advancing age. Not surprisingly, the progression is slower for mandibular extractions because they take longer to erupt (see Fig 7-12), and the crossover occurs around age 30 years.[14] These data show that waiting until a patient is 20 years

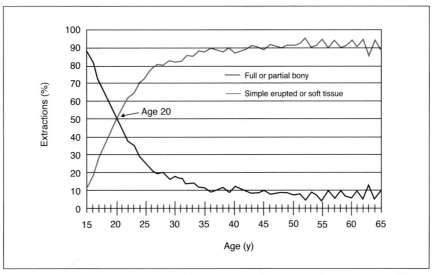

Fig 7-11 Proportion of maxillary third molar extractions claimed as full or partial bony extractions versus simple erupted or soft tissue extractions, by age, for persons insured by Delta Dental Plan of Michigan, 1997.[14]

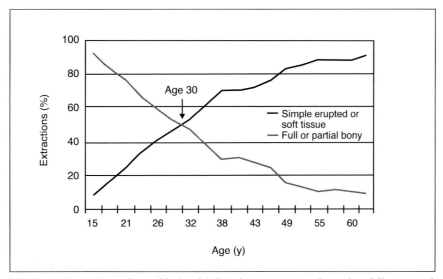

Fig 7-12 Proportion of mandibular third molar extractions claimed as full or partial bony extractions versus simple erupted or soft tissue extractions, by age, for persons insured by Delta Dental Plan of Michigan, 1997.[14]

or older to extract third molars will have a substantial effect on the total cost of the procedure as well as the trauma sustained by the patient, both of which are QOL issues. Therefore, the age of the patient at the time of extraction, as well as the type of extraction, should also be considered if third molar extraction rates are to be accurate measures of QOL.

Professionally Applied Topical Fluoride

Another example of a traditional QOL indicator that may be questionable today is the professionally applied topical fluoride measure. The tremendous decline in caries prevalence in the economically developed world is so clearly attributable to fluoride that it is easy to assume that if a little fluoride is good, more is better. However, data from children who are beneficiaries of dental insurance programs in the United States population fail to demonstrate the link between high frequency of professionally applied topical fluoride and reduced levels of caries.[15] This finding results from the interrelated factors of (1) regular exposure to fluoride from a number of sources, notably drinking water and toothpaste, in addition to the professional applications and (2) the low level of caries activity in the population under study. Given these facts, it seems unlikely that high rates of regular professional application of topical fluoride would correlate with reduced decay and a related improvement in QOL, especially when one considers the large proportion of insured children who receive such treatments and the small proportion of these that are prone to caries.

Quantifiable Comparison of QOL Among Individuals

An issue that has been underexplored is the quantifiable comparison of QOL among individuals. This involves trade-off calculations among alternative policies, with a determination being made about whether one approach leads to a greater QOL improvement than would another. In the long term, it is not enough to determine whether the QOL of an individual can be improved by a particular procedure. One must also assess whether alternative uses of the same amount of money would further improve QOL, not only for that one individual, but for society at large.

Determining Need for Preventive Procedures: Rate of Caries Progression in Children

Figure 7-13 illustrates how the rate of caries progression in children has slowed over the years. The results of a landmark study[16] on the rate of caries progression in children in a nonfluoridated community (Kingston, NY) who were followed longitudinally from 1944 to 1960 showed that about a third of the occlusal surfaces in permanent first molars had become decayed or filled within a year of eruption (Fig 7-13). This rate of caries progression is staggering in comparison with current rates. This study stated that if a tooth is going to become decayed, it does so within 3 or 4 years after eruption—a statement that was held to be true until recently. The study showed that over 10% of the premolars, other than the mandibular first premolar, became decayed or filled within a year of eruption. For the mandibular first premolar, the rate was a little under 5%.[16] The remaining information in Fig 7-13 is derived from national surveys from the early 1970s to the mid-1990s, and requires some extrapolation from cross-sectional data.[6,9–11] However, these estimates are reasonable enough to show the magnitude of the change that has taken place since the 1944 to 1960 data were collected. The probability that a given sound occlusal surface is going to be decayed or filled within a year of eruption has decreased from 35% for the permanent first molars to approximately 5%. Evidence from insurance data indicates that the rate continues to decline even further.

The implications of this change are profound, especially for preventive procedures such as sealants. Approximately four million children

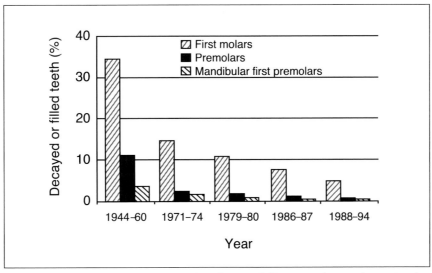

Fig 7-13 Percentage of sound occlusal surfaces in different tooth types becoming decayed or filled within 1 year of eruption. Trends from five different data sets between 1944 and 1994 are shown. Data from US Public Health Service[6,9–11] and Carlos and Gittelsohn.[16]

are born every year in the United States. As these children grow up, about 32 million molars erupt in any given year. If all of these molars were sealed at $25 a tooth, $800 million would be spent in a given year just for this procedure. Based on data from insurance claims today, without sealants approximately 4% to 5% of those teeth would be decayed in any given year. The alternative to sealing them all is therefore to place restorations at a total cost of $64 million per year, assuming $50 per decayed tooth for the restorations. This means that during the course of a year, for every dollar that would be spent on sealants, only $0.08 would be spent on restorations, and these savings would accumulate over time. The difference is even larger if premolars are included, because the rate at which these teeth become decayed is much lower than it is for molars. Therefore, universal sealing would be a highly expensive undertaking, and the expense would be unlikely to result in lower caries levels.

This example shows that many beneficial preventive procedures, including those that

have been repeatedly demonstrated to be effective, may not be justified in all cases. Therefore, to gauge true improvement in QOL, one has to evaluate not only the efficacy of the procedure in regards to health, but also whether it is more beneficial than an alternative that might be more cost-effective or otherwise have a greater positive effect on other areas of QOL.

Determining What Should Be Covered by Dental Insurance

Although it is commonly thought that the insurance carrier pays for dental care, the insurance carrier merely administers the reimbursement procedures. The group who collectively pays the premium must decide if it is willing to pay the extra premium to cover a particular procedure for those who chose to get it. If a purchasing group wants orthodontics, crowns, fixed partial dentures, and sealants for children, all of this is reflected in the premium that is set for the group. If the issue relates to a government-funded program (eg, whether prescription drugs should be covered under Medicare), then society as a whole, through its elected representatives, has to make the decision.

One way to confront the health care issue of what should or should not be covered by insurance is to ask patients if they would be willing to pay for a procedure out of their own pockets. Another interesting experiment would be to give people the choice of either having a dental procedure paid for by insurance or receiving the cash equivalent of the fee to spend in any way they choose. It is likely that some people would prefer to take the money for certain procedures and buy something else. Therefore, it can be concluded that such procedures are not worth much to the patient. As purchasers of insurance and as a society, our real concerns must be the efficient use of money in health care. It is possible that some of the dollars spent on health care could produce a greater improvement in QOL if spent some other way.

Conclusions

Public health and QOL are inextricably bound together. Better oral health does lead to better QOL; when oral health is evaluated using basic measures such as tooth retention or the severity of caries, the connection seems obvious. However, the issue becomes complicated when making decisions on how to best direct resources toward improving the oral health, and therefore the QOL, of the population.

References

1. World Health Organization. Constitution of the World Health Organization. Geneva: World Health Organization, 1946:3.
2. Locker D. Concepts of oral health, disease and the quality of life. In: Slade GD (ed). Measuring Oral Health and Quality of Life. Chapel Hill: University of North Carolina, 1997.
3. Winslow CEA. The untilled fields of public health. Mod Med 1920;2:183–191.
4. Institute of Medicine. The Future of Public Health. Washington DC: National Academy Press, 1988.
5. US Public Health Service, National Center for Health Statistics. Edentulous Persons, United States 1971. DHEW Publication No (HRA) 74-1516, Series 10, No. 89. Government Printing Office, 1974.
6. US Public Health Service, National Center for Health Statistics. Use of Dental Services and Dental Health, United States, 1986. DHHS Publication (PHS) 88-1593, Series 10, No. 165. Government Printing Office, 1988.
7. US Department of Health and Human Services, National Center for Health Statistics. Third National Health and Nutrition Examination Survey, 1988-94. Public use data file 7-0627. Government Printing Office, 1997.
8. US Public Health Service, National Center for Health Statistics. Decayed, Missing, and Filled Teeth in Adults, United States, 1960-62. PHS Publication 1000, Series 11, No. 23. Government Printing Office, 1967.
9. US Public Health Service, National Center for Health Statistics. Decayed, Missing, and Filled Teeth Among Persons Aged 1-74, United States 1971-74. DHHS Publication (PHS) 81-1678, Series 11, No. 223. Government Printing Office, 1981.
10. US Public Health Service, National Institute of Dental Research. The Prevalence of Dental Caries in United States Children, 1979-80. NIH Publication 82-2245. Government Printing Office, 1981.
11. US Public Health Service, National Institute of Dental Research. Oral Health of United States Children. NIH Publication 89-2247. Government Printing Office, 1989.
12. US Public Health Service, National Center for Health Statistics. Decayed, Missing, and Filled Teeth Among Youths 12-17 years, United States. DHEW Publication (HRA) 75-1626, Series 11, No. 144. Government Printing Office, 1974.
13. Dean HT, Arnold FA, Jay P, Knutson JW. Studies on mass control of dental caries through fluoridation of the public water supply. Public Health Rep 1950; 65:1403–1408.
14. Eklund SA, Pittman JL. Third-molar removal patterns in an insured population. J Am Dent Assoc 2001;132: 469–475.
15. Eklund SA, Pittman JL, Heller KE. Professionally applied topical fluoride and restorative care in insured children. J Public Health Dent 2000;60:33–38.
16. Carlos JP, Gittelsohn AM. Longitudinal studies of the natural history of caries, II: A life-table study of caries incidence in the permanent teeth. Arch Oral Biol 1965;10:739–751.

Oral Health and Quality of Life in Children

Marita Rohr Inglehart, Dr phil habil

Sara L. Filstrup, DDS, MS

Angela Wandera, BDS, MS

In June 2000, the Surgeon General of the United States held a conference entitled "The Face of the Child: Children and Oral Health."[1] The goals of this conference were to highlight the findings of the Surgeon General's report on oral health,[2] increase awareness of the significance of oral health issues for children's lives, engage the child health and welfare community and the public in a discussion of these issues, and promote partnerships and community collaborations to eliminate disparities in children's oral health and access to care.[1] More than 700 participants from approximately 80 collaborating agencies, organizations, and academic institutions attended the conference. Their backgrounds were in such various fields as dentistry, medicine/pediatrics, nursing, education, law, ethics, and history. They represented the government, research institutions, parent and advocacy groups, and the private sector. This conference and the March 2000 workshop that paved the way for it were true turning points in oral health issues for US children. The main findings

of the conference clearly and unequivocally point out that children's oral health is important to their overall health and well-being, and that dental and oral disease and disorders can have a profound impact on the quality of children's lives. This chapter on oral health–related quality of life (OHRQOL) in children provides clinicians with a framework for understanding the significance of these issues.

Children and Health-Related Quality of Life

Pediatric patients differ from most adult patients in at least two significant ways. First, they do not necessarily self-regulate their behavior concerning health promotion and health care. A toddler does not make the decision to wear warm clothes when it is cold, eat a well-balanced diet, and seek care for health problems. It is the primary caregiver's responsibility to take care of these needs. Simply assessing a child's quality of life (QOL) is therefore not sufficient to ultimately get children the health care they need to achieve a positive QOL; it is also important to consider the child's caregiver when discussing health-related quality of life (HRQOL) issues. Although a health care provider may be able to assess a child's QOL, it is the caregiver who ultimately needs to understand how to prevent health problems, how to educate the child about these facts, and how to assess if there is a problem that needs attention. The second major difference between children and adult patients is the qualitative difference between children's and adults' perceptions and assumptions about the world and their experiences. For example, when a 3-year-old child plays hide-and-seek, she might just lie down in plain sight of the child who is the seeker and cover her eyes. Based on this child's egocentric view of the world, this behavior is absolutely sensible and appropriate. The child believes that if she cannot see the seeker, the seeker will not be able to see her. This is a simple example of how children's assumptions about the world and their behavior differ from those of adults. Communicating with children about their health, their health care, and their HRQOL therefore has to be uniquely tailored toward the child's developmental stage.

Given these challenges associated with interacting with pediatric patients, it is not surprising that research on children's HRQOL has a short history. Before 1990, researchers largely focused on indicators of mortality and morbidity when they assessed children's health status and the outcomes of treatments,[3,4] despite excellent work in the 1970s that discussed the importance of assessing children's health more comprehensively.[5,6] The first measurement instrument proposed for use in population-based studies was published in 1979,[7] and methodological and conceptual challenges were identified and discussed in the 1980s.[8] Despite these efforts, research on children's HRQOL was struggling. Some researchers used instruments developed for adults when studying children[9]; others globally compared the QOL of children with different health problems with that of healthy children.[10,11]

This situation began to change in 1990 when the Child Health Questionnaire (CHQ) was published.[12] The CHQ considers 14 dimensions of health that range from physical functioning and bodily pain to self-esteem and mental health. Currently there is one version that is completed by the child, and three versions of various lengths (98, 50, and 28 items) that are completed by the parents or primary caregivers. A large body of methodological studies has shown the reliability and validity of this scale.[12] Moreover, it can serve as an excellent model of how a similar instrument could be conceptualized and developed in the oral health sciences. It offers a way to assess the perceptions of the child and the family about the child's HRQOL, and it takes into account the multidimensionality of this concept.

Given the fact that instruments to assess children's HRQOL exist, the increase in the volume of published research on this topic during the past decade is not surprising. Most of this research is directed at measuring the QOL of children with specific diseases such as asthma,[13] seizure disorders,[14] chronic headaches,[15] cancer[16] and its treatment,[17] or sleep disorders.[18] A search for ongoing research projects with the National Institutes of Health Computer Retrieval of Information on Scientific Projects (CRISP) conducted between May 1 and May 5 of the year 2000 resulted in 183 hits for the query "quality/life/children." This indicates that the amount of ongoing research concerned with children's HRQOL is quite impressive. However, *oral* health–related QOL research is only now starting to develop, despite the significance of oral diseases in children's lives.

Children and Oral Health–Related Quality of Life

Caries is the single most common chronic childhood disease.[2,19–21] Dental caries in children is 5

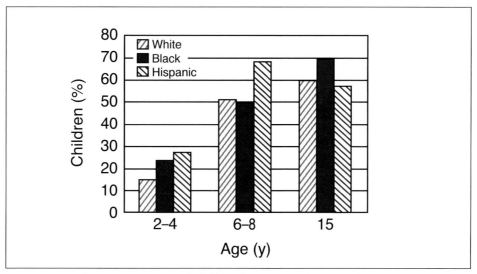

Fig 8-1 Dental caries experience of children by age and ethnic/racial background. Baseline data are from the 1988–94 data set from the third National Health and Nutritional Examination Survey.[20]

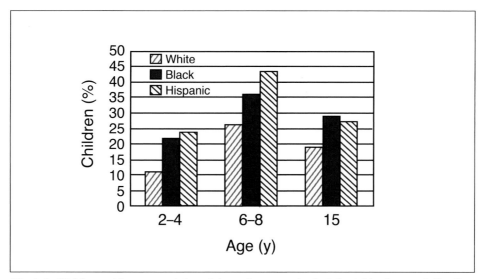

Fig 8-2 Children with untreated dental decay by age and ethnic/racial background. Baseline data are from the 1988–94 data set from the third National Health and Nutritional Examination Survey.[20]

times more common than hay fever and 14 times more common than chronic bronchitis.[2,19] On average, it affects 18% of young children between 2 and 4 years of age, 52% of children between 6 and 8 years of age, and 61% of adoles-cents by the age of 15 years. As shown in Fig 8-1, these percentages vary by ethnicity and race. The percentage of children with untreated dental decay is substantial (Fig 8-2), and preventive measures such as applying dental sealants

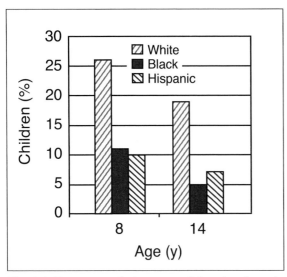

Fig 8-3 Frequency of placement of dental sealants in children by age and racial/ethnic background. Baseline data are from the 1988–94 data set from the third National Health and Nutritional Examination Survey.[20]

are still largely underutilized (Fig 8-3). As shown in Figs 8-2 and 8-3, these figures also differ significantly among different racial/ethnic groups.

If caries occurs before a child is 72 months old, it is referred to as early childhood caries (ECC). This relatively new term encompasses all dental caries occurring in the primary dentition of young children.[21] In the past, this pattern was referred to as labial caries, caries of incisors, rampant caries, nursing bottle caries, and baby bottle tooth decay.[22] Lack of agreement on definitions and diagnostic criteria for ECC most likely hindered efforts to combat it in the past.[23] However, this situation changed in April 1999 when the National Institute of Dental and Craniofacial Research, the Health Resources and Services Administration, and the Health Care Financing Administration sponsored a workshop on ECC. The participants of this workshop reviewed the methods used to diagnose dental

caries in the primary teeth and proposed case definitions and diagnostic criteria for future research projects regarding dental caries in preschool-aged children.[24] The term ECC is defined as the presence of one or more decayed (noncavitated or cavitated lesions), missing (owing to caries), or filled surfaces in any primary tooth. Figure 8-4 shows a child's healthy dentition; Fig 8-5 shows moderate ECC.

The term *severe* ECC refers to atypical, progressive, acute, rampant, or virulent patterns of decay. Severe ECC results in devastating tooth destruction (Figs 8-6 and 8-7). Patients with severe ECC typically first present to the dentist between the ages of 15 and 48 months. They commonly enter the health care system through emergency services. Caregivers usually state that their child's teeth break down or chip away, and might mention a familial pattern of weak or poor teeth. These children have multiple decayed teeth in the posterior and anterior regions and experience pain, which interferes with their daily activities such as eating, sleeping, and playing with others. Soft tissue pustules, furuncles, and draining fistulae accompany the rotted teeth as the bacteria traverse the pulpal chamber to the root apex and seep into the surrounding bone, causing acute or chronic infections and manifesting as soft tissue or gingival lesions (Fig 8-8).

ECC develops on all teeth and all surfaces. However, data from the third National Health and Nutrition Examination Survey (NHANES III) show that there is a typical pattern of tooth susceptibility. The continuum from the most common to the least common sites of caries prevalence in primary teeth of 3-year-old children is as follows: *(1)* occlusal surfaces of molars, *(2)* maxillary incisors, *(3)* buccal and lingual surfaces of molars, *(4)* mesial and distal surfaces of molars, *(5)* maxillary canines, and *(6)* mandibular canines and incisors.[21] The ECC prevalence rates differ as a function of income of caregiver, age, sex, race/ethnicity, and medical status. Children at high risk of developing caries are from low-income and minority families and/or have special health care needs.[1,25]

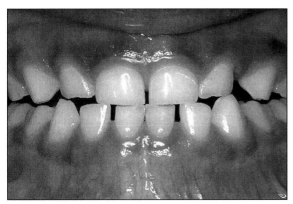

Fig 8-4 Healthy dentition of a young child.

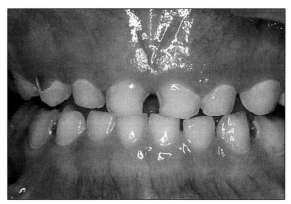

Fig 8-5 Moderate ECC.

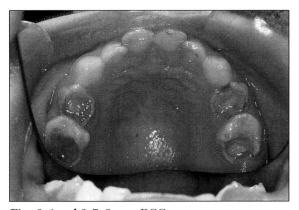

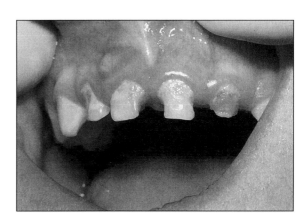

Figs 8-6 and 8-7 Severe ECC.

Fig 8-8 Severe ECC with early facial cellulites.

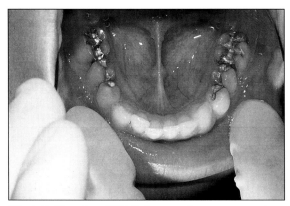

Fig 8-9 Transfer of ECC decay to the permanent dentition.

Consequences of Oral Disease

Research shows that young children who develop caries at an early age run a high risk of further caries development in the primary dentition and are likely to develop caries in the permanent dentition (Fig 8-9). In a longitudinal study of the development of dental caries in children aged 2.5 to 3.5 years, it was found that 92% of the children with caries at baseline developed new caries lesions during the 1-year follow-up period, compared with 29% of children who were caries-free at baseline.[26] A similar result was found in a study with children in a Head Start program (mean age, 3.8 years). These children were categorized at baseline as caries-free, having pit and fissure caries, or having maxillary anterior caries. After 2 years, children who presented at baseline with maxillary anterior or pit and fissure caries had a mean posterior decayed, missing, and filled (DMF) tooth score of more than 7. This score was four times the score of children who had been caries-free at baseline.[27] The same patterns of findings are reported by other researchers as well.[28–30] Therefore, it seems reasonable to postulate that ECC has a lifetime impact on a child's oral health status.

ECC is also a major reason for emergency visits and hospitalization of infants and young children.[31] The reported proportions of child emergency visits attributable to caries range from 17% to 49%.[32–34] For approximately half of the children aged 3.5 years and younger, an emergency appointment because of ECC is the first contact with a dentist.[33] These data show the importance of providing information about early and preventive dental care for children to the families of these young patients.

In addition to the direct impact of ECC on a child's future oral health status and the likelihood that this child might have to endure emergency appointments because of severe pain and discomfort, attention recently has been given to the biopsychosocial impact of ECC on a child's life. Research shows that rampant caries is one of the factors causing insufficient development in children who have no other medical problems.[35] ECC adversely affects the growth of a child's body, specifically body weight and height.[35,36] Children with ECC are significantly more likely than other children to weigh less than 80% of their ideal weight and thereby fall into the group of children who are described as showing a "failure to thrive."[35] There are several explanations for this finding. First, the onset of dental pain and infection may alter a child's eating habits, thereby affecting body weight and height.[36] Second, increased pain might also affect a child's glucocorticoid production. Third, disturbed sleep patterns may decrease the production of growth hormones. Fourth, the overall increased metabolic rate during the course of infection may retard normal growth and development in patients with ECC.[35]

Oral disease has also been shown to affect school attendance and results in days with restricted activity. Researchers found that oral disease and dental visits result in substantial levels of work loss and school days off in the US population.[37,38] Results of the National Health Interview Survey show that 117,000 hours of school were lost per 100,000 school-aged children in 1989.[38] It is interesting to note that these hours of school missed might be distributed disproportionally among different segments of the US population. For those children who visit the dentist routinely and preventively, the time per visit could range from 30 to 60 minutes per treatment, including travel time. These visits might even be scheduled in advance and at times when a child does not attend school. However, for those children without routine and preventive dental care, oral problems may result in lengthy and/or multiple appointments. Research shows that children from US families with a yearly income of $10,000 to $19,000 missed more school time compared with children from higher income groups (11.7 vs 4.7 days per 100 children per year, respectively).[39] In addition, the caregivers of these children might have had to miss work because of their children's dental visits. These data indicate that the burden of time lost because of dental visits may be the heaviest for those families who can least afford it.

The aforementioned research shows that ECC is likely to affect a child's future oral health, lead to an increased likelihood of emergency department visits, and put a burden on families and children. Research also demonstrates that a child's oral health status is closely associated with his or her OHRQOL.[40] A first pilot investigation evaluating the effect of severe ECC on the QOL of children between 36 and 44 months of age demonstrates the significant impact of severe ECC on children's well-being.[41] This research shows that severe ECC not only leads to pain and discomfort, but also affects the quality and quantity of food that the child eats and his or her sleep. Based on these first studies on children's OHRQOL it seems obvious that future research is needed to assess children's oral health status and treatment outcomes in a more complete and patient-centered way instead of focusing merely on indicators assessing the health of the oral cavity. Raising parents' awareness of how powerfully dental caries affects their child's QOL could be a first step in motivating parents to engage in oral health promotion, which includes making dental visits for preventive care as well as the treatment of caries at an early stage (unpublished data, 2002).

Assessing Children's Oral Health–Related Quality of Life

Four dimensions are relevant when considering children's OHRQOL. First, functional factors such as whether children can chew and bite play an essential role. Pain and discomfort because of oral health problems are a second component of children's OHRQOL. Psychologic factors, in particular whether children like the appearance of their teeth and how oral health affects their self-esteem, are a third aspect of children's OHRQOL. Finally, social aspects such as whether children's oral health interferes with their school and play activities must also be considered (unpublished data, 2002).

If one agrees that these four aspects should be included when assessing OHRQOL, the next question is how to develop a measurement instrument that is reliable, valid, and can be used for children at different stages of development. One consideration discussed in the literature is whether children themselves need to respond to such an instrument or whether parents or caregivers would be able to judge a child's QOL.[42–44] Research shows that health care professionals, parents, and children can differ in their views of a child's HRQOL. This finding might lead to the conclusion that only children themselves can and should provide a subjective evaluation of their own QOL. However, this approach does not consider the ultimate role that parents play in connecting children with the dental and medical care they need. Asking parents questions about their child's QOL can serve as a wake-up call for parents. It provides an opportunity to raise awareness in parents or caregivers about a child's situation. Parents or guardians are ultimately responsible for educating their children about oral health promotion and arranging dental visits.[45]

In the tradition of the CHQ,[12] OHRQOL instruments to which children themselves respond as well as surveys that parents/caregivers and even healthcare providers can use to assess a child's QOL should be developed. This approach has two advantages. First, answering several concrete questions about a child's situation might make a child's problems salient and thus raise parents' awareness of their child's situation. Second, encountering potential discrepancies in the answers provided by parents, children, and providers may prove beneficial. Research on the child-parent-dentist triad shows that misperceptions exist (unpublished data, 2002).[47] For example, parents' assessment of their child's dental fear is significantly correlated with the parents' dental fear. However, the parents' assessment of their child's fear is uncorrelated with dentists' ratings of the child's behavior in the dental chair. It is important to understand that these discrepancies are not methodological or measurement problems. They reflect subjective reality as perceived by the individuals involved in the situation. A discussion of these discrepancies can provide an opportunity to increase understanding of the situation and ultimately will lead to improved communication and better care for the child.

A second methodologic concern when assessing QOL in children is to decide which question/answer format should be chosen for children in different developmental stages. If children are affected by ECC early in their lives, it is crucial to give them a voice at this time. Preliminary research has been conducted on measuring HRQOL in children between 1 and 5 years of age.[46] However, research on pain measurement in children is most informative for understanding how to measure QOL in an age-appropriate manner. This research shows that children are able to report their distress quite accurately at as young as 5 years of age.[47] However, the ability to describe pain develops along with the child's cognitive development from concrete, perceptually bound descriptions to more abstract, generalized descriptions.[48] Based on these developmental considerations, an OHRQOL scale for children aged 4 years and older and their parents was developed in English and Spanish versions (unpublished data, 2002). It consists of eight questions concerned with functional aspects ("My child has difficulty chewing," "My child has difficulty biting hard"), psychologic aspects ("My child is happy with

his/her teeth," "My child has a nice smile"), and pain/discomfort ("My child's teeth are sensitive to hot and/or cold," "My child's teeth are sensitive to sweets," "My child had a toothache or pain during the last year," "My child has a toothache or pain now"). Several questions that explored how toothaches can potentially interfere with the child's ability to sleep, learn at school, and play and interact with others were included. Data from 203 children (age range, 4 to 16 years; mean age, 8.2 years) show that children as young as 4 years old are able to answer such questions if a "yes/no" answer format is used. Data from 50 parents who accompanied their children to a dental practice in an inner city location show that these parents are able to respond to these questions. The Parent Oral Health Quality of Life Scale uses a Likert scale answer format with five categories, ranging from "strongly disagree" to "strongly agree."[49] The reliability and validity of these scales used in the first pilot studies were tested in additional studies (unpublished data, 2002).[42,50]

Future Directions

Oral and craniofacial conditions that require health care providers' attention are common among children and adolescents.[1,2] Dental caries is just the most common problem. Chapter 9 discusses the importance of providing optimal care for children with special needs. It is important to understand that cleft lip and palate is one of the most common birth defects and that many other genetic syndromes, developmental disabilities, and diseases have oral health–related aspects.[51] Dental care is the most prevalent unmet health care need for children,[52] and children from poor and/or minority families are especially vulnerable.[53]

One way to address these issues would be to focus the attention of all persons involved on the degree to which OHRQOL of children with unmet dental needs is impaired. It is important to educate parents/primary care providers, dental as well as general health care providers, and teachers/child care personnel about the way poor oral health can affect a child's QOL. Parents have to realize that more than "just a baby tooth that will fall out anyway" is involved when their young child has a "toothache." They have to understand that this toothache is a health problem that can lead to future dental problems; general health problems; and problems with the child's social, academic, and emotional adjustment in life. Dental health care providers' education has to become patient-centered and include careful instruction about the special issues involved in providing care for children and adolescents.[54] General health care providers need to understand how oral health problems can affect a child's general health and QOL. Medicine and dentistry have to work together in a close and supportive team approach. Ultimately, research on children's OHRQOL can help to demonstrate the "burden of illness" caused by oral diseases, which might be useful for changing health policy.[55] It can contribute to determining priorities for care[56] and identifying priority groups for public health interventions.[55] A focus on children's OHRQOL could be the catalyst leading to the changes needed to ultimately improve children's oral health in the United States.

References

1. National Institute of Dental and Craniofacial Research. Surgeon General's Conference on Children and Oral Health. 12–13 June 2000, Washington, DC. Available at: http://www.nidcr.nih.gov/sgr/children/children.htm. Accessed August 29, 2001.

2. National Institute of Dental and Craniofacial Research. Oral Health in America: A Report of the Surgeon General—Executive Summary. Available at: http://www.nidcr.nih.gov/sgr/execsumm.htm. Accessed August 29, 2001.

3. American Medical Association. Profiles of Adolescents Health Series, I: Adolescents—How Healthy Are They? Chicago: American Medical Association, 1990.

4. Office of Technology Assessment. Adolescent Health, I: Summary and Policy Options. Government Printing Office, 1991.

5. Grave G, Pless IB. Chronic Childhood Illness: Assessment of Outcomes. DHEW Publication NIH 76-877. Government Printing Office, 1974.

6. Walker DK, Richmond JB. Monitoring Child Health in the United States: Selected Issues and Policies. Cambridge, MA: Harvard University Press, 1984.

7. Eisen M, Ware JE, Donald CA, Brook RH. Measuring components of children's health status. Med Care 1979;17:902–921.

8. Starfield BH. Child health status and outcome of care: A commentary of measuring the impact of medical care on children. J Chronic Dis 1987;40(suppl 1):1095–1155.

9. Bradlyn AS, Harris CV, Warner JE, Ritchey AK, Zaboy K. An investigation of the validity of the quality of well-being scale with pediatric oncology patients. Health Psychol 1993;12:246–250.

10. Stein REK, Jessop DJ. Functional status II (R): A measure of child health status. Med Care 1990;28:1041–1055.

11. Starfield B, Bergner M, Ensminger M, et al. Adolescent health status measurement: Development of the child health and illness profile. Pediatrics 1993;91:430–435.

12. Landgraf JM, Abetz L, Ware JE. Child Health Questionnaire (CHQ): A User's Manual. Boston: HealthAct, 1999.

13. Juniper EF. Quality of life in adults and children with asthma and rhinitis. Allergy 1997;52:971–977.

14. Arunkumar G, Wyllie E, Kotagal P, Ong H, Gilliam F. Parent- and patient-validated consent for pediatric epilepsy quality-of-life assessment. Epilepsia 2000;41: 1474–1484.

15. Bandell-Hoekstra I, Abu-Saad H, Passchier J, Knipschild P. Recurrent headache, coping, and quality of life in children: A review. Headache 2000;40: 357–370.

16. Guyatt G. Measuring health-related quality of life in childhood cancer: lessons from the workshop [discussion]. Int J Cancer Suppl 1999;12:143–146.

17. Barrera M, Boyd-Pringle L, Sumbler K, Saunders F. Quality of life and behavior adjustment after pediatric bone marrow transplantation. Bone Marrow Transplant 2000;26:427–435.

18. Franco RJ, Rosenfeld R, Rao M. Quality of life for children with obstructive sleep apnea. Otolaryngol Head Neck Surg 2000;123(part 1):9–16.

19. Evans CA, Kleinman DV. The Surgeon General's Report on America's Oral Health: Opportunities for the dental profession. J Am Dent Assoc 2000;131:1721–1728.

20. Centers for Disease Control. Data 2010: The Healthy People 2010 database. Available at: http://198.246. 96.90/HP2010/index.htm. Accessed August 23, 2001.

21. Kaste LM, Drury TF, Horowitz AM, Beltran E. An evaluation of NHANES III estimates of early childhood caries. J Public Health Dent 1999;59:198–200.

22. Ismail AI, Sohn W. A systematic review of clinical diagnostic criteria of early childhood caries. J Public Health Dent 1999;59:171–191.

23. Horowitz H. Research issues in early childhood caries. Community Dent Oral Epidemiol 1998; 26(suppl 1):67–81.

24. Drury TF, Horowitz AM, Ismail AI, Maertens MP, Rozier RG, Selwitz RH. Diagnosing and reporting early childhood caries for research purposes. J Public Health Dent 1999;59:192–197.

25. Vargas CM, Crall JJ, Schneider DA. Sociodemographic distribution of pediatric dental caries: NHANES III, 1988-1994. J Am Dent Assoc 1998;129:1229–1238.

26. Grindefjord M, Dahllöf G, Modéer T. Caries development in children from 2.5 to 3.5 years of age: A longitudinal study. Caries Res 1995;29:449–454.

27. O'Sullivan DM, Tinanoff N. The association of early dental caries patterns with caries incidence in preschool children. J Public Health Dent 1996;56: 81–83.

28. Johnsen DC, Gerstenmaier JH, DiSantis TA, Berkowitz RJ. Susceptibility of nursing-caries children to future approximal molar decay. Pediatr Dent 1986;8: 168–170.

29. Al-Shalan TA, Erickson PR, Hardie NA. Primary incisor decay before age 4 as a risk factor for future dental caries. Pediatr Dent 1997;19:37–41.

30. Gray MM, Marchment MD, Anderson RJ. The relationship between caries experience in deciduous molars at 5 years and in first permanent molars of the same child at 7 years. Community Dent Health 1991; 8:3–7.

31. Sheller B, Williams BJ, Lombardi SM. Diagnosis and treatment of dental caries-related emergencies in a children's hospital. Pediatr Dent 1997;19:470–475.

32. Majewski RF, Snyder CW, Bernat JE. Dental emergencies presenting to a children's hospital. ASDC J Dent Child 1988;55:339–342.

33. Fleming P, Gregg TA, Saunders ID. Analysis of an emergency dental service provided at a children's hospital. Int J Paediatr Dent 1991;1:25–30.

34. Schwartz S. A one-year statistical analysis of dental emergencies in a pediatric hospital. J Can Dent Assoc 1994;60:959–968.

35. Acs G, Lodolini G, Kaminsky S, Cisneros GJ. Effect of nursing caries on body weight in a pediatric population. Pediatr Dent 1992;14:302–305.

36. Ayhan H, Suskan E, Yildirim S. The effect of nursing or rampant caries on height, body weight and head circumference. J Clin Pediatr Dent 1996;20:209–212.

37. Reisine ST. Dental health and public policy: The social impact of disease. Am J Public Health 1985;75:27–30.

38. Gift HC, Reisine ST, Larach DC. The social impact of dental problems and visits. Am J Public Health 1992; 82:1663–1668.

39. Hollister MC, Weintraub JA. The association of oral status with systemic health, quality of life, and economic productivity. J Dent Educ 1993;57:901–912.

40. Chen M, Hunter P. Oral health and quality of life in New Zealand: A social perspective. Soc Sci Med 1996; 48:1213–1222.

41. Low W, Tan S, Schwartz S. The effect of severe caries on the quality of life in young children. Pediatr Dent 1999;21:325–326.

42. Theunissen N, Vogels T, Koopman H, et al. The proxy problem: Child report versus parent report in health-related quality of life research. Qual Life Res 1998;7: 387–397.

43. Levi RB, Drotar D. Health-related quality of life in childhood cancer: Discrepancy in parent-child reports. Int J Cancer Suppl 1999;12:58–64.

44. Parsons SK, Barlow SE, Levy SL, Supran SE, Kaplan SH. Health-related quality of life in pediatric bone marrow transplant survivors: According to whom? Int J Cancer Suppl 1999;12:46–51.

45. Inglehart MR, Tedesco LA. The role of the family in preventing oral diseases. In: Cohen LK, Gift HC (eds). Disease Prevention and Oral Health Promotion: Sociodental Sciences in Action. Copenhagen: Munksgaard, 1995:271–307.

46. Fekkes M, Theunissen NC, Brugman E, et al. Development and psychometric evaluation of the TAPQOL: A health related quality of life instrument for one to five year old children. Qual Life Res 2000;9:961–972.

47. Ross DM, Ross SA. Childhood pain: The school-aged child's viewpoint. Pain 1984;20:179–191.

48. Gaffney A, Dunne EA. Developmental aspects of children's definition of pain. Pain 1986;26:105–117.

49. Watson DO, Inglehart MR, Bagramian RA. Oral health promotion and underrepresented minority children and parents: An empirical study. Presented at the American Association for Dental Research Meeting, Chicago, March 2000.

50. Filstrup, SC. The Effects of Early Childhood Caries (ECC) and Restorative Treatment on Children's Oral Health Related Quality of Life—The Parent's/Guardian's and the Child's Perspective [thesis]. Ann Arbor: University of Michigan School of Dentistry, 2001.

51. Gorlin RJ, Cohen Jr MM, Levin LS. Syndromes of the Head and Neck, ed 3. New York: Oxford Univ Press, 1990:693–895.

52. Newacheck PW, Hughes DC, Hung YY, Wong S, Stoddard JJ. The unmet health needs of America's children. Pediatrics 2000;105(4 part 2):989–997.

53. US General Accounting Office. Oral Health: Dental Disease Is a Chronic Problem Among Low Income Populations. General Accounting Office Publication GAO/HEHS-00-72. Government Printing Office, 2000.

54. Mouradian WE. The face of a child: Children's oral health and dental education. J Dent Educ 2001;65: 821–831.

55. Patrick D, Erickson PR. Health Status and Health Policy. New York: Oxford Univ Press, 1993.

56. Gift HC. Quality of life: An outcome of oral health care? J Public Health Dent 1996;56:67–68.

CHAPTER 9

Oral Health–Related Quality of Life in Children and Adolescents with Special Health Care Needs

Marcio A. da Fonseca, DDS, MS

The Federal Maternal and Child Health Bureau's Division of Services for Children with Special Health Care Needs has defined special care children as "those who have or are at increased risk for a chronic physical, developmental, behavioral, or emotional condition and who also require health and related services of a type or amount beyond that required by children generally."[1] The definition was intentionally made broad and inclusive to focus on the prevention of both primary and secondary disabilities, and to encourage a greater commitment to the task of effective intervention in the lives of these children.[1] The 1994 National Health Interview Survey (NHIS) showed that 18% of US children younger than 18 years had a chronic physical, developmental, behavioral, or emotional condition that required health-related services beyond that used by children in general.[2]

Disability in children is defined as a long-term reduction in the ability to conduct social role activities, such as school or play, because of a chronic physical or mental condition.[3] The 1992–94 NHIS revealed that an estimated 6.5% of all noninstitutionalized US children had some degree of disability. The most common disabilities were respiratory diseases (especially asthma) and impairments of speech, special sense, and intelligence, particularly mental retardation.[3] The prevalence of disabilities was higher for children older than 5 years; boys; African-Americans; and children from low-income, less-educated, and/or single-parent families.[2,3] These children were restricted in their daily activities more than 2 weeks per year on average, causing substantial effects on the educational and health care systems.[3] Further analysis of the NHIS showed the strong association of economic and social disadvantage with higher prevalence of disability. It is therefore of paramount importance to target prevention and rehabilitation efforts toward these children and their families to ameliorate the impact of the disabling conditions and reduce their lifelong consequences, including the associated financial costs.[2,3] It is known that members of racial and ethnic minority groups, persons of lower socioeconomic status, and those who are medically compromised are also at increased risk for the development of oral diseases.[4] The 1995 NHIS survey showed that four of five uninsured children with special health care needs came from middle- to lower-income families, and dental care was their most prevalent unmet need.[5]

Securing Dental and Oral Care

Access to dental care is highly correlated with income. Dental care is less likely to be covered by third-party insurance, and its deductibles and coinsurance payments are usually higher than are those for medical or surgical care.[6] The 1994 National Access to Care Survey showed that more individuals in fair or poor health (16.1%) had unmet dental needs than did persons in good or excellent health (7.7%). Unmet dental care wants were greater among those individuals who had chronic conditions. The main reasons given by these individuals for not securing dental care were inability to pay for insurance or dental services, and/or inability to find a dentist who accepted their insurance.[6] When respondents in the general population were questioned about five health care services (medical/surgical care, prescription drugs, eyeglasses, dental care, and mental health services), dental care was the highest reported unmet want.

The law requires that dental professionals provide similar treatment to patients with special care needs as they do for healthy individuals. However, many families face difficulties in finding dental professionals who are willing to take their medically-compromised child as a patient because of the following reasons[4,7–19]:

1. Physical limitations of the dental practice.
2. Time-consuming appointments (longer visits may be needed because of the patient's limited ability to cooperate, the need for consultation with physicians, etc).
3. Financial reimbursement may not be viewed as commensurate with the amount of time and effort spent on providing dental services.

For instance, many dental professionals do not participate in Medicaid programs because of their frustration with the amount of paperwork and discontentment with the reimbursement rates. These lower rates, in turn, may encourage clinicians to provide care of a lower quality. Moreover, providers accepting Medicaid patients may be looked upon with less esteem by policy makers, other patients, and dental colleagues.

4. Lack of adequate training on the part of the dental professional or belief that these children should only be treated in a hospital environment.
5. Lack of education regarding the patient's condition and unwillingness to learn about it. Approximately 75% of dentists do not treat patients with a disability because of their medical and behavioral issues.
6. Lack of hospital privileges necessary to provide care in the operating room for certain types of patients.
7. Lack of training of auxiliary staff.
8. Guardianship and consent issues.
9. The dental professional's fear of disease transmission (acquired immunodeficiency syndrome [AIDS], hepatitis, etc), becoming socially stigmatized for treating the patient, and/or loss of business. He or she may also personally disapprove of the individual's behavior that led to the development of the disease or condition (societal attitudes and stereotypes).
10. Belief that existing dental practice standards need to be modified extensively to care for these patients.
11. The dentist's own feelings of inadequacy.
12. The low ratio of pediatric dentists to children (approximately 1.2:100,000).

Family attitudes in relation to oral health and dental care raise additional issues that may interfere with provision of dental care to the medically compromised child. Some of the relevant factors here are as follows[17,20,21]:

1. Ignorance about the relationship between oral and systemic health

2. Oral health being a low priority in relation to many other medical issues
3. Weariness of dealing with multiple health care professionals
4. Assumption that the child has no oral/dental problems
5. Fatalistic attitude toward dental disease
6. Caretakers' attitudes toward dental care
7. The anxiety of the caretaker/guardian over the dental visit
8. Geographic distance to the dental center
9. Lack of transportation
10. Overindulging the child with sweets and cariogenic snacks and lack of enforcement of good oral hygiene habits

Caretakers who understand the importance of a healthy oral cavity may face discouraging barriers such as the need for ongoing excessive advocacy and continued involvement even after the child has reached adulthood. They might perceive a lack of sensitivity exhibited by the dental professional and a lack of networking of care providers that leaves families on their own to seek and coordinate appropriate care. Furthermore, a willingness to treat does not necessarily translate into availability of care.[4,7,15,17] Finances are also a significant barrier to obtaining dental care, and are cited as the primary reason for lack of coverage for three of every four uninsured children.[5,6] For older children and adolescents, fear, anxiety, dislike of the dentist, and negative attitudes toward dentistry are also issues that delay seeking care.[18,19]

In the case of institutionalized patients, caretakers may be reluctant to provide oral hygiene care because of the need to probe into the oral cavity and feelings of discomfort with saliva and gingival bleeding. Furthermore, their lack of training in oral health care and hygiene and their fear of provoking disruptive behavior may also contribute to poor oral care.[21]

Dental insurance coverage does not necessarily equate with full access to services. Certain procedures may not be considered medically necessary by the insurance companies because they may consider them optional or unrelated to the patient's overall health.[4,5] A good example is the refusal to cover expenses associated with general anesthesia and hospitalization for dental rehabilitation of children and adolescents who cannot receive, withstand, or cooperate with dental care delivery in a regular dental setting. The denial of coverage for dental care in the operating room causes a significant financial burden to the families. Most of these families cannot afford to pay for these expenses, which leads to further compromise of the child's oral health and quality of life (QOL). Furthermore, language and cultural barriers may also interfere with access to health care and insurance. Communication skills in a foreign language, different cultural perspectives in relation to chronic childhood conditions, and understanding insurance eligibility and enrollment processes have become growing challenges in the United States.[5]

All of these factors lead to several negative consequences that affect the patient's QOL. These consequences include the following[17,22]:

1. Periodic preventive dental examinations are curtailed.
2. The choice of providers is restricted.
3. The quality of the services may be inferior to those provided for healthy individuals.
4. There may be long intervals between visits, leading to crisis-oriented dental and oral care.
5. The costs to repair the effects of oral disease that could have been prevented or treated at an earlier stage are higher.

The magnitude of lost productivity and its effects on society are great. The difficulties of obtaining dental care at a local level leads to work loss by the caretakers who often have to travel great distances to have their children treated. Often, caretakers who lose time from work are those members of society who can least afford it.[23] Studies have found, however, that communities that sought to coordinate care with local agencies and dental schools or hospital dental clinics had fewer barriers to access to dental treatment for special care populations.[9,13,18,20]

These studies also found that the children and adults with special needs in these communities showed a better attendance rate pattern than the average population.

Oral and Systemic Health and QOL

Because oral diseases are treatable and usually not life threatening, they have been erroneously perceived as having little relationship to other measures of health, often being viewed as minor annoyances in the social and economic context.[23,24] However, oral and systemic health are closely related. The implications of poor oral health status for the patient's QOL are clear, particularly in children with special health needs: pain, restricted food choices because of a decreased ability to chew and/or swallow, reduced nutritional intake leading to failure to thrive, poor esthetics, impaired speech with consequent social withdrawal, adverse drug-related side effects in the oral cavity, and sequelae from oral infections and poor oral hygiene on systemic health.[23,25] If left untreated, oral diseases result in morbidity, disability, and dysfunction, leading to behavioral, psychologic, and social QOL issues.[4] Studies have demonstrated that the gravity of the medical condition is correlated with the severity of dental disease, which in turn is increased significantly in disabled individuals.[7,24] There is a strong correlation between deterioration of oral health and deterioration of general health.[23] Furthermore, many drugs that are prescribed to treat systemic conditions trigger oral side effects such as gingival hyperplasia (eg, nifedipine, cyclosporine, phenytoin) and xerostomia, increasing the risk of developing caries and opportunistic infections. To complicate matters, many pediatric medications have high amounts of sugar (eg, nystatin, digoxin, clotrimazole troches).[26] Although many interdisciplinary health care teams have made oral care a matter of attention in their practice, most pediatricians and family physicians still ignore its im-

portance and fail to provide anticipatory guidance and referral to dental professionals.

Many systemic conditions have oral manifestations that increase the risk of oral disease, which in turn is a risk factor for a number of systemic conditions. There is growing evidence that oral microorganisms can cause or complicate an array of systemic diseases if they enter the bloodstream.[27] Optimal oral health contributes to the success of surgeries to correct congenital malformations (eg, cardiac anomalies) as well as bone marrow and solid organ transplants. It is imperative that candidates for these procedures have their oral cavity examined before undergoing surgery to diagnose and treat any potential sources of infection that could threaten a positive outcome of the medical procedures.[27–30] Problems such as abscessed teeth, caries lesions, and poor gingival health must be dealt with in a timely fashion so that the oral cavity can heal before proceeding with the transplant or surgery to decrease the risk of infection and complications.[28–30] Pediatric patients who have certain cardiac anomalies, even after correction, may be at risk for infective endocarditis caused by oral bacteria during a dental procedure.[23,27,29,30] In a study of oral health in children with cardiac diseases, Hallett and colleagues[29] found that compared with healthy children, these children suffered poorer oral health, had significantly more teeth treated endodontically, and had more untreated caries. In addition, these children had less-than-optimal professional and home oral care, and only 31% were educated about preventive dental behavior.

Children who receive chemotherapy and/or radiotherapy may develop mucositis (Fig 9-1). Mucositis can affect the whole gastrointestinal tract, interfering with the patient's oral intake and comfort level; even the medical treatment may need to be interrupted until the patient recovers.[28,31] Spontaneous gingival bleeding and opportunistic oral infections are also common occurrences in these patients.[28,31–33] Patients who receive radiation therapy to the head and face may develop temporomandibular joint problems, muscular trismus, and xerostomia, all of

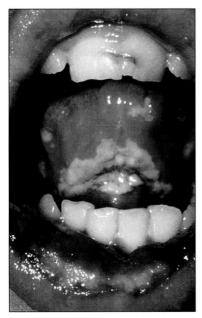

Fig 9-1 Mucositis caused by chemotherapy and radiotherapy.

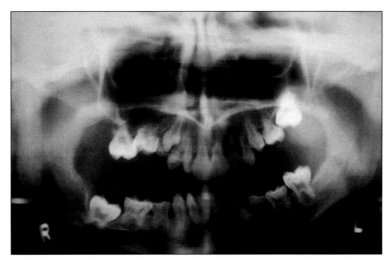

Fig 9-2 Disturbances in dental development after administration of chemotherapy and radiotherapy to an 18-month-old patient prior to bone marrow transplantation.

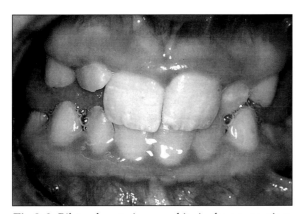

Fig 9-3 Bilateral posterior open bite in the same patient seen in Fig 9-2.

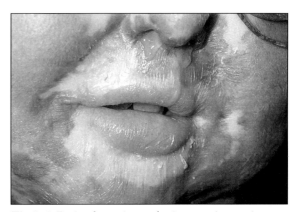

Fig 9-4 Perioral scarring and microstomia seen in a severe case of graft-vs-host disease.

which affect the patient's nutrition, oral hygiene, and caries risk.[34] Possible long-term sequelae from the administration of chemotherapeutic agents and radiation therapy to young patients, particularly those under 6 years of age, include disturbance of the dental development and malocclusion (Figs 9-2 and 9-3).[34–37] Patients who receive a nonautologous bone marrow transplant or one from a donor who is not an identical twin may develop oral graft-vs-host disease which can bring about oral pain, dryness, disruption of nutrition, and reduced mouth opening secondary to perioral scarring, among other problems (Fig 9-4).[38,39] Oral lesions, periodontal disease, opportunistic infections, and parotid swelling also affect young patients with AIDS.[40–42]

Children and adolescents with liver disease experience changes in the oral mucosa because

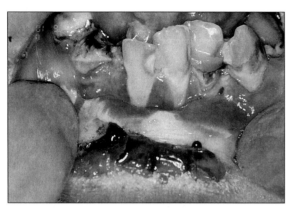

Fig 9-5 Rampant caries and oral bullae in a young patient with epidermolysis bullosa.

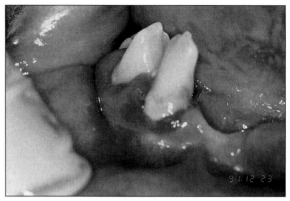

Fig 9-6 Periodontal disease in an adolescent with Down syndrome.

of vitamin and metabolite deficiencies, oral bleeding secondary to impaired vitamin K synthesis, hypoplastic crowns, and tooth discoloration from prolonged jaundice or accumulation of blood products.[40] Patients with bleeding dyscrasias (hemophilias, von Willebrand disease, etc) need a strong preventive dental program to avoid complications related to dental treatment such as soft tissue hematomas from anesthetic blocks and prolonged bleeding from tooth extractions.[43] Strong dental preventive efforts are also of paramount importance for patients diagnosed with epidermolysis bullosa, a condition characterized by mechanical fragility and blistering of the skin.[44] In some cases, the oral mucosa is affected and patients are unable to chew hard foods or brush their teeth because the mechanical friction of the brush or the hard texture of the foods can cause painful bullae, leading to perioral scarring and microstomia. Consequently, these patients are at a high risk of developing rampant dental caries, oral infections, and poor nutrition (Fig 9-5).[44,45]

Caries and periodontal disease are concerns in children diagnosed with cerebral palsy and mental retardation because of their inability to maintain oral hygiene efficiently or their failure to cooperate with the caretaker's provision of care. Many are also seizure-prone and take phenytoin, which can induce gingival over-

growth. Bruxism, malocclusion, dental trauma, drooling, and consequent perioral skin rashes are common in this population.[40] Although many studies have shown that dental caries prevalence in children with mental and/or physical handicaps is often no greater than in healthy children, the former usually present fewer filled teeth and more extractions as well as poorer gingival status and more malocclusion.[46–49] The malocclusion seen in these children can lead to improper chewing of foods and put them at higher risk for traumatic injuries to the maxillary incisors, further compromising their QOL.[47,48] The periodontal condition may be further compromised by bruxism and anterior open bites.[7] Similar problems are seen in children with muscular dystrophy.[40] Patients with Down syndrome present unique facial and oral features that can significantly affect their QOL. Problems such as a small oral cavity, fissured tongue, mouth breathing, poor oral muscular function and swallowing, congenitally missing teeth, malocclusion, and periodontal disease can cause early loss of teeth and eventual development of dental caries (Fig 9-6).[40,50,51] Pediatric patients with diabetes also display a high prevalence of periodontal problems and are predisposed to xerostomia, delayed wound healing, and opportunistic infections.[27,40] Moreover, the presence of periodontal disease is felt to influence a reduced glycemic control.[27] Periodontitis can also affect the successful outcome of joint and organ replacement and renal dialysis.[27] Provision of optimal oral care can decrease risks to the health of these children and have a positive impact on their well-being.

Compared with other body parts, the mouth and face are more visible and involved in communication and social exchanges.[23] Improvement in the appearance of the teeth and face are therefore of great psychologic, social, and emotional benefit for the patients, having a positive impact on their QOL. Children with cleft lip and palate, ectodermal dysplasia, amelogenesis and dentinogenesis imperfecta, and craniofacial anomalies, to cite just a few disorders, need close dental supervision throughout their life. The effects of fetal alcohol syndrome on the craniofacial complex are well documented.[40,52] Affected children present a characteristic facies with microcephaly, short palpebral fissures, depressed midface, flat nasal bridge, short philtrum, thin upper lip, and micrognathia. Although these features tend to improve with age, the patient's behavior is usually a challenge not only in the dental office, but also in society.[52]

Summary

The issues discussed herein are just some highlights of how oral and systemic health are intricately related. Little research has been done to evaluate the association between pediatric patients with special health care needs and oral disease, QOL issues, and financial burden to the family and society as a whole. However, it is clear that the barriers to access to dental care have to be eliminated. Having access to dental care will positively affect these patients' QOL, and it would decrease the financial costs to society through less hospitalization, lower treatment costs, and fewer days of work loss for the caretakers.

Changes must be made on many levels to increase these patients' opportunities to receive optimal oral health care. For example, it would be beneficial to change the undergraduate dental curriculum to include extensive didactic and clinical experience in working with this patient population. If graduating dental students feel unprepared to treat these patients, during their professional career they may erroneously believe that these patients should only be seen by specialists or in a hospital dental clinic.[12,13,15,21,53] Moreover, many dental professionals do little to counter their own professional inadequacy and prejudices, and, in some instances, even reinforce them.[4] Glick and Burris[11] have suggested that the most promising single source of behavioral changes in dentists is the dental professionals themselves. This is because the clear articulation of professional norms and acceptable attitudes leads dentists to understand them as legitimate.[11] In places where Medicaid fees have been increased and its bureaucracy cut, patients with special needs have seen their choices of providers increase.[8,10] Similarly, some state dental associations, together with their communities, have won the right to include general anesthesia for dental rehabilitation as an insurance benefit for their pediatric population. Unfortunately, many researchers in the area of health services predict a continuing decline in access to oral health care as federally funded programs shrink and the responsibility is shifted to the state level.[19]

References

1. McPherson M, Arango P, Fox H, et al. A new definition of children with special health care needs. Pediatrics 1998;102:137–140.
2. Newacheck PW, Strickland B, Shonkoff JP, et al. An epidemiologic profile of children with special health care needs. Pediatrics 1998;102:117–123.
3. Newacheck PW, Halfon N. Prevalence and impact of disabling chronic conditions in childhood. Am J Public Health 1998;88:610–617.
4. Crall JJ. Delivery systems for preschool children. Dent Clin North Am 1995;39:897–907.
5. Newacheck PW, McManus M, Fox HB, Hung YY, Halfon N. Access to health care for children with special health care needs. Pediatrics 2000;105:760–766.
6. Mueller CD, Schur CL, Paramore LC. Access to dental care in the United States. J Am Dent Assoc 1998;129:429–437.

7. Tesini DA, Fenton SJ. Oral health needs of persons with physical or mental disabilities. Dent Clin North Am 1994;38:483–498.

8. Capilouto E. The dentist's role in access to dental care by Medicaid recipients. J Dent Educ 1988;52:647–652.

9. New availability and access to dental care for the disabled: NFDH programs. Spec Care Dentist 1982;2(2):51–52.

10. Nainar SMH, Tinanoff N. Effect of Medicaid reimbursement rates on children's access to dental care. Pediatr Dent 1997;19:315–316.

11. Glick M, Burris S. The professional responsibility for care. Oral Dis 1997;3(suppl 1):S221–S224.

12. Perlman S. Helping special olympics athletes sport good smiles. An effort to reach out to people with special needs. Dent Clin North Am 2000;44:221–229.

13. Glassman P, Miller CE, Lechowick J. A dental school's role in developing a rural, community-based, dental care delivery system for individuals with developmental disabilities. Spec Care Dentist 1996;16(5):188–193.

14. Shuman SK, Bebeau MJ. Ethical and legal issues in special patient care. Dent Clin North Am 1994;38:553–575.

15. Burtner AP, Jones JS, McNeal DR, Low DW. A survey of the availability of dental services to developmentally disabled persons residing in the community. Spec Care Dentist 1990;10(6):182–184.

16. American Academy of Pediatric Dentistry. Rationale and justification for requiring medical plan reimbursement for hospital costs associated with general anesthesia when provided in the course of dental treatment for the young and special needs. Spec Care Dentist 1995;15:203.

17. Finger St, Jedrychowski JR. Parents' perception of access to dental care for children with handicapping conditions. Spec Care Dentist 1989;9(6):195–199.

18. Russell GM, Kinirons MJ. A study of the barriers to dental care in a sample of patients with cerebral palsy. Community Dent Health 1993;10:57–64.

19. Gordon SM, Dionne RA, Snyder J. Dental fear and anxiety as a barrier to accessing oral health care among patients with special health care needs. Spec Care Dentist 1998;18(2):88–92.

20. Leahy J, Lennon MA. The organization of dental care for school children with severe mental handicap. Community Dent Health 1986;3:53–59.

21. Faulks D, Hennequin M. Evaluation of a long-term oral health program by carers of children and adults with intellectual disabilities. Spec Care Dentist 2000;20(5):199–208.

22. Garrard SD. Health services for mentally retarded people in community residences: Problems and questions. Am J Public Health 1982;72:1226–1228.

23. Hollister MC, Weintraub JA. The association of oral status with systemic health, quality of life, and economic productivity. J Dent Educ 1993;57:901–912.

24. Rosenberg D, Kaplan S, Senie R, Badner V. Relationships among dental functional status, clinical dental measures, and generic health measures. J Dent Educ 1988;52:653–657.

25. White BA. The costs and consequences of neglected medically necessary oral care. Spec Care Dentist 1995;15(5):180–186.

26. Feigal RJ, Gleeson MC, Beckman TM, Greenwood ME. Dental caries related to liquid medication intake in young cardiac patients. ASDC J Dent Child 1984;51:360–362.

27. Slavkin HC. Does the mouth put the heart at risk? J Am Dent Assoc 1999;130:109–113.

28. da Fonseca MA. Pediatric bone marrow transplantation: Oral complications and recommendations for care. Pediatr Dent 1998;20:386–394.

29. Hallett KB, Radford DJ, Seow WK. Oral health of children with congenital cardiac diseases: A controlled study. Pediatr Dent 1992;14:224–230.

30. Duncan WJ. Congenital cardiac disease and contemporary dental care of the pediatric patient: A cardiologist's point of view. J Can Dent Assoc 1992;58:208–212.

31. Peterson DE, Elias EG, Sonis ST. Head and Neck Management of the Cancer Patient. Boston: Martinus Nijhoff Publishing, 1986.

32. Peterson DE. Oral infection. Support Care Cancer 1999;7:217–218.

33. Heimdahl A. Prevention and management of oral infections in cancer patients. Support Care Cancer 1999;7:224–228.

34. da Fonseca MA. Long-term oral and craniofacial complications following pediatric bone marrow transplantation. Pediatr Dent 2000;22:57–62.

35. Dahllöf G, Forsberg CM, Ringdén O, et al. Facial growth and morphology in long-term survivors after bone marrow transplantation. Eur J Orthod 1989;11:332–340.

36. Goho C. Chemoradiation therapy: Effect on dental development. Pediatr Dent 1993;15:6–12.

37. Näsman M, Björk O, Söderhäll S, Ringdén O, Dahllöf G. Disturbances in the oral cavity in pediatric long-term survivors after different forms of antineoplastic therapy. Pediatr Dent 1994;16:217–223.

38. Woo SB, Lee SJ, Schubert MM. Graft-vs.-host disease. Crit Rev Oral Biol Med 1997;8:201–216.

39. da Fonseca MA, Schubert M, Lloid M. Oral aspects and management of severe graft-vs-host disease in a young patient with beta-thalassemia: Case report. Pediatr Dent 1998;20:57–61.

40. Cooley RO, Sanders BJ. The pediatrician's involvement in prevention and treatment of oral disease in medically compromised children. Pediatr Clin North Am 1991;38:1265–1288.

41. Chigurupati R, Raghavan SS, Studen-Pavlovich DA. Pediatric HIV infection and its oral manifestations: A review. Pediatr Dent 1996;18:106–113.

42. Kline MW. Oral manifestations of pediatric human immunodeficiency virus infection: A review of the literature. Pediatrics 1996;97:380–388.

43. Garfunkel AA, Galili D, Findler M, Lubliner J, Eldor A. Bleeding tendency: A practical approach in dentistry. Compend Contin Educ Dent 1999;20:836–844.

44. Wright JT. Comprehensive dental care and general anesthetic management of hereditary epidermolysis bullosa. A review of fourteen cases. Oral Surg Oral Med Oral Pathol 1990;70:573–578.

45. Fine JD, Eady RA, Bauer EA, et al. Revised classification system for inherited epidermolysis bullosa: Report of the Second International Consensus Meeting on diagnosis and classification of epidermolysis bullosa. J Am Acad Dermatol 2000;42:1051–1066.

46. Nunn JH. The dental health of mentally and physically handicapped children: A review of the literature. Community Dent Health 1987;4:157–168.

47. Vigild M. Prevalence of malocclusion in mentally retarded young adults. Community Dent Oral Epidemiol 1985;13:183–184.

48. Pope JE, Curzon ME. The dental status of cerebral palsied children. Pediatr Dent 1991;13:156–162.

49. Hallett KB, Lucas JO, Johnston T, Reddihough DS, Hall RK. Dental health of children with cerebral palsy following sialodochoplasty. Spec Care Dentist 1995;15(6):234–238.

50. Hennequin M, Faulks D, Veyrune JL, Bourdiol P. Significance of oral health in persons with Down syndrome: A literature review. Dev Med Child Neurol 1999;41:275–283.

51. Reuland-Bosma W, van Dijk J. Periodontal disease in Down's syndrome: A review. J Clin Periodontol 1986;13:64–73.

52. Streissguth AP, Aase JM, Clarren SK, Randels SP, LaDue RA, Smith DF. Fetal alcohol syndrome in adolescents and adults. JAMA 1991;265:1961–1967.

53. Romer M, Dougherty N, Amores-Lafleur E. Predoctoral education in special care dentistry: Paving the way to better access? ASDC J Dent Child 1999;66:132–135, 185.

Oral Health–Related Quality of Life and Older Adults

David P. Sarment, DDS, MS

Toni C. Antonucci, PhD

The Surgeon General's report on oral health in the United States published in the year 2000 indicates that one is not healthy without good oral health.[1] This important document states that oral health is broader than just dental health, and that it is intimately related to systemic diseases. Pointing to oral health disparities in the US population, the report states that older adults in particular are prone to multiple oral and systemic diseases that ultimately impair their quality of life (QOL). Not surprisingly, this has led to further development of the field of geriatric dentistry.

Geriatric dentistry refers to the provision of care for patients 65 years or older. With increased life expectancies, as seen in Western industrialized countries, this field of specialization has become increasingly important. Improvement in medical care will allow older patients to maintain an active and pleasant life at more advanced ages. These patients are also maintaining their natural dentition much longer than did previous generations, and research shows that their QOL is affected by their oral status in many ways. For ex-

ample, patients with complete dentures may not be able to function fully. Their chewing ability may decrease, leading to a loss of confidence, which in turn may lead to isolation from others. This is especially harmful for older adults because having a good social network is of great significance for their general and psychologic health. As this segment of the US population continues to grow, it becomes increasingly important for dental care providers to improve their understanding of older adults and evaluate their treatment in a patient-centered focus, using QOL as the ultimate treatment outcome.

Sociodemographic Background

In 1997, 13% of the United States population was 65 years or older, and 4 million were older than 85 years. It is estimated that these numbers will double in the next 30 years to reach 70 million persons older than 65 years by the year 2030. Approximately 60% of older adults are

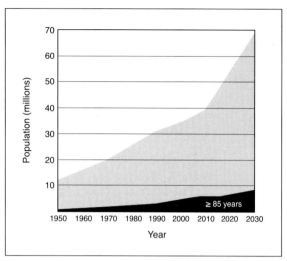

Fig 10-1 United States population 65 years and older. Data from Centers for Disease Control and Prevention.[2]

women, and this percentage increases in the age group above 85 years to 70% (Fig 10-1). On average, 65-year-old men and women live an additional 16 and 19 years, respectively.[2]

About one third of the elderly population assesses its health as fair or poor, with limitations in normal activities. Approximately half of them report at least one disability. Activities of daily living are impaired for more than 4 million older adults, and this percentage increases sharply in people 80 years and older. These patients are more likely than younger patients to present with chronic diseases that require multiple medications. In 1995, about 80% of adults 70 years or older had a least one of the common chronic diseases related to age. Osteoporosis was found in 60% of women and 50% of men, one third had hypertension, and 25% had heart disease. About 10% had chronic respiratory difficulties, approximately 10% had diabetes, and 4% reported a form of cancer.[2] A commonly overlooked fact is that depression is more frequent among older adults than in any other age group (approximately 6%).[3] It is a severe disease that is often related to other systemic diseases and may even lead to suicide.[3] Despite

this high prevalence rate of diseases, it is interesting to note that there seems to be a discrepancy between the health status as measured by the medical profession and the self-reported well-being of older people.[4]

Estrogen replacement therapy and multiple antihypertensive agents are among the most prescribed medications in this population. Anxiolytic and antidepressant drugs are also quite prevalent. It is important to remember that many medications such as calcium channel blockers or anxiolytics have major effects on the oral cavity. Approximately 30% of all drugs are sold to older people, and 9 out of 10 adults older than 65 years use at least one medication. In addition, this group uses about one third of all over-the-counter medications.

General information on QOL and oral health status is available and is becoming increasingly recognized in the treatment of older patients.[5,6] Seven percent of people 65 years and older reported experiencing tooth pain twice in the last 6 months.[7] One third of all older adults present with at least one caries lesion, and one third is edentulous (Figs 10-2 and 10-3). Edentulism decreased by about 20% in the 1980s, while yearly dental visits increased by about 10% in that same period to reach 52% in the early 1990s.[8] Dental caries is the leading cause of tooth loss, but periodontal diseases affect 41% of older people.[9] This high prevalence rate is a function of the accumulation of periodontal loss and is not because of a greater susceptibility to the disease. Periodontal diseases can cause tooth loss and may be causal factors for other systemic diseases such as cardiovascular diseases or diabetes.[1] In addition, oral cancers are much more common in older patients.

Psychosocial Considerations

Social Relationships

The dental health care provider is included among the social relationships of an older person. Social relations can help maximize the health and well-being of older adults. Research

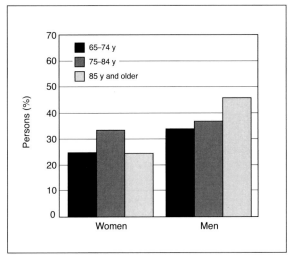

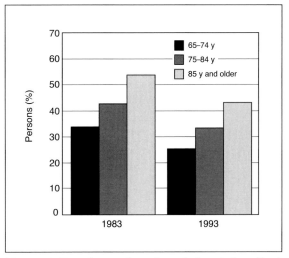

Fig 10-2 Percentage of dentate, noninstitutionalized persons 65 years and older with untreated coronal and root caries by age and sex (United States, 1988–94). Data from Centers for Disease Control and Prevention.[2]

Fig 10-3 Prevalence of total tooth loss (edentulism) among noninstitutionalized persons 65 years and older (United States, 1983–93). Data from Centers for Disease Control and Prevention.[2]

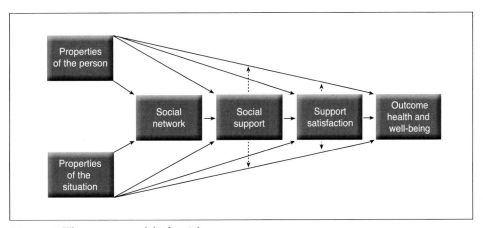

Fig 10-4 The convoy model of social support.

conducted in 1979 showed that people with close social connections are less likely to die early than are people without social ties.[10–12] This association between social relations and morbidity was demonstrated in a study where individuals sought diagnosis and treatment for cancer.[13] Several other studies have shown a similar relationship between social support and morbidity rates associated with cardiovascular disease.[14–16]

Utilization of health care services is also a function of social relations. Among hospitalized patients, those who have good social relations require less time in the hospital[17] and less pain medication.[18] People with close social ties are less likely to develop dementia[19] and use emergency department facilities less frequently.[20]

One patient-centered approach to understanding oral health and QOL is the convoy model of social relations (Fig 10-4).[21] This model proposes that patients are best understood within the framework of a life span. This implies that individuals are influenced by their past and present experiences and even by future anticipated experiences. The convoy model suggests that antecedent characteristics of the person and the situation influence the social experiences of the individual, including their social networks, social support, and support satisfaction. Together these factors influence outcomes such as health and QOL.

This model suggests that a dental health care provider needs to be aware of a multitude of factors that influence a patient's reaction in the dental chair. This patient carries with him or her the experience of the present day, as well as the experience of an entire lifetime, which includes all previous dental care experiences. These experiences will influence any reaction in a given situation. For example, a patient facing treatment for periodontal disease might be aware that gum disease is common in his or her family, that family members in previous generations could not afford care, or that treatment was not yet available. This patient may have expected to lose all teeth, and might rejoice when realizing that treatment can change this expected fate. However, another older person faced with the same condition and proposed treatment might consider this to be a disaster and a personal failure if all the other members of the family were proud of their strong and healthy teeth. In fact, this patient might be especially saddened by the fact that he or she will be the first member of the family to ever require such a treatment. This example illustrates how patients' personal histories influence their attitude toward an event and how past social exchanges can shape an older person's adjustment and coping mechanism with the current oral health experience.

The convoy model of social relations[21] can help one to understand the factors that affect health and QOL. These factors include antecedent conditions, namely the properties of the person and the situation, as well as social network factors, social support, and social satisfaction (see Fig 10-4). Properties of the person refer to those individual sociodemographic characteristics that define the person, such as age, sex, race, income, or religion. It is not difficult to understand how these properties can influence a patient's life experiences.

Properties of the situation refer to role expectations, life events, health crises, health events, and daily obstacles. These properties of the situation clearly influence expectations and experiences, particularly for an older person, who is much more likely to have experienced numerous significant life events. Even if these events did not occur recently, they may have had a negative or detrimental impact. Accumulated health events shape the response of an older person to dental treatment. Older people increasingly may come to see all health events as negative, at best construing such events as an opportunity merely to regain a prior level of competence. The older person is particularly vulnerable because this scenario replays itself in various situations across numerous arenas, eg, physical, environmental, and social. Thus, the older patient who seeks care from a dentist for a minor oral health problem may also have recently experienced a significant heart problem, a minor but very painful foot problem, a recent move from the family home to an apartment, and the loss of a spouse. While these are events of which the oral health professional might not be aware, they can have a negative impact on the outcome of treatment, no matter how competently the treatment is delivered. Therefore, it is important for both health and QOL reasons that the health care professional has a full understanding of the patient's personal properties and the properties of the situation because they influence the achievement and maintenance of a successful oral health–related quality of life (OHRQOL).

In addition to considering personal factors and factors of the situation, the convoy model of social relations[21] stresses the significance of understanding social relations when predicting health and QOL. Figure 10-5 illustrates normal social support networks. The individual, in this case the patient, is the person in the middle of the concentric circles. Those persons to whom the patient feels closest are in the inner circle. Close family members and best friend(s) might fall in this circle. The second and third circles are reserved for those people to whom the individual feels less close. Social relationships tend to remain relatively stable over long periods. This fact relates in particular to those persons who are in the inner circles of a patient's social network, which under normal circumstances would not include a dentist or other health care professionals. However, in the face of a health care crisis, a health care professional can easily become a more central figure in the social network. For example, an older person may be unable to get his or her dentures to fit properly and therefore refuse to participate in a certain event because he or she is too embarrassed or in too much pain to socialize. During such times, seemingly trivial or unimportant circumstances can become critical and the persons who can help the individual cope with that specific circumstance become instantly significant because of the social support they can provide.

The term "social support" refers to what is exchanged. Aid, affect, and affirmation are the three kinds of support that people exchange. Aid is the essential, tangible exchange of instrumental supports, such as that provided by the oral health care provider. The patient may be in pain, have a broken tooth, or require a cavity to be filled, and the oral health care provider can specifically address these needs. Affect refers to the affective or emotional exchange of support. Feeling supported by a health care provider can significantly affect both the immediate and long-term well-being and health of the patient. Affect is support of an emotional and caring type, whereas affirmation, the third type of support, is more cognitive. Affirmation is confirmation by the support provider that the person's values, attitudes, and beliefs are shared. For example, a dentist might support a patient by agreeing that it is important for an 85-year-old person to have his or her own natural teeth.

Another critical element of social relations is how the individual evaluates them. This aspect of social relations has been termed "support satisfaction." It is helpful to health care providers to know how satisfied patients have been with their health care. Understanding patients' evaluations of prior experiences can help the health care provider to design an experience that is

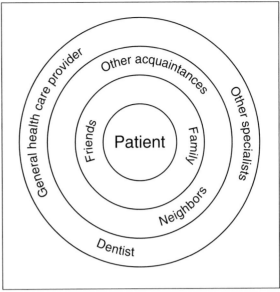

Fig 10-5 Model of a patient's social support networks. During a health care crisis, a health care professional may move to one of the inner circles of the support network.

consistent with previous satisfactory experiences, or to address past problems in a manner likely to enhance the current experience.

General Issues

Although it is not desirable to stereotype older patients, it is important to consider some common characteristics. For example, considering the historical context in which these patients had their first experiences with oral health care sheds light on the fact that these patients may see the health care professional as an authority figure. This fact could affect communication. For example, these patients might believe that it is inappropriate to ask questions. While this behavior may seem like good patient behavior on the surface, it can cause problems. For example, a patient might be fearful of an upcoming procedure, but feels uncomfortable asking about it. This lack of communication can prevent the opportunity to alleviate these fears. Other patients might interpret the need for a procedure inappropriately and will not have such misinterpretations corrected because of their reluctance to ask the relevant questions. In such cases, oral health care professionals could relieve significant worries and concerns if the patients would only ask the appropriate questions.

Interactions with formal health care providers can also take on increased importance for older adults because the number of informal daily social interactions often declines with age. It is, therefore, important for the health care provider not to interact in a hurried manner with the patient. This is especially important when considering the increasing probability of comorbidities with age. If a health care provider does not use an adequate amount of time to assess the general health situation of a patient, serious problems can arise.

It can be useful to think of health and the consequent need for health care as existing along a continuum with three basic stages, namely the precrisis period, the crisis period, and the postcrisis period. Social relationships can benefit the individual in how well he or she copes with each of these stages on the health care continuum. Support from others can be helpful in precrisis situations by encouraging preventive behaviors, such as brushing, flossing, exercising, and regular checkups. The health care provider can carefully explain the usefulness of these activities and discuss with the patient how these behaviors could be most easily integrated into the patient's life. In the case of regular checkups, the health care provider could offer to send a reminder postcard or place a phone call to help arrange the appointment. Crisis situations, such as when the patient is about to undergo a major treatment, require in-depth preparation. It is helpful to allow the patient to have time to adjust to what will happen. Older patients can often cope better if they have advance warning and believe that their health care provider is supporting them.

An example of a postcrisis event is a follow-up interaction that occurs after a procedure has taken place. Such postcrisis support could take the form of information provided to patients that helps them to fully recover or that can speed up their recovery. It is during this period that a health care provider might have a chance to engage a patient in new health behaviors. The support and encouragement provided by a health care provider can be especially important at this critical moment. A positive attitude that communicates a health professional's faith in the individual's ability to meet a new challenge can be very important. Similarly, it is important not to allow patients to engage in any ageist reasoning, eg, to believe that they are too old to change or that change would be fruitless at this late point in life. Older people can find creative ways to maintain those aspects of life that are important to them. This fact is described in the theory of selective optimization with compensation, which suggests that older individuals should focus on fewer behaviors (select) to facilitate better performance (optimize) and engage in behaviors that offset specific negative effects of age (compensate).[22] Although people in every age cohort engage in selective optimization with compensation, older people are more likely to do so because their capabilities are often questioned.

OHRQOL among older people is a complex phenomenon informed by the life history of the individual and the nature of his or her social relations. Personal and situational characteristics of patients, their general history of social relations, and their specific history of relationships with health care providers are important factors influencing their current OHRQOL. It can be beneficial to the health care provider to evaluate the significance of these relationships at different stages of the health continuum. Health care providers play an active role in helping their patients maintain optimal OHRQOL.

Research Findings

OHRQOL is a complex multifactorial entity.[23] A global approach is required for any research on OHRQOL, especially in certain groups of patients.[24] When treating older adults, one may assume that the association between oral health and QOL decreases because of the overwhelming importance of other health issues. However, research findings suggest otherwise.[25]

Three factors are usually most important for an older adult's OHRQOL: lack of pain, ability to maintain hygiene, and a disease-free mouth.[26] Oral health affects a patient's daily life in his or her physical and psychosocial interactions. Furthermore, older patients are unique in their ability to cope with changes as a normal process of aging. Therefore, specific tools are required to better assess and address their OHRQOL. In a series of studies, Atchison and colleagues[27–29] developed and evaluated the Geriatric Oral Health Assessment Index, which was developed in collaboration with different groups of older patients in an attempt to capture specific needs related to functional impairment (Box 10-1). Note the inclusion of negative and positive questions.

Such a tool is useful in evaluating patients, identifying needs of patient subgroups such as those who are covered by a specific type of insurance or receive community care, and measuring outcomes of treatments such as the placement of complete dentures. Ultimately, prospective clinical trials are necessary to definitively examine how different dental treatments affect patients' QOL.[30] However, based on current findings, it is likely that a significant relationship will be found between older adults' oral health status and their QOL. Locker and colleagues[31] recently found evidence that QOL is affected significantly by oral health when they prospectively measured self-rated oral health and general well-being. In another study of self-reported OHRQOL conducted in Veterans Affairs medical centers, Jones and colleagues[32] found that older people complained less than younger patients. However, self-perceived oral health was better when more teeth were present and when dental treatment was sought. Oral health correlated significantly with the degree to which normal daily activities were impaired, the degree of systemic diseases, and patient reports of self-perceived oral health.

Factors such as a higher number of retained teeth, regular visits to the dentist, and a higher

Box 10-1 Specific items from the Geriatric Oral Health Assessment Index[27]
Eat without discomfort
Limit foods—dental problems
Trouble biting, chewing
Trouble speaking
Uncomfortable eating in front of people
Nervous/self-conscious
Limit social contacts
Worry/concern
Use medication for teeth
Teeth and gums sensitive
Pleased with looks
Swallow comfortably

socioeconomic background usually correlate positively with oral health and OHRQOL.[33–35] This finding suggests that older patients do not get used to and accept impaired oral conditions and that they suffer from impaired oral health if no preventive or restorative measures are implemented. Research also shows that oral health may be an indicator of general health and QOL. For instance, the dental provider may detect depressive disorders by finding poor oral hygiene and decreased interest in oral comfort and esthetics.[36]

Oral Health Care and QOL

Only a few studies have measured the impact of dental treatment on QOL. However, it is reasonable to assume that removal of pain and an improvement of function through restorative and/or prosthetic means should improve the ability of older patients to function, interact with others, and perform normal daily activities. Petersen and colleagues[37] conducted a prospective study while implementing free dental services in a community. They showed that as dental visits increased, the patients' oral care improved, and they reported an improved QOL over time. This result is also supported by re-search on the outcomes of treatment of patients with medical conditions. Signs of systemic prob-lems are numerous in the mouth. When these diseases are treated, QOL changes. In addition, QOL of patients with chronic diseases may be improved when oral conditions are addressed.[38]

Dentures

A common clinical question is if and when clin-icians can recommend that a remaining poor dentition be extracted and a denture placed in-stead. Both the patient and the dental provider must decide whether QOL will be improved. In this particular scenario, one may believe that a denture may serve the patient better because of the removal of pain and improved esthetics. However, it is important to note that the mainte-nance of a stable natural dentition is best for all parameters of QOL.[39] In addition, objective out-comes are difficult to obtain and are mostly lim-ited to chewing or masticatory functioning. For instance, the patient-perceived ability of chew-ing is often good and may not deteriorate with time. Because the incidence rate of self-reported poor chewing is low (approximately 10%),[40] it is difficult to assess the impact of treatment be-cause even significant differences could become statistically invisible. Furthermore, in the case of dentures, it is difficult to detect complaints,[41,42] and causal factors are not obvious to most ex-aminers unless a design fault is present.[43]

Implant-Retained Dentures

Modern dental implants were first designed for retention or replacement of poorly retentive full mandibular dentures. Their use has long been advocated and documented. However, the ad-vantages of such devices have been objectively measured only recently.[44] QOL related to implant-retained removable dentures is a good model for studying the impact of oral improve-ments on general well-being because this re-search shows that the implant-retained dentures greatly improve a patient's chewing abilities.

Dental implants are mostly root form, bone-anchored (osseointegrated) devices that support teeth or dentures. In the case of dentures, and particularly mandibular prostheses for resorbed jaws,[45] the extreme mobility of traditional den-tures is eliminated. This can lead to a significant improvement in oral health–related functions.

It has been difficult to evaluate the outcomes of this treatment protocol because of the low number of patient complaints. Other obstacles include high cost, the need for surgical proce-dures, and the fact that patients may not foresee a possible improvement. Therefore, few patients will spontaneously express a desire for such procedures[45] unless they have complaints about their existing prostheses.[46] In addition, profes-sional explanations might bias patients. How-ever, early trials reported a net improvement in multiple QOL-related parameters when patients with poor dentures were provided with implant-retained fixed restorations.[44] This finding was supported by other evaluations.[47–50] Patients re-port successful integration of their prosthesis to the point where they see it as their own body part. Surrogate measures such as bite force, food comminution, or chewing abilities are also improved when implants are used to stabilize a denture.[51–54] These factors contribute to an in-creased overall perception of comfort, which in turn will improve social relationships as the pa-tient develops a sense of security. These events will then lead to an increased QOL. A net improvement is particularly evident when an implant-retained overdenture is used on at-rophic mandibles.[55–57]

Expectations play a role in OHRQOL because the pretreatment status greatly determines the patient's satisfaction with the outcome.[58–60] For instance, in a comparison of new well-fitting dentures with new implant-retained dentures similar results can be seen with regard to satis-faction.[61] However, this finding does not imply that treatment outcomes are alike. Another com-plicating factor is the maintenance of an im-provement. A relapse can be seen in self-reported satisfaction with the treatment because the treatment outcome is no longer a new experience. Short-term satisfaction with a treatment and improved QOL may also decrease over time because of increasing expectations at the end of the treatment phase. Therefore, using long-term evaluations may be a better approach to assessing the true outcomes of treatments.[62]

The use of QOL outcomes as they pertain to different treatment approaches is important for public health purposes if a possible implementation for the general population is under investigation. In a study of more than 5,000 edentulous patients whose treatment with implant-retained dentures would have been covered by their insurance carrier, Cune and colleagues[48] found that only a few patients received this treatment. This was despite the fact that there were a large number of dissatisfied denture wearers, and that the satisfaction of patients treated with implants was high. Indeed, there is a discrepancy between patient experiences and population-based evaluations, despite the fact that an improvement of oral functioning has an important effect on QOL, and can improve patients' general health status.

Future Research

Research is still needed to measure specific QOL outcomes for older people.[63] An adequate evaluation of OHRQOL in older adults could lead providers to design the best treatment plans for this patient population. Importantly, improved oral health will allow these older patients to maintain or improve their self-confidence, have active social lives, and continue to engage in diverse daily activities. This outcome is likely to affect these patients' general health as well. It might allow for a better control of chronic diseases, such as diabetes or hypertension, that can be partially improved with adequate nutrition and physical activity. Clinical decisions such as maintenance of a poor natural dentition vs placement of a denture, or fabrication of a new denture vs advanced implant placement are currently largely based on subjective clinical experiences. Providing clinicians with outcome data

from prospective studies could better inform the dental community about the best possible care for older patients. In the end, patients' QOL is the ultimate treatment outcome on which every provider should focus.

References

1. US Department of Health and Human Services. Oral Health in America: A Report of the Surgeon General—Executive Summary. Rockville, MD: US Department of Health and Human Services, National Institute of Dental and Craniofacial Research, National Institutes of Health, 2000.
2. Centers for Disease Control and Prevention. Health and Aging Chartbook. DHHS publication PHS 99-1232-1. Washington, DC: Centers for Disease Control and Prevention, 1999.
3. National Institutes of Health. Older Adults: Depression and Suicide Facts. NIH Publication 01-4593. Government Printing Office, 2001.
4. Ingerslev J. 85-year-olds in Denmark: The socio-psychological conditions and general health and disorders in a representative group of 85-year-old Danes. Dan Med Bull 1992;39:207–211.
5. Gift HC, Atchison KA. Oral health, health, and health-related quality of life. Med Care 1995;33(suppl): NS57–NS77.
6. Kiyak HA. Successful aging: Implications for oral health. J Public Health Dent 2000;60:276–281.
7. Vargas CM, Macek MD, Marcus SE. Sociodemographic correlates of tooth pain among adults: United States, 1989. Pain 2000;85:87–92.
8. Vargas CM, Kramarow EA, Yellowitz JA. The oral health of older Americans. Hyattsville, MD: National Center for Health Statistics, 2001:3.
9. Brown L, Brunelle JA, Kingman A. Periodontal status in the United States, 1988-91: Prevalence, extent, and demographic variation. J Dent Res 1996;75:672–683.
10. Berkman LF, Syme SL. Social networks, host resistance, and mortality: A nine-year follow-up study of Alameda county residents. Am J Epidemiol 1979;109:186–204.
11. Blazer DG. Social support and mortality in an elderly community population. Am J Epidemiol 1982;115:684–694.
12. House JS, Robbins C, Metzner HL. The association of social relationships and activities with mortality: Prospective evidence from the Tecumseh community health study. Am J Epidemiol 1982;116:123–140.
13. Antonucci TC, Kahn RL, Akiyama H. Psychosocial factors and the response to cancer symptoms. In: Yancik R, Yates JW (eds). Cancer in the Elderly: Approaches to Early Detection and Treatment. New York: Springer Publishing, 1989:40–52.

14. Medalie JH, Goldbourt U. Angina pectoris among 10,000 men. II. Psychosocial and other risk factors as evidenced by a multivariate analysis of a five year incidence study. Am J Med 1976;60:910–921.

15. Berkman LF, Vaccarino V, Seeman TF. Gender differences in cardiovascular morbidity and mortality: The contribution of social networks and support. Ann Behav Med 1993;15:112–118.

16. Taylor CB, Bandura A, Ewart CK, Miller NH, DeBusk RF. Exercise testing to enhance wives' confidence in their husbands' cardiac capability soon after clinically uncomplicated acute myocardial infarction. Am J Cardiol 1985;55:635–638.

17. Wan TTH, Weissert WG. Social support networks patient status, and institutionalization. Res Aging 1981;3: 240–256.

18. Kulik JA, Mahler HI. Social support and recovery from surgery. Health Psychol 1989;8:221–238.

19. Fratiglioni L, Wang H, Ericsson K, Maytan M, Winblad B. Influence of social network on occurrence of dementia: A community-based longitudinal study. Lancet 2000;355:1315–1319.

20. Coe RM, Wolinsky FD, Miller DK, Prendergast JM. Elderly persons without family support networks and use of health services: A follow-up report on social network relationships. Res Aging 1985;7:617–622.

21. Kahn RL, Antonucci TC. Convoys over the life course: Attachment, roles, and social support. In: Baltes PB, Brim O (eds). Life Span Development and Behavior. New York: Academic Press, 1980;3:253–286.

22. Baltes PB. Psychological perspectives on successful aging: A model of selective optimization with compensation. In: Baltes PB (ed). Successful Aging: Perspectives from the Behavioral Sciences. Cambridge, MA: Cambridge Univ Press, 19901–19934.

23. Gift HC, Atchison KA, Dayton CM. Conceptualizing oral health and oral health-related quality of life. Soc Sci Med 1997;44:601–608.

24. Weintraub JA. Uses of oral health related quality of life measures in public health. Community Dent Health 1998;15:8–12.

25. McGrath C, Bedi R. The importance of oral health to older people's quality of life. Gerodontology 1999;16: 59–63.

26. MacEntee MI, Hole R, Stolar E. The significance of the mouth in old age. Soc Sci Med 1997;45:1449–1458.

27. Atchison KA. Development of the geriatric oral health assessment index. J Dent Educ 1990;54:680–687.

28. Atchison KA, Matthias RE, Dolan TA, et al. Comparison of dentist and patient ratings of oral health in dentate elders. J Public Health Dent 1993;53:223–230.

29. Kressin NR, Atchison KA, Miller DR. Comparing the impact of oral disease in two populations of older adults: Application of the geriatric oral health assessment index. J Public Health Dent 1997;57:224–232.

30. Gibson G, Niessen LC. Research issues related to the oral health status of aging veterans. Med Care 1995;33 (11, suppl):NS45–NS56.

31. Locker D, Clarke M, Payne B. Self-perceived oral health status, psychological well-being, and life satisfaction in an older adult population. J Dent Res 2000; 79:970–975.

32. Jones JA, Kressin NR, Spiro A 3rd, et al. Self-reported and clinical oral health in users of VA health care. J Gerontol A Biol Sci Med Sci 2001;56:M55–M62.

33. McGrath C, Bedi R. A study of the impact of oral health on the quality of life of older people in the UK: Findings from a national survey. Gerodontology 1998;15:93–98.

34. McGrath C, Bedi R. Can dental attendance improve quality of life? Br Dent J 2001;190:262–265.

35. Locker D, Slade G. Oral health and the quality of life among older adults: The oral health impact profile. J Can Dent Assoc 1993;59:830–844.

36. Friedlander AH, Mahler ME. Major depressive disorder: Psychopathology, medical management and dental implications. J Am Dent Assoc 2001;132:629–638.

37. Petersen PE, Nortov B. The effect of a three-year trial of a community dental care program for aged pensioners in Denmark [in Danish]. Ugeskr Laeger 1995; 157:2712–2716.

38. Ghezzi EM, Ship JA. Systemic diseases and their treatments in the elderly: Impact on oral health. J Public Health Dent 2000;60:289–296.

39. Appollonio I, Carabellese C, Frattola A, Trabucchi M. Dental status, quality of life, and mortality in an older community population: A multivariate approach. J Am Geriatr Soc 1997;45:1315–1323.

40. Ow RK, Loh T, Neo J, Khoo J. Perceived masticatory function among elderly people. J Oral Rehabil 1997; 24:131–137.

41. Kotkin H. Diagnostic significance of denture complaints. J Prosthet Dent 1985;53:73–77.

42. Kotkin H, Slabbert JC, Becker PJ. The prognostic value of denture complaints. Int J Prosthodont 1993;6: 341–345.

43. Brunello DL, Mandikos MN. Construction faults, age, gender, and relative medical health: Factors associated with complaints in complete denture patients. J Prosthet Dent 1998;79:545–554.

44. Albrektsson T, Blomberg S, Brånemark A, Carlsson GE. Edentulousness—An oral handicap. Patient reactions to treatment with jawbone-anchored prostheses. J Oral Rehabil 1987;14:503–511.

45. Salonen MA. Assessment of states of dentures and interest in implant-retained prosthetic treatment in 55-year-old edentulous Finns. Community Dent Oral Epidemiol 1994;22:130–135.

46. Kotkin H, Slabbert JC, Becker PJ, Carr L. Perceptions of complete dentures by prospective implant patients. Int J Prosthodont 1998;11:240–245.

47. Cune MS, de Putter C, Hoogstraten J. Treatment outcome with implant-retained overdentures: II, Patient satisfaction and predictability of subjective treatment outcome. J Prosthet Dent 1994;72:152–158.

48. Cune MS, de Putter C, Hoogstraten J. Characteristics of 5410 edentulous implant candidates and the treatment they receive. Community Dent Oral Epidemiol 1995;23:110–113.

49. Cune MS, de Putter C, Hoogstraten J. A nationwide evaluative study on implant-retained overdentures. J Dent 1997;25(suppl 1):S13–S19.

50. Cibirka RM, Razzoog M, Lang BR. Critical evaluation of patient responses to dental implant therapy. J Prosthet Dent 1997;78:574–581.

51. Fontijn-Tekamp FA, Slagter AP, van't Hof MA, Geertman ME, Kalk W. Bite forces with mandibular implant-retained overdentures. J Dent Res 1998;77:1832–1839.

52. Geertman ME, Slagter AP, van Waas MA, Kalk W. Comminution of food with mandibular implant-retained overdentures. J Dent Res 1994;73:1858–1864.

53. Geertman ME, Boerrigter EM, van't Hof MA, et al. Two-center clinical trial of implant-retained mandibular overdentures versus complete dentures-chewing ability. Community Dent Oral Epidemiol 1996;24:79–84.

54. Geertman ME, Slagter AP, van't Hof MA, van Waas MA, Kalk W. Masticatory performance and chewing experience with implant-retained mandibular overdentures. J Oral Rehabil 1999;26:7–13.

55. Worthington P, Rubenstein JE. Problems associated with the atrophic mandible. Dent Clin North Am 1998;42:129–160.

56. Boerrigter EM, Geertman ME, Van Oort RP, et al. Patient satisfaction with implant-retained mandibular overdentures. A comparison with new complete dentures not retained by implants—A multicentre randomized clinical trial. Br J Oral Maxillofac Surg 1995;33:282–288.

57. Boerrigter EM, Stegenga B, Raghoebar GM, Boering G. Patient satisfaction and chewing ability with implant-retained mandibular overdentures: A comparison with new complete dentures with or without preprosthetic surgery. J Oral Maxillofac Surg 1995;53:1167–1173.

58. Allen PF, McMillan AS, Walshaw D. Patient expectations of oral implant-retained prostheses in a UK dental hospital. Br Dent J 1999;186:80–84.

59. Allen PF, McMillan AS, Walshaw D. A patient-based assessment of implant-stabilized and conventional complete dentures. J Prosthet Dent 2001;85:141–147.

60. Allison PJ, Locker D, Feine JS. The relationship between dental status and health-related quality of life in upper aerodigestive tract cancer patients. Oral Oncol 1999;35:138–143.

61. Bouma J, Boerrigter LM, Van Oort RP, van Sonderen E, Boering G. Psychosocial effects of implant-retained overdentures. Int J Oral Maxillofac Implants 1997;12:515–522.

62. Awad MA, Locker D, Korner-Bitensky N, Feine JS. Measuring the effect of intra-oral implant rehabilitation on health-related quality of life in a randomized controlled clinical trial. J Dent Res 2000;79:1659–1663.

63. Oral health for aging veterans. Making a difference: Priorities for quality care research agenda. Med Care 1995;33(11, suppl):NS6–NS15.

CHAPTER 11

Oral Health–Related Quality of Life: Does Gender Matter?

Marita Rohr Inglehart, Dr phil habil

Susan F. Silverton, MD, PhD

Jeanne C. Sinkford, DDS, PhD

Gender exerts a powerful force on a child's life from the moment he or she is born. It affects the child's biologic, personal, and social development and shapes opportunities and challenges the child will face in a given society and culture. This chapter explores how it also affects oral health, oral health care, and oral health–related quality of life (OHRQOL), and whether it is adequately considered in the education of future oral health care providers.

Sex vs Gender

In 2001, the Institute of Medicine's Committee on Understanding the Biology of Sex and Gender Differences published a major report entitled "Exploring the Biological Contributions to Human Health—Does Sex Matter?"[1] This report was based on extensive literature reviews and numerous invited presentations. Its overarching conclusions were:

1. Sex matters on all levels of biologic organization (from the cell to the organism), throughout the life cycle ("from womb to tomb"), and in regard to health.
2. The study of sex differences is evolving into a mature science that should be supported, and future research on the role of sex should include longitudinal and interdisciplinary studies.
3. Barriers to the advancement of knowledge about sex differences in health and illness exist and must be eliminated.

One of the 14 recommendations of this exciting and important contribution to understanding the role of sex and gender in human health is to clarify how the terms *sex* and *gender* are used. The authors suggest use of the term *sex* as a "classification according to the reproductive organs and functions that derive from the chromosomal complement"; while *gender* should be used to refer to a "person's self-representation as male or female, or how that person is responded

111

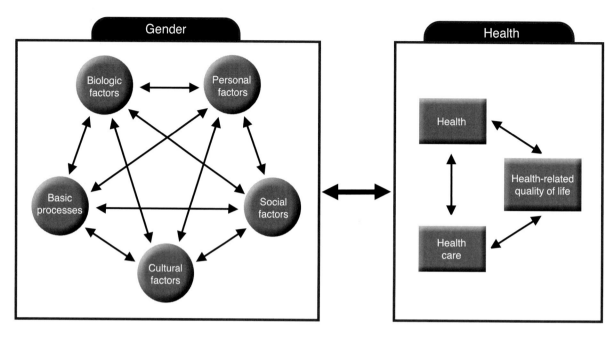

Fig 11-1 Overview of the factors involved in gender and health.

to by social institutions on the basis of the person's gender presentation."[1] Following this recommendation and the definitions described, this chapter will focus on how gender—and not sex—affects health, health care, and quality of life. While a person's sex is closely tied to biologic determinants, the term *gender* will be used in this chapter to refer to the result of a complex interplay of biologic, psychologic, social, and cultural forces. Figure 11-1 illustrates the many ways in which these aspects are interrelated to create the ultimate outcome of gender; it also demonstrates graphically the close interrelationship of gender and health.

Recent research on gender and stress can be used to illustrate this perspective. Historically, it was widely accepted that stress had a physiologic as well as a psychologic and social dimension.[2] However, gender differences in stress responses were largely ignored. This situation changed with the publication of some recent research findings that show that both the physiologic and psychologic aspects of stress and coping are a function of gender.[3] Males as well as

females tend to show a "flight-or-fight" response to stress. However, females' responses also include a pattern of "tend-and-befriend" behavior. Tending consists of nurturing activities that protect oneself and one's offspring, reduce stress, and promote safety. For example, one study showed that children reported more nurturing and love from their mothers on days when their mothers experienced more work stress compared to days when their mothers experienced less work stress, while fathers seemed to withdraw from their children on stressful workdays.[4,5] Befriending involves creating, maintaining, and utilizing social networks that may help in stressful situations. Research shows that, compared with men, women throughout the life cycle seek, give, and receive more social support, and are more satisfied with the support they receive.[6–8]

In addition to describing these behavioral responses, the researchers analyzed the ongoing physiologic changes that occurred during stressful situations in men and women. They found neuroendocrine evidence that suggests that oxytocin, in connection with female reproductive hormones, and endogenous opioid peptide mechanisms might actually drive these behavioral responses.[3] The significant body of research findings that show gender differences in personality[9] and the role of personality as a moderator of stress,[2] as well as the significant impact of cultural forces that cause stress and shape responses,[10] can be added to complement the picture. This example illustrates how the factors and the relationships between these factors shown in Fig 11-1 create the concept of gender and how an application of this complex concept can ultimately contribute to a comprehensive understanding of the relationship between gender and stress. Women and men's stress and coping are clearly the result of an intricate interplay of biologic factors, basic psychologic processes that unfold in the context of these biologic conditions, personal styles, and social and cultural conditions. This chapter argues that women and men's health status, health care, and health-related quality of life (HRQOL) are affected by gender to an equally powerful degree.

Gender and Health Research

In 1990, the Office of Research on Women's Health (ORWH) was established at the National Institute of Health (NIH). This development was in response to a report by the US General Accounting Office, mandated by the Congressional Caucus on Women's Issues, that showed that women were routinely excluded from medical research supported by NIH.[11] While guidelines for the inclusion of women had been in place at NIH since 1986, women were largely underrepresented in research studies. The two major arguments used to justify this neglect of women were that experimental treatments and clinical interventions might have negative effects on undetected or future pregnancies, and that the menstrual cycle could confound research results.[11] Putting this latter argument into the context of health care is interesting. Given

the fact that half of the population is women, the realization that the menstrual cycle might influence, for example, the effectiveness of a new medication should lead to the conclusion that this influence needs to be carefully analyzed in order to understand these effects and guarantee the effectiveness of the medication for women as well as men. However, instead of intensifying the research efforts to understand the exact nature of these "interferences," this argument caused women to be excluded from research.

Prior to 1990, the one area of health research in which women's health issues were studied was reproductive health. This situation has changed since 1990, and especially since 1993, when the guidelines for the inclusion of women and minorities in NIH-funded research became legally binding in the NIH Revitalization Act. Since then, researchers have been required to include women in all clinical research, and to design clinical trials in a way that determines whether the studied variables affect women and minorities differently than they do other research participants.[11] Recent analyses of the frequencies of inclusion of men and women in medical research show that while women are still underrepresented in cardiovascular research, they seem to be overrepresented in cancer research.[12,13] However, the overall trend seems to indicate that gender now is included and analyzed as a factor in most clinical studies.

Gender, Health, Health Care, and HRQOL

Three general trends are quite apparent in the relationships between gender, health, health care, and HRQOL. First, women and men have significantly different life expectancies across all ethnic/racial groups.[14] In 1997, the estimated life expectancy of a new born baby boy was 73.6 years and for a baby girl it was 79.2 years.[15] While more boys than girls are conceived and born on average, the mortality rate for males is higher at every age.[16] At age 65, the gender ratio is 5 women to 4 men, and this discrepancy increases over time to a ratio of 5 women to 2 men in the 85- to 89-year-old age range.[17] This differential in mortality rates might be a result of biologic causes. However, lifestyle factors and risk-taking behavior are also clearly related to this outcome. Men are more likely to smoke,[18] drink alcohol,[19] be involved in homicides or accidents,[20] commit suicide,[21] or die from AIDS.[22] Understanding how biologic factors interact with basic psychologic processes (such as engaging in addictive behavior) and are moderated by personal styles and social and cultural conditions seems therefore crucial when analyzing women and men's mortality data.

Second, women and men differ in the degree to which they are affected by different diseases. One catchy title of a book review on women's health read "Men sweat, women starve: Gender affects health."[23] Variations to this title could be "Women get depressed,[24,25] men abuse alcohol,"[26] or "Women get abused,[27] men get killed,"[28] or "Women have pain,[29] men have high blood pressure."[1] While none of these titles should be interpreted as indicating absolute dichotomies, the titles represent an attempt to capture the fact that the incidence rates of various diseases are quite different for men and women. It is beyond the scope of this chapter to catalogue all the many ways in which women and men differ in their probability to be affected by given diseases. However, it is clear that the causes for these various gender differences need to be better understood and explored with a biopsychosocial perspective in mind.[1]

Third, women and men also differ in their experiences with health care and in their HRQOL. An analysis of the frequencies with which men and women utilize health care services shows, for example, that women have a higher frequency of physician visits than do men.[30] Women and men also differ in their chances to receive certain surgical or pharmacologic treatments.[16] Satisfaction with medical treatment[31] and quality of life (QOL) outcomes after being treated for certain diseases are also a function of gender.

Studies of men and women with cardiovascular problems show clear gender differences in HRQOL. For example, research on patients undergoing coronary artery bypass surgery shows that women do not only have a higher mortality rate 5 years after the surgery than men, but that women reported suffering more in terms of physical limitations, chest pain, and other HRQOL issues when compared with men.[32] The same research also showed that men reported greater improvements in QOL associated with physical activities such as walking than did women.[32] Among patients in a study of left ventricular dysfunction trials, women with heart failure again reported lower general life satisfaction, physical functioning, and social and general health scores when compared with men.[33–35] Gender differences in HRQOL are also found in such diverse areas of health as alcohol dependency treatment,[36] HIV infection,[37,38] and irritable bowel syndrome.[39,40]

HRQOL research itself is still such a research-oriented enterprise that it is not surprising that research on gender differences in QOL are still in an early stage. Although research findings show that there are gender differences in HRQOL, the causes and implications of these differences are largely unexplored and not theoretically understood. Further research is necessary to gain a better understanding of how gender affects health and health care and how the QOL of both men and women is affected by these aspects of their lives.

Gender, Oral Health, Oral Health Care, and OHRQOL

In 1995, Chesney and Ozer[41] proposed a comprehensive paradigm to study the content areas of women's oral health. This model is exemplary in its attempt to capture the complexity of the issues involved and can easily be revised to include QOL considerations. The authors argue for the significance of studying oral diseases that affect most women and those that are more common in women than in men, the relationship between women and the oral health care system, gender influences on health risk, societal influences on women's health, systemic influences on oral health, and oral influences on systemic health. Given the fact that gender differences in oral health indicators are not impressive,[42,43] this paradigm points to the broader picture in which gender and oral health need to be studied.

Gender differences in tooth loss, dental caries, and periodontal disease in the US show that tooth loss of men and women is comparable; women are more likely to have coronal caries than men; men are more likely to have root surface caries than women; and men have more gingivitis, recession, and loss of attachment than do women.[42,43] However, compared with men, women have higher percentages of temporomandibular joint disease[44] and some other oral diseases such as certain alterations in gland dysfunction, alterations in taste, and pregnancy-associated changes.[42,45]

Concerning oral health care utilization, the same picture as was described for general health care emerges. Women are more likely to seek preventive dental care and report a higher rate of preventive dental behavior such as toothbrushing.[46,47] Despite the fact that gender differences in malocclusion are small,[48] women are also more likely than men to seek surgical orthodontic treatment,[49] and men (boys) are less likely than women (girls) to have orthodontic treatment.[50] However, this pattern of women utilizing oral health care services at a higher rate than men is moderated by several structural factors. For example, women are more likely to live in poverty than men, and this affects oral health care utilization.[51] If women struggle with life-threatening diseases such as HIV, they are likely to underutilize oral health care services.[52] These facts imply that given comparable structural situations, women might be even more likely to seek oral health care services when needed as compared with men.

Additionally, new research focuses on understanding the relationship between general health and oral health. This research shows, for example, that there is a relationship between certain oral diseases and some general health conditions, such as cardiovascular disease,[53] postmenopausal bone loss,[54] eating disorders,[55] perinatal outcomes,[56] and low birth weight.[57,58] The effect of gender-specific considerations for medication, such as the effects of hormone replacement therapy for oral health[59,60] and the special considerations during pregnancy,[61] are also well documented.

Less systematically documented are findings that provide information about the relationship between gender and OHRQOL. There is clear evidence that patients perceive a relationship between oral health and QOL[62] and that this relationship is moderated by gender.[63] Women perceive oral health as having a greater impact on their QOL than do men. On the negative side, compared to men, women report more frequently that oral health causes them pain, embarrassment, and financial hardship; while on the positive side, women more frequently perceive oral health as enhancing their life quality, their moods, their appearance, and their general well-being in comparison to men.[63] Considering interactions between patients and dental care providers, it is important to understand that there are gender differences in the QOL before, during, and after a dental interaction. For example, men predict more pain before they have periodontal surgery than do women; however, compared with women, men remember less pain after periodontal surgery.[64] During a dental procedure, male patients differ from female patients not only in their immune system response to anxiety and stress,[65] but also in the way in which interaction with the provider can cause increased anxiety and lead to future avoidance of treatment.[66] After a treatment, research shows that women might report a longer recovery[67] and, in some instances, lower global QOL ratings than do men.[68] Gender differences in the degree to which oral health affects QOL over the life span and in old age are also quite interesting.[69]

In summary, it is evident that gender is a crucial factor in oral health and oral health care research, as well as in clinical practice. On average, men and women might not differ dramatically in their overall oral health. However, the utilization of health care services is clearly dependent on gender influences, as are treatment outcomes and OHRQOL. Special circumstances such as poverty, violence, and physical and mental diseases might be more prevalent among men or women, and these circumstances will then affect oral health and health care statistics. Dental researchers, as well as dental practitioners, need to be aware of the significant role that gender plays in their professions and take advantage of the increasing number of available resources that provide access to information about these important matters.[70,71]

Gender and Dental Education

Given the significance of gender for oral health, oral health care, and OHRQOL, an important question is whether future health care providers are adequately educated about these gender considerations. This question was investigated in a 1997 study that was conducted to determine what is taught about women's health and oral health issues in US and Canadian predoctoral dental programs and to assess the way in which these topics are addressed.[72–74] The background for this study was provided by findings from a survey conducted in February 1995 by the American Association of Medical Colleges (AAMC) with all 142 medical schools in the United States and Canada. The goal of this survey was to determine what was taught about women's health issues in medical school curricula.[75] Following the lead of the AAMC, the American Association of Dental Schools (now the American Dental Education Association [ADEA]) mailed a revised version of this survey to 54 United States and 10 Canadian dental schools in May 1997. The overall response rate was 87.5%. Of the 54 US dental schools, 51 (94%) responded; 5 of the 10 Canadian schools completed the survey. The 124 women's health and gender-related topics were organized into nine content areas:

1. General social themes and gender (6 items)
2. Biologic and basic science considerations (10 items)
3. Developmental and psychosocial themes (25 items)
4. Health behavior and health promotion (13 items)
5. Sexual and reproductive function (9 items)
6. Selected conditions prevalent in women (30 items)
7. Impact of medications (7 items)
8. History, physical examination, and communication skills (12 items)
9. Selected topics of concern to women (12 items)

For each of the topics included, the dental school leadership was asked to indicate (a) whether the topic is covered as part of the required or elective curriculum; (b) in which academic period of the predoctoral dental program the issues are covered; (c) how this material is presented (as a lecture, in a small group or laboratory, case based, or as a tutorial); (d) by which disciplines the material is covered; and (e) which methods of assessing the outcomes (such as by multiple choice questions, oral examination, observation, or objective structured clinical exam) are used.

As an introduction to the results, it is interesting to note that while the respondents were quite willing to provide answers, it became obvious from follow-up communications with academic leaders in the schools that often students were the best source of information on how gender-related topics were covered in the curriculum. This fact indicates that in many dental school curricula gender considerations are not consciously and purposefully included. Not surprisingly, only one of the US schools had a women's health education office or program, and only three of the US schools and none of the Canadian schools had a mechanism to assist faculty in increasing their competence in women's health and in incorporating women's health and gender-related issues into their teaching.

Table 11-1 Topics most frequently included in US dental school curricula*

Topic	Schools (%) addressing topic
Taking an appropriate medical and medication history	90
Normal and abnormal female biology	88
Effects of aging population on oral health care needs and services	88
The impact of poverty/socioeconomic status on health status and access to health care	86
The impact of poverty/socioeconomic status on oral health status and access to oral health care	86
The impact of race/ethnicity/culture on health status, health beliefs and behaviors, and health care utilization	84
The impact of race/ethnicity/culture on oral health status, oral health beliefs and behaviors, and oral health care utilization	84
Temporomandibular disorder	84
Antibiotics	84
HIV testing and counseling	84
Normal and abnormal female physiology	84
Gender differences in the epidemiology of oral diseases and disease rates	84
HIV and related disorders	84
Sjögren syndrome	84

*From a sample of 50 US schools.

Table 11-1 provides a list of topics that were most frequently included in US dental school curricula. Overall, it is encouraging to find that general medical topics were clearly included in dental curricula. Dental schools have also been exemplary in the inclusion of the impact of HIV and related disorders. Temporomandibular joint disease and Sjögren syndrome are also included in all but eight of the US dental school curricula. However, as can be seen in Table 11-2, a list of the most frequently excluded topics shows that issues surrounding female sexuality (lesbian health issues, female sexuality, sexual dysfunction, gender orientation, and sexual orientation) are the most frequently omitted topics.

The results show significant positive efforts on the part of dental schools to provide appropriate training for future practitioners. However, they also demonstrate a lack of conscious inclusion of gender in many dental school curricula. This fact also became obvious when the average responses to statements concerning the significance of women's health issues were analyzed. Respondents were asked to rate the degree to which they agreed with statements based on a 5-point scale, with 5 indicating strong agreement and 1 indicating strong disagreement. On the positive side, it became clear that there is support for such statements as "Educating future dental health care providers about women's health issues is important" (mean, 4.02), and "Educating future health care providers about women's health issues would contribute to their future professional effectiveness" (mean, 4.02). However, the average response to statements about an increase in coverage of these issues in dental curricula is less encouraging. The average response to the statement "Major efforts will be

Table 11-2 Topics most frequently excluded from US dental school curricula*	
Topic	**Schools (%) addressing topic**
Lesbian health issues	8
Female sexuality	16
Sexual dysfunction	20
Gender identification and sexual orientation	24
Women's health issues within and across ethnic groups	24
Women's oral health issues within and across ethnic groups	24
Health consequences of disabilities in women	24
Oral health consequences of disabilities in women	26
Intentional and unintentional injuries	26
Adolescent pregnancy and parenting	26
Legal and ethical issues in women's health	28
Premenstrual syndrome	28
Effects of maternal health and health practices on the health of the fetus and newborn	28

*From a sample of 50 US schools.

made to increase the coverage of women's health issues in our school's curriculum" was only 2.82, with 15 of the 50 schools disagreeing with this statement. The average response to "Future curriculum changes will aim at increasing the coverage of women's health issues in our school's curriculum" was 3.02, with 11 schools disagreeing and only 3 schools agreeing strongly with this statement.

These results show that infusion of gender concerns in dental school curricula is not yet achieved, and is not likely to occur in the near future. This finding will affect the ability of future practitioners to appropriately treat their patients, and is likely to result in barriers to health and oral health care for women. To be effective, future dental school curricula must include education about the role of gender for the oral health, oral health care, and OHRQOL of men and women throughout their life cycle and in all different social/cultural groups.

Conclusion

Research shows that oral health is a function of gender, that oral health care is affected by the patients and the provider's gender, and that OHRQOL depends on a person's gender. NIH research policies drive gender inclusion in all basic and clinical research studies. However, increasing efforts are necessary to infuse gender considerations into dental education and the daily professional life of clinicians. Predicted dental faculty shortages[76] might open the door for more female dental faculty, and these changes might affect the degree to which gender will be considered as an important factor when treating patients. However, further careful efforts will be necessary to assure that female patients, practitioners, and dental educators have a positive QOL in dentistry.[77]

References

1. Wizeman TM, Pardue ML (eds). Exploring the biological contributions to human health—Does sex matter? Washington, DC: National Academy Press, 2001.

2. Inglehart MR. Reactions to critical life events—A social psychological perspective. New York: Praeger, 1991.

3. Taylor SE, Klein LC, Lewis BP, Gruenewald TL, Gurung RAR, Updegraff JA. Biobehavioral responses to stress in females—Tend-and-befriend, not fight-or-flight. Psychol Rev 2000;107:411–429.

4. Repetti RL. The effects of daily job stress on parent behavior with preadolescents. Presented at the biennial meeting of the Society for Research on Child Development, Washington, DC, April 1997.

5. Repetti RL, Wood J. Effects of daily stress at work on mothers' interactions with preschoolers. J Fam Psychol 1997;11:90–108.

6. Copeland EP, Hess RS. Differences in young adolescents' coping strategies based on gender and ethnicity. J Early Adolescence 1995;15:203–219.

7. Belle D. Gender differences in the social moderators of stress. In: Barnett RC, Biener L, Baruch K (eds). Gender and Stress. New York: Free Press, 1987:257–277.

8. Tamres LK, Janicki D, Helgeson VS. Sex differences in coping behavior: A meta-analytic review and an examination of relative coping. Pers Soc Psychol Rev 2002;61:12–30.

9. Feingold A. Gender differences in personality: A meta-analysis. Psychol Bull 1994;116:429–453.

10. Schmitt MT, Branscombe NR, Kobrynowicz D, Owen S. Perceiving discrimination against one's gender group has different implications for well-being in women and men. Pers Soc Psychol Bull 2002;28:197–210.

11. Pinn V. Catalyst for Change. Women's Health at NIH. National Institute of Health. News & Features. NIH Publication 98-3516. Bethesda, MD: NIH Office of Communications, 1998.

12. Meinert CL, Gilpin AK, Unalp A, Dawson C. Gender representation in trials. Control Clin Trials 2000;21:462–475.

13. Lee PY, Alexander KP, Hammill BG, Pasquali SK, Peterson ED. Representation of elderly persons and women in published randomized trials of acute coronary syndromes. JAMA 2001;286:708–713.

14. Leigh WA, Lindquist MA. Women of Color Health Data Book. NIH Publication No. 98-4247. Hyattsville, MD: Office of Research on Women's Health, US Department of Health and Human Services, 1998.

15. Ventura SJ, Anderson RN, Martin JA, Smith BL. National statistics reports: Births and deaths. Preliminary data for 1997. Hyattsville, MD: National Vital Statistics Reports, 1998.

16. Rodin J, Ickovics JR. Women's health. Review and research agenda as we approach the 21st century. Am Psychol 1990;5:1018–1034.

17. Hobbs FB, Damon BI (eds). 65+ in the United States. US Bureau of the Census. Numerical Growth. Changes in age composition. Government Printing Office, 1998.

18. National Center for Health Statistics. Health. United States, 1999, with Health and Aging Chart Book. Publication PHS-99-1232. Hyattsville, MD: National Center for Health Statistics, 1999.

19. Kilbey MM, Sobeck JP. Epidemiology of alcoholism. In: Travis CB (ed). Women and Health Psychology. Mental Health Issues. Hillsdale, NJ: Lawrence Erlbaum, 1988:91–107.

20. Kochanek KD, Hudson BL. Monthly vital statistics report: Advance report of final mortality statistics, 1992. DHHS Publication 92-1120. Hyattsville, MD: US Department of Health and Human Services, Public Health Service, 1995.

21. Cutright P, Fernquist R. The relative gender gap in suicide: Social integration, the culture of suicide and period effects in 20 developed countries, 1955–1994. Soc Sci Res 2001;30(special issue):76–99.

22. Blechman EA, Brownell KD (eds). Behavioral Medicine and Women. A Comprehensive Handbook. New York: Guilford, 1998.

23. Golub S. Men sweat, women starve: Gender affects health. Contemp Psychol 1995;40:269.

24. Cave LJ. Hopeful news for women suffering from mental disorders. National Institute of Health. News & Features. NIH Publication No. 98-3516. Bethesda, MD: NIH Office of Communications, 1998.

25. Ali A, Toner BB. Gender differences in depressive response: The role of social support. Sex Roles 1996;35:281–293.

26. Howard JM, Martin SE, Mail PD, Hilton ME, Taylor ED (eds). Women and Alcohol: Issues for Prevention Research. NIAAA Research Monograph 32, NIH Publication 96-3817. Bethesda, MD: National Institute of Health, 1996.

27. Davidson HA. Child abuse and domestic violence: Legal connections and controversies. Fam Law Q 1995;29:357–373.

28. Travis CB. Health psychology. Focus on women's health. Psychol Sci Agenda March/April 1994:10–12.

29. LeResche L. Gender considerations in the epidemiology of chronic pain. In Crombie IK, Croft PR, Linton SJ, LeResche L, Von Korff M (eds). Epidemiology of pain. Seattle: IASP, 1999: 43–52.

30. Woodwell DA. Advance data: National Ambulatory Medical Care Survey. 1996 Summary. DHHS Publication PHS No. 97-1250. Hyattsville, MD: National Center for Health Statistics, 1997.

31. Scholle SH, Weisman CS, Anderson R, Weitz T, Freund KM, Binko JA. Women's satisfaction with primary care: A new measurement effort from the PHS National Centers of Excellence in Women's Health. Womens Health Issues 2000;10:1–8.

32. Herlitz J, Wicklund I, Sjoland H, et al. Relief of symptoms and improvement of health-related quality of life five years after coronary artery bypass graft in women and men. Clin Cardiol 2001;24:385–392.

33. Riedinger MS, Dracup KA, Brecht ML, Padilla G, Sarna L, Ganz PA. Quality of life in patients with heart failure: Do gender differences exist? Heart Lung 2001;30(2):105–116.

34. Verrill D, Barton C, Beasley W, Brennan M, Lippard M, King C. Quality of life measures and gender comparisons in North Carolina Cardiac Rehabilitation Program. J Cardiopulm Rehabil 2001;21:37–46.

35. Carhart RL Jr, Ades PA. Gender differences in cardiac rehabilitation. Cardiol Clin 1998;16:37–43.

36. Foster JH, Peters TJ, Marshall EJ. Quality of life measures and outcome in alcohol dependent men and women. Alcohol 2000;22:45–52.

37. Cederfjall C, Langius-Eklof A, Lidman K, Wredling R. Gender differences in perceived health-related quality of life among patients with HIV infection. AIDS Patient Care STDs 2001;151:31–39.

38. Schor-Posner G, Lecusay R, Miguez-Burbano MJ, et al. Quality of life measures in the Miami HIV-1 infected drug abusers cohort: Relationship to gender and disease status. J Subst Abuse 2000;11:395–404.

39. Simren M, Abrahamsson H, Svedlund J, Bjornsson ES. Quality of life in patients with irritable bowel syndrome seen in referral centers versus primary care: The impact of gender and predominant bowel pattern. Scand J Gastroenterol 2001;36:545–552.

40. Lee OY, Mayer EA, Schmulson M, Chang L, Naliboff B. Gender-related differences in IBS symptoms. Am J Gastroenterol 2001;96:2184–2193.

41. Chesney MA, Ozer EM. Women and health: In search of a paradigm. Womens Health Res Gender Behav Policy 1995;1:3–26.

42. Redford M. Beyond pregnancy gingivitis: Bringing a new focus to women's oral health. J Dent Educ 1993;57:742–748.

43. Redford M, Drury TF. Gender differences in oral disease patterns among US adults [abstract 2879]. J Dent Res 1997;76(special issue):373.

44. Lipton JA, Ship JA, Larach-Robinson D. Estimated prevalence and distribution of reported orofacial pain in the United States. J Am Dent Assoc 1993;124:115–121.

45. Redford M, Jeffcoat M, Silverton S. Oral health. Excerpt from the Oral Health Working Group Presentation. Research on Women's Health for the 21st Century. In: Silverton SF, Sinkford JC, Inglehart MR, Tedesco L, Valachovic R (eds). Women's health in the dental school curriculum. Report of a survey and recommendations. NIH publication 994399. Washington, DC: US Public Health Service, National Institutes of Health, Office of Research on Women's Health, Health Resources and Services Administration, 1999.

46. Weintraub JA. Gender differences in oral health research: Beyond the dichotomous variable. J Dent Educ 1993;57:753–758.

47. Swank ME, Vernon SW, Lairson DR. Patterns of preventive dental behavior. Public Health Rep 1986;101:179–184.

48. US Department of Health, Education and Welfare, Public Health Service, Human Resources Administration. An assessment of the occlusion of teeth of children 6 to 11 years. DHEW Publication (HRA) 74-1612. Vital and Health Statistics Series 11, Number 130. Government Printing Office, 1983.

49. Profitt WR, Phillips C, Dann C. Who seeks surgical-orthodontic treatment? Int J Adult Orthod Orthognath Surg 1990;5(3):153–160.

50. National Caries Program, NIDR. Dental treatment needs of United States children 1979-80. The national dental caries survey. NIH Publication 82-2246. Government Printing Office, 1982.

51. Kuthy RA, Salsberry PJ, Nickel JL, Policvka BJ. Dental utilization of low income mothers. J Public Health Dent 1998;58:44–50.

52. Shiboski CH, Palacio H, Neuhaus JM, Greenblatt RM. Dental care access and use among HIV infected women. Am J Public Health 1999;89:834–839.

53. Beck JD, Slade G, Offenbacher S. Oral disease, cardiovascular disease and systemic inflammation. Periodontol 2000 2000;23:110–120.

54. Jeffcoat MK, Lewis CE, Reddy MS, Wang CY, Redford M. Post-menopausal bone loss and its relationship to oral bone loss. Periodontol 2000 2000;23:94–102.

55. Spigset O. Oral symptoms in bulimia nervosa. Acta Odontol Scand 1991;49:335–339.

56. Carl DL, Roux G, Matacale R. Exploring dental hygiene and perinatal outcomes: Oral health implications for pregnancy and early childhood. AWHONN Lifelines 2000;4:22–27.

57. Dassanayake AP. Poor periodontal health of the pregnant woman as a risk factor for low birth weight. Ann Periodontol 1998;3:206–212.

58. Jeffcoat MK, Geurus NC, Reddy MS, Cliver SP, Goldernberg RL, Hauth JC. Periodontal infection and preterm birth: Results of a prospective study. J Am Dent Assoc 2001;132:875–880.

59. Allen IE, Monroe M, Connelly J, Cintron R, Ross SD. Effect of postmenopausal hormone replacement therapy on dental outcomes: Systematic review of the literature and pharmacoeconomic analysis. Manag Care Interface 2000;13(4):93–99.

60. Reinhardt RA, Payne JB, Maze CA, Patil KD, Gallagher SJ, Mattson JS. Influence of estrogen and osteopenia/osteoporosis on clinical periodontitis in postmenopausal women. J Periodontol 1999;70:823–828.

61. Moore PA. Selecting drugs for the pregnant dental patient. J Am Dent Assoc 1998;129:1281–1286.

62. McGrath C, Bedi R. Can dental attendance improve quality of life? Br Dent J 2001;190(5):262–265.

63. McGrath C, Bedi R. Gender variations in the social impact of oral health. J Ir Dent Assoc 2000;46(3):87–91.

64. Eli I, Baht R, Kozlovsky A, Simon H. Effect of gender on acute pain prediction and memory in periodontal surgery. Eur J Oral Sci 2000;108:99–103.

65. Koga C, Itoh K, Aoki M, et al. Anxiety and pain suppress the natural killer cell activity in oral surgery outpatients. Oral Surg Oral Med Oral Pathol Oral Radiol Endod 2001;91:654–658.

66. Weiner AA, Forgione A, Weiner LK, Hwang J. Potential fear provoking patient experiences during treatment. Gen Dent 2000;48:466–471.

67. Conrad SM, Blakey GH, Shugars DA, Marciani RD, Phillips C, White RP Jr. Patients' perception of recovery after third molar surgery. J Oral Maxillofac Surg 1999;57:1288–1294.

68. Allison PJ, Locker D, Wood-Dauphinee S, Black M, Feine JS. Correlates of health-related quality of life in upper aerodigestive tract cancer patients. Qual Life Res 1998;7:713–722.

69. McGrath C, Bedi R. The importance of oral health to older people's quality of life. Gerodontology 1999;16:59–63.

70. Studen-Pavlovich D, Ranalli DN. Evolution of women's oral health. Dent Clin North Am 2001;45:433–442.

71. Holt K, Kraft K, DeFrancis B, Coble S (eds). Women's Oral Health Resource Guide. Arlington, VA: National Center for Education in Maternal and Child Health, 2001.

72. Silverton SF, Sinkford JC, Inglehart MR, Tedesco L, Valachovic R. Women's Health in the Dental School Curriculum. Report of a Survey and Recommendations. NIH Publication 99-4399. Washington, DC: US Public Health Service, National Institutes of Health, Office of Research on Women's Health, 1999.

73. Silverton SF, Sinkford JC, Inglehart MR, Tedesco L. Women's health and oral health—A neglected topic in dental education? Presented at the annual meeting of the American Dental Education Association, Washington, DC, March 1999.

74. Silverton SF, Inglehart MR. Integrating Learning in the Fourth Year of Predoctoral Education: How is it done? Presented at the annual meeting of the American Dental Education Association, Vancouver, Canada, March 2000.

75. Sumaya CV, Pinn VW, Blumenthal SJ. Women's Health in the Medical School Curriculum: Report of a Survey and Recommendations. HHS Publication HRSA-A-OEA-96-1. Rockville, MD: US Public Health Service, National Institutes of Health, Office of Research on Women's Health, Health Resources and Services Administration 1997.

76. Haden NK, Beemsterboer PL, Weaver RG, Valachovic RW. Dental school faculty shortages increase: An update on future dental school faculty. J Dent Educ 2000;64:657–673.

77. Silverton SF. Women's health and oral health implications of the curriculum study. Dent Clin North Am 2001;45:603–612.

CHAPTER 12

Effects of Race and Ethnicity on Oral Health–Related Quality of Life

George W. Taylor, DMD, MPH, DrPH

Linda V. Nyquist, PhD

Wenche S. Borgnakke, DDS, MPH, PhD

Marilyn W. Woolfolk, DDS, MPH

In the broader context of general health, racial and ethnic disparities have persisted despite improving health in the US population as a whole. These trends in general health are paralleled in measures of oral health.[1] A comprehensive model of oral health that includes quality of life (QOL) indicators should consider constructs that take into account racial and ethnic disparities. The introduction of a comprehensive model of oral health raises the critical question of whether members of different ethnic, racial, and cultural groups define and value oral health and the consequences of oral diseases and conditions in similar ways. The answers to these questions will help evaluate the extent and consequences of oral health problems in various segments of the population. They will also help determine priorities for and the design of programs that are targeted at improving oral health and oral health–related quality of life (OHRQOL) for all segments of society.

A comprehensive definition of health includes both objective indicators of disease states and the subjective experience of these conditions. Extensive discussions of the conceptualization and measurement of OHRQOL are included in chapters 1, 3, 4, and 5. The organizing framework used in this chapter for evaluating health and the subjective experience of health in people of various races and ethnicities is the conceptual model of oral health proposed by Locker.[2] The beginning point in this model is a state of disease that disrupts the functioning of the biologic systems. This impairment leads to functional limitations and discomfort/pain that can create a disability. This disability can ultimately cause a disruption of social functions (handicap) if not adequately addressed. Although the links among the different components of this model are depicted as unidirectional, no necessary causality is implied. The advantage of using this model is the inclusion of the subjective experiences of the individual as consequences of objective disease states. This conceptual framework is therefore well suited to considering OHRQOL. However, this model does not include any antecedent factors that might contribute to the current disease status. A more complete understanding of the factors influencing the development and progression of oral diseases in people of various races and ethnicities will be critical when developing programs to improve oral health and well-being at the individual as well as the group level.

This chapter provides a review of data on the oral health status of people from various racial and ethnic groups. The consequences of these findings will be discussed. At the end of the chapter, outcomes of a research project that investigated many theoretic and empiric constructs and their impact on oral health and experiences of African Americans and whites in the Detroit tri-county area are presented.

Oral Health in Various Racial and Ethnic Groups

There is considerable evidence that the general health of Americans has improved markedly over the past decades. Despite the general improvements at the population level, there still persist disparate rates of mortality, morbidity, and disability among different racial and ethnic groups.[3–7] The situation concerning oral health is not different. The research findings presented herein, unless noted otherwise, are based on the most recent population-based epidemiologic surveys summarized in the Surgeon General's report on oral health in America.[1] As noted in this report, data for American Indians and Alaskan Natives come from the Indian Health Service, which serves approximately 60% of the members of these groups. Methods of analyses used range from simple exploration of racial and ethnic differences in rates of oral diseases and conditions to more complex, multivariate procedures that permit statistical control of factors that may vary with race and ethnicity. The latter designs allow researchers to assess whether changing these factors would attenuate any observed race differences. Virtually all of this research is

cross-sectional in design; therefore, there is no definitive information about the causes of any observed differences.

Caries Experience

Three factors are strongly associated with the experience of dental caries in the United States: poverty, age, and race/ethnicity. In childhood, adolescence, and adulthood, the percentage of people living in poverty who have at least one untreated decayed tooth is approximately twice the percentage of those living above the poverty level. Among children 2 to 9 years of age with untreated decayed primary teeth, the effect of poverty is most pronounced among nonHispanic whites and is attenuated in other racial and ethnic groups. Mexican Americans living in poverty have the highest percentage of untreated primary teeth with decay (70.5%), while their counterparts living above the poverty level have 56.9% of primary teeth with active decay. Among nonHispanic black children, primary teeth with untreated decay have been found in 67.4% of those below poverty level and 56.1% of those above poverty level. NonHispanic white children have the lowest rates of decay in primary teeth for children both below (57.2%) and above (37.3%) the poverty level. These children show the greatest impact of poverty on their rates of decay. In children ranging in age from 12 to 17 years, Mexican American adolescents living in poverty again have the highest rates of untreated decay with almost half of their permanent teeth (47.2%) on average affected by active decay. Mexican American adolescents living in families that are above the poverty level have substantially fewer teeth (23.1%) with untreated decay. Among nonHispanic black adolescents, family income has little impact. The adolescents in this group living below poverty level have an average of 43.6% of their teeth in active decay, while those living above the poverty level have a similar percentage of permanent teeth (41.7%) with untreated decay. This rate of active decay is more than three times greater than the rate among nonHispanic white adolescents living above the poverty level (12.1%). NonHispanic white adolescents living below the poverty level have less than half the rate of decay (20.7%) than do Mexican Americans and nonHispanic blacks. The caries experience of American Indian and Alaskan Native children served by the Indian Health Service is markedly different from that of the general population. They have five times the rate of dental decay in primary teeth and two to three times the rate of untreated decay. Almost one third of these children living on or near reservations reside in households with incomes below the poverty level.

The effects of poverty and race/ethnicity are also evident in the rates of untreated decay in adults. NonHispanic blacks and Mexican Americans living in poverty have the highest rates of untreated decay, with 46.7% and 46.9% of these groups having decayed and filled teeth, respectively. NonHispanic whites have the lowest average rates of teeth with active decay, regardless of whether they are living below (27.0%) or above the poverty level (8.6%). Among nonHispanic black adults, having above-subsistence income reduces rates of active decay from 46.7% to 30.2%. Mexican American adults show a much greater reduction in active decay (46.9% vs 21.9%) with above-poverty income.

Despite the overall decrease in the prevalence of dental caries among the US population in recent decades, there are still profound disparities associated with poverty and race/ethnicity. The effect of poverty per se is not uniform across all ages within each racial/ethnic grouping. Thus, such simple dichotomies of family income cannot sufficiently explain differences in caries experience. More complex models of the impact of income and other contributing factors will be required to further our understanding of the phenomenon and begin efforts to eliminate these differences. The pervasive effects of race/ethnicity, particularly among children and adolescents in the United States, foreshadow continuing disparities in oral health in the future. Dental caries is preventable and, if left untreated, has a well-documented course leading ultimately to tooth loss.

Periodontal Diseases

Another preventable cause of tooth loss is periodontal disease. Most epidemiologic studies use a clinical measure of periodontal status—the loss of periodontal attachment. Generally, severity of disease increases with increased loss of attachment and number of sites affected. Across most population groups, mean attachment loss increases with age. Severe disease, defined as a loss of attachment of 6 mm or more at one or more sites, varies with socioeconomic status, age, and race/ethnicity. The pattern of the effect of socioeconomic status, with highest rates of disease occurring at the lowest socioeconomic level, is evident at all age levels.

Among adults aged 30 to 49 years, a larger percentage of nonHispanic blacks (12.4%) have severe periodontal disease than do Mexican Americans (6.2%) or nonHispanic whites (5.7%). Rates of disease increase substantially across all racial/ethnic groups in persons aged 50 to 69 years. NonHispanic blacks in this age group still have the highest rates of disease (31.2%), followed closely by Mexican Americans (28.2%). NonHispanic whites also demonstrate higher rates of disease at age 50 to 69 years (16.9%) than at younger ages, but maintain lower rates than other racial/ethnic groups of comparable age. Among those aged 70 years and older, racial/ethnic disparities are most pronounced. Again, nonHispanic blacks have the highest percentage (47.1%) of individuals with at least one site with loss of periodontal attachment of 6 mm or more. Among Mexican Americans in this age group, severe disease affects 32%. The lowest rate of disease in individuals older than 70 years occurs among nonHispanic whites (24.1%).

Gingival bleeding, an indicator of inflammation, also differentially occurs in racial/ethnic groups. More Mexican Americans (63.6%) have gingival bleeding than do nonHispanic blacks (55.7%) or nonHispanic whites (48.6%). At the more extreme end of the spectrum of periodontal conditions is aggressive periodontitis, a rapidly progressive disease that usually occurs in persons younger than 35 years. Among 13- to 17-year-olds, substantially more African American youths (10.0%) have aggressive periodontitis than do Hispanic adolescents (5.0%) or non-Hispanic white adolescents (1.3%).

Tooth Loss

As shown earlier, nonHispanic blacks and Mexican Americans have the highest rates of untreated caries and periodontal conditions. However, when one considers rates of edentulism among persons 18 years and older, a larger percentage of nonHispanic whites (10.9%) have lost all of their teeth than nonHispanic blacks (8.0%) or Mexican Americans (2.4%). Poverty level is related to edentulism among nonHispanic blacks (9.9% of persons living below the poverty level vs 6.9% of those living above the poverty level) and nonHispanic whites (18.7% of persons living below the poverty level vs 9.8% of those living above the poverty level), but has virtually no impact on rates among Mexican Americans (2.1% of persons living below the poverty level vs 2.2% of those living above the poverty level). This apparent paradox of edentulism rates in the general adult population can be understood if one considers two facts: (1) the rates increase with age and (2) there are racial/ethnic differences in life expectancy. Almost a third of Americans aged 65 years and older are edentulous. Because of lower life expectancies among Hispanics and African Americans, population surveys of adults aged 18 years and older will have relatively higher proportions of people from these groups in younger age groups, in whom edentulism is less prevalent, than in older age groups, in whom edentulism is more prevalent.

Although edentulism can affect daily functioning at all age levels, its impact may be more severe among older adults who often have multiple chronic diseases that may also compromise their functioning and well-being. When focusing on rates of edentulism in the older population (65 years and older), different patterns emerge for racial/ethnic groups. Based on Centers for

Disease Control and Prevention data from 46 states participating in the 1995–97 Behavioral Risk Factor Surveillance System,[8] nonHispanic blacks aged 65 years and older have the highest rates of edentulism (31.9%), followed by non-Hispanic whites (24.1%), and Hispanics (18.2%). Also evident in these data are wide fluctuations in the prevalence of edentulism among the 46 states surveyed, from a low of 13.9% in Hawaii to a high of 47.9% in West Virginia.

Loss of all permanent teeth as well as the development and treatment of dental caries and periodontal conditions are influenced by access to and utilization of dental care, attitudes of both patients and their dental care providers, and prevailing standards of care.[9] These factors may vary with race/ethnicity, socioeconomic status, and geographic region in the United States. All of these factors also reflect more complex, underlying processes that contribute to disparities in preventable oral health conditions.

Oral Cancers

Cancers in the oral cavity and pharynx develop in approximately 1.2 million American adults each year. The 5-year survival rate for people with these cancers (52%) is lower than survival rates for prostate, breast, colon, melanoma and several other cancers, and has not improved in the last 25 years (see chapter 14). Although early detection of oral cancers increases the 5-year survival rate to 81.3%, only 35% of these cancer cases are diagnosed at an early, localized stage.

Black men have the highest incidence rates of oral and pharyngeal cancers, namely 20.8 cases per 100,000, compared with white (14.9), American Indian and Alaskan Native (10.2), and Hispanic (8.8) men. Women are less likely to develop oral and pharyngeal cancers than are men. Black and white women have the same incidence rates (6.0 per 100,000). Access, utilization, and treatment issues influence survival rates and stage at diagnosis. Five-year survival rates of patients with oral and pharyngeal cancers vary by race/ethnicity as they do in many other kinds of cancer. Fewer black patients with cancer (34%) survive 5 years compared with white patients (56%). A smaller percentage of oral or pharyngeal cancers are diagnosed at the most treatable, localized stage in black patients (19%) than in white patients (38%), and a larger percentage of distant-stage cancers are diagnosed in black patients (15%) than in white patients (8%). Regardless of stage of diagnosis, the 5-year survival rates are lower for black patients than they are for white patients.

Dental Care Utilization

Many of the disparities in oral health noted are potentially ameliorated with professional dental care. Although estimates of utilization vary depending on the time interval surveyed and whether the reason for visit (preventive or symptomatic) is specified, the patterns of relative differences among racial/ethnic groups remain similar. The most recent review of dental services utilization patterns over 20 years is based on the 1977 National Medical Care Expenditure Survey, the 1987 National Medical Expenditure Survey, and the 1996 Medical Expenditure Panel Study.[10] Utilization was defined as one or more dental visits during a given year. Overall, the percentages of community-dwelling persons of all ages who made a dental visit did not increase significantly from 1977 (41.05%) to 1987 (42.43%) and 1996 (43.19%). The percentages of those patients who made a dental visit differed in age, gender, socioeconomic, and racial/ethnicity groupings. Although the disparity in visits of nonHispanic blacks and whites attenuated somewhat over the 20 years, according to the most current data (1996), substantially smaller percentages of blacks (26.73%) and Hispanics (29.86%) visited a dentist than did whites (47.84%).

One of the more broad-based studies of utilization of dental services that evaluated a number of ethnic groups and risk factors for underutilization is the International Collaborative Study of Oral Health Outcomes (ICS-II), which was conducted at research sites in the US.[11] Dental care utilization was determined by asking respondents when they had last received dental care. Comparisons were made among whites and African Americans in Baltimore, Navajo and Lakota served by the Indian Health Service, and whites and Hispanics in San Antonio, TX, in two age cohorts: 35 to 44 years and 65 to 74 years. Dentate Native Americans, Hispanics, and African Americans in both age cohorts reported significantly fewer dental contacts in the previous year than did white adults, with rates ranging from a high of 80.4% of middle-aged white adults in Baltimore to a low of 28.5% of older Navajo adults. Multivariate analyses found that dentate status, having a usual source of care, and oral pain were associated with the number of dental contacts in all ethnic groups. Different patterns of risk factors for underutilization emerged in each of the ethnic groups, suggesting that the most effective utilization promotion programs would be designed in a culture-specific way.

Racial/ethnic disparities in oral health conditions in conjunction with different rates of utilization suggest that dental care needs are not being uniformly met. More direct evidence of unmet dental care needs and a comparison of these needs with unmet medical needs are available in data from the 1994 National Access to Care Survey.[12] Respondents indicated if they wanted dental care but could not get it in the past 12 months and if there was an unmet medical or surgical care want during the same period. Unmet dental care wants were more prevalent (8.5% of the population) than unmet medical or surgical care wants (5.6%). Almost twice as many African Americans (15.0%) reported unmet dental care wants as did whites (7.4%) and Hispanics (8.2%). Fair or poor health status, poverty, type and lack of insurance, age, gender, and geographic region also influenced rates of unmet dental care wants. Almost 55% of those adults having unmet wants tried to obtain dental care. Of these individuals, 36.8% indicated that the main reason they did not obtain care was because they could not afford it.

Among the 45% of the population who did not try to obtain dental care when they wanted it, 71.4% indicated that it was mainly because they could not afford care. Regardless of whether an attempt was made to obtain dental care, 43.7% of those reporting a need indicated that they had limited their activities for longer than a day because of their dental problem.

Many of the epidemiologic data described earlier evaluate oral health conditions in racial and ethnic groups because they are population-based studies, which necessarily include individuals from all segments of society. Although the national surveys have sufficient sampling of Hispanic and African American populations to permit comparisons with white samples, most do not provide sufficient information to assess subgroups within racial or ethnic groupings. In addition, regional or state-level data are seldom available to more effectively target high-risk groups. Finally, few studies are specifically designed to consider oral health and related factors in a comprehensive manner within a racial or ethnic category.

Prevalence of oral health conditions in different segments of society reflects in part dental care contacts in the past as well as dental care needs of the future. Racial/ethnic disparities in the development of oral diseases as well as the opportunities for receiving care are influenced by macro-level variables of societal structure or organization. Variations in oral health and dental care utilization or unmet dental care needs that occur by region of the country and state of residence suggest that optimal health can be constrained or facilitated by societal structures. Closely entwined with the societal influences on oral health are those processes determined at the level of the individual embedded in a cultural context. Culture-specific values, beliefs, normative standards, and traditions all operate within individuals to influence how health is defined, which events are viewed as health problems, what might be done to prevent such problems, and what actions will be taken if health problems are identified. To date, few studies have examined race/ethnicity in concert with the individual-level objective and subjective measures that comprise a comprehensive model of oral health and QOL. Virtually no studies have systematically integrated more macro-level dimensions in empirical investigations of oral health models.

Studies on Racial/Ethnic Differences in OHRQOL

Although numerous studies with racial/ethnic information include certain components of OHRQOL, few collect objective measures of oral health status and measures of QOL assessed with validated measurement instruments. The measure of OHRQOL used most frequently in studies of racial/ethnic differences is the Oral Health Impact Profile (OHIP).[13] This instrument assesses self-reported dysfunction, discomfort, and disability caused by problems related to the mouth, teeth, or dentures.

In the Piedmont 65+ Dental Study in North Carolina, racial differences in both objective oral health and perceived impact were observed at the 3-year follow-up when participants were 70 years or older.[14] Dentate black respondents in this sample had more episodic dental visits and poorer oral health, including more unreplaced tooth loss, untreated carious roots and coronal surfaces, root fragments, and periodontal disease. Older black respondents reported more frequent impact on 22 of the 49 items comprising the OHIP when compared with older white respondents. The summary measure of total impact also varied by race, with older black respondents reporting more impact than did older white respondents. However, when the data were controlled for average periodontal pocket depth, the number of root fragments, and whether dental visits were episodic or regular, the differences among these older black and white adults in total impact of oral problems were not significant.

The social impact of oral health status has also been compared across groups in three countries.[15] Adults 65 years and older from metropolitan and rural areas in Australia and Canada and older black and white adults in the Piedmont region of North Carolina had oral examinations and completed the 49-item OHIP questionnaire. Six groups of respondents were thus compared. Among the dentate older adults, more black respondents in North Carolina reported frequent impact on 41 items than did those in the five other patient groups. The older adults in North Carolina reported the most extreme overall social impacts of oral problems, with black respondents reporting the greatest impact and white respondents reporting the lowest impact among the six groups. A twofold difference in social impact between black and white respondents persisted after statistically controlling the oral status, including number of missing teeth and retained root fragments, maximum pocket depth, number of decayed root surfaces, and number of problem-oriented dental visits.

The few studies published on racial/ethnic differences in OHRQOL serve to highlight the dearth of information currently available for comprehensive models of oral health in all segments of society. The data consistently show racial/ethnic disparities in many objective indicators of patients' oral health status. The knowledge of the consequences of these conditions on the daily lives and experiences is currently limited to older black and white adults living in North Carolina. Clearly, advancements in comprehensive models of oral health will require much more extensive research that considers the full spectrum of cultural variation in the United States.

OHRQOL in African American and White Individuals

The data presented herein come from a probability sample designed to accrue a large number of African Americans. A broad range of objective measures of oral health status was obtained in an in-home dental examination, and a similar breadth of subjective and sociodemographic measures was obtained in a 65-minute interview conducted at the home of the respondents.

The study population was a disproportionate probability sample of adults aged 18 years or older living in housing units in the Detroit tri-county area. Sampling was done using stratified, clustered, area probability sampling techniques based on 1990 census tracts. For analyses aimed at comparing African Americans with whites and to separate the effects of race or ethnicity from socioeconomic status, the sampling design was disproportionate, with African Americans, particularly African Americans in high-income census tracts, being oversampled. Weights used in the analyses were corrected for the disproportionate sampling so that weighted results are representative of adults living in the Detroit tri-county area. Data were collected in face-to-face interviews in 1994. The response rate for the interview was 71% (n = 787). Interview questions were designed to represent predisposing sociodemographic characteristics, predisposing health beliefs, enabling resources, and health behaviors included in models predicting health care utilization.[16–18]

At the time of the interview, respondents were invited to participate in a second phase of the study, a 65-minute in-home dental examination. A total of 577 respondents (73.3%) were examined. Modified National Institute of Dental Research examination criteria were used.[19] Tooth loss, prosthetic replacements, and root fragments were recorded. Coronal and root surfaces were examined for caries and restorations. Probing was not done for individuals reporting a history of heart murmur, artificial heart valve, or joint replacement. Gingival bleeding and calculus were noted. Pocket depth was measured at four sites on each tooth present. Excluded from the analyses were 79 individuals who had no natural dentition, had a health history contraindicating probing, or were of Hispanic origin.

Respondents also completed the 49-item OHIP questionnaire at the time of the oral examination.[13] The seven dimensions of the scale represent a theoretic hierarchy of the social impacts of oral disorders in Locker's model of oral

Table 12-1 Demographic characteristics of the study sample

Characteristics	No. of African American adults* (weighted %)	No. of white adults[†] (weighted %)
Age[‡] (y)		
18–29	64 (27.4)	49 (22.6)
30–39	86 (23.8)	54 (19.5)
40–54	75 (25.8)	72 (31.2)
55–64	39 (13.1)	23 (8.5)
≥ 65	30 (9.9)	55 (18.3)
Gender		
Male	113 (43.8)	112 (47.2)
Female	181 (56.2)	141 (52.8)
Income (US $)		
< 20,000	111 (35.1)	62 (17.6)
20,000–39,999	80 (27.1)	55 (20.2)
40,000–69,999	69 (25.8)	71 (30.5)
≥ 70,000	34 (12.0)	65 (31.7)
Education (y)		
< 12	58 (22.0)	32 (11.1)
12	85 (32.3)	89 (33.5)
13–15	99 (29.4)	58 (25.2)
≥ 16	52 (16.3)	74 (30.2)

*N = 294 (26.3%).
[†]N = 253 (73.7%).
[‡]Among African American adults, range = 18–85 y; among white adults, range = 19–93 y.

health.[2] These dimensions are functional limitation, physical pain, psychologic discomfort, physical disability, psychologic disability, social disability, and handicap.

The following sections will (1) describe the prevalence of oral conditions in nonHispanic African American and white adults, (2) assess factors associated with the oral conditions in each group, (3) identify differences in social impact of these conditions (OHIP subscales), and (4) determine whether differences in impact between nonHispanic African Americans and white Americans persist after controlling for oral health as well as other demographic and psychosocial factors.

Table 12-1 displays the demographic characteristics of the nonHispanic African American and white adults in the sample. The respondents ranged in age from 18 to 93 years and the

distribution was roughly equal in the two groups. Slightly more than half of those respondents in each group were women. The income and education distributions show that white respondents in this population-based sample had on average higher education levels and higher incomes than did the African American respondents. This finding was similar to that observed in the overall US population.

Two measures of the oral health of the groups presented in Tables 12-2 and 12-3 suggest that racial disparities in caries experience and periodontal disease existed among the groups in our sample. As seen in Table 12-2, white respondents actually had a higher average number of decayed and filled teeth (DFT score) than did African American respondents. However, a closer examination of the components of this measure indicates that African Americans had

Table 12-2 Caries experience of African American and white study participants

Caries	African American participants (SD)	White participants (SD)	P value
Mean DFT*	7.80 (5.6)	10.90 (6.8)	< .001
Mean DT†	2.50 (3.4)	1.10 (2.7)	< .001
%D‡ of DFT	37.50 (37.6)	12.50 (24.7)	< .001
Root fragments	0.20 (0.8)	0.05 (0.4)	.004

*DFT, Decayed and filled teeth.
†DT, Decayed teeth.
‡D, Decayed.

Table 12-3 Clinical indicators of periodontal disease in African American and white respondents

Periodontal disease indicators	African American participants	White participants	P value
Mean percentage of teeth with gingival bleeding (SD)	19.2 (21.0)	10.0 (13.7)	< .001
Mean percentage of teeth with calculus (SD)	35.4 (32.2)	17.9 (25.7)	< .001
No. of participants with severe periodontitis (weighted %)	44.0 (19.2)	26.0 (11.6)	.044

on average over twice as many teeth with active decay as did white respondents, who had more teeth with restorations. The percentage of DFT scores representing decayed teeth that required treatment (%D of DFT) was almost three times higher in African Americans compared with white participants. Thus, differences were found in treatment needs and treatment received, which potentially implicate differential access to care and resources. The number of root fragments also varies based on racial differences. Root fragments usually result from a carious process that has destroyed a substantial portion of the crown of the tooth. In persons receiving regular dental care, root fragments would have been removed or caries would not have progressed to destroy the crown. Therefore, a much higher proportion of retained root fragments in African Americans suggests different patterns of dental care.

Gingival bleeding is an index of gingival inflammation. There are typically two common types of periodontal disease in this population, gingivitis and periodontitis, both of which are bacterially induced. Periodontal disease leads to destruction of the tooth attachment, inflammation, and in severe cases, loss of teeth. Percentage of teeth with gingival bleeding, a measure of periodontal status, was almost twice as high in African American participants as compared with their white counterparts (see Table 12-3). Similarly, the mean percentage of teeth with calculus was higher among African American adults than white adults. A dichotomous

Table 12-4 African American and white participants responding "very often," "often," or "sometimes" to OHIP subscale items

Subscale	African American participants (%)	White participants (%)
Functional limitation		
Difficulty chewing*	32.8	17.2
Trouble pronouncing words*	14.0	5.0
Tooth does not look right*	52.5	27.3
Looks affected	27.3	16.4
Breath stale*	52.2	30.0
Sense of taste worsened*	19.1	4.6
Food catching in teeth	86.6	77.3
Digestion worsened*	15.4	2.8
Dentures not fitting properly*	9.2	2.5
Physical pain		
Painful aching	27.5	18.2
Sore jaw	13.6	10.7
Headaches	10.4	5.7
Teeth sensitive to hot and cold	57.0	45.0
Toothache	21.3	13.3
Painful gums	27.1	15.9
Uncomfortable to eat*	39.7	23.3
Sore spots in mouth	27.2	17.5
Uncomfortable dentures*	10.2	2.4
Psychologic discomfort		
Worried about dental problems	36.8	24.5
Self-conscious due to teeth*	35.5	19.6
Miserable due to dental problems*	19.6	10.4
Uncomfortable about appearance*	35.7	19.1
Tense due to problems with teeth*	22.1	10.1
Physical disability		
Speech unclear*	12.2	4.1
People misunderstood words*	13.3	4.3
Less flavor in food*	11.8	3.4
Unable to brush properly	21.3	10.3
Avoid eating some foods*	30.4	16.5
Diet unsatisfactory	8.3	2.2
Unable to eat with dentures	5.4	1.1
Avoid smiling*	22.4	5.5
Meals been interrupted	9.4	4.2
Psychologic disability		
Sleep been interrupted	8.0	4.2
Upset due to problems with teeth	11.5	9.7
Difficult to relax	11.7	5.5
Felt depressed*	12.2	3.9
Concentration affected	4.8	2.9
A little embarrassed	23.9	11.5

Table 12-4 (cont) African American and white participants responding "very often," "often," or "sometimes" to OHIP subscale items

Subscale	African American participants (%)	White participants (%)
Social disability		
Avoid going out	2.5	0.4
Less tolerant of spouse or family	3.2	1.3
Trouble getting along with others	1.0	0.4
A little irritable	3.5	3.1
Difficulty doing usual activities	3.4	1.3
Handicap		
General health worsened*	6.2	1.0
Suffered financial loss	2.7	3.4
Unable to enjoy others' company*	7.1	1.5
Life less satisfying	6.1	1.5
Totally unable to function	1.5	0.2
Unable to work to capacity	3.3	1.2

*$P = .001$.

measure of severe periodontitis was constructed based on the presence of five or more sites with attachment loss of 5 mm or more, with one of those sites having probing pocket depth of 5 mm, an indication of inflammation. Using this measure, a significantly higher proportion of African Americans were classified as having severe periodontitis.

Thus, in this sample, group differences in oral health existed. Data from the OHIP allow us to explore whether these racial disparities in disease are also evident in measures of the social impact of oral conditions. Respondents indicated whether the problem described in each statement and attributed to the condition of their teeth, gums, or dentures had been experienced "very often," "fairly often," "sometimes," "hardly ever," or "never" in the previous 3 months. Table 12-4 presents the percentages of respondents reporting an impact of "very often," "fairly often," or "sometimes" for each item in the seven OHIP subscales. As can be seen in the Table 12-4, for 48 of the 49 items, a higher percentage of African American respondents reported that the problem had affected them than did white re-

spondents. The table indicates which differences were statistically significant ($P < .001$).

Based on the conceptual model of oral health by Locker,[2] one immediate consequence of oral disease and impairment is functional impairment, the loss of function at the level of body parts or organ systems. On the OHIP functional limitation scale, more African Americans reported problems with chewing, pronouncing words, having a tooth that does not look right, having stale breath, a worsening sense of taste and digestion, and dentures not fitting properly than did white respondents. A second consequence of disease and impairment is pain or discomfort. Compared with white respondents, more African Americans indicated on the OHIP physical pain scale that it was uncomfortable to eat and that their dentures were uncomfortable. A larger proportion of African American than white respondents also reported problems on the OHIP psychologic discomfort scale. The items showing significant differences on this subscale were "being self-conscious due to teeth," "uncomfortable about appearance," and "tense due to problems with their teeth, gums,

Table 12-5 OHIP total scores* and self-rated oral health and general health

Self-rated scores	African American respondents' OHIP total scores*	White respondents' OHIP total scores*
Oral health		
Excellent	–2.20	–2.90
Good	–0.10	–1.50
Fair	5.10	3.00
Poor	11.60	10.60
General health		
Excellent	0.24	–1.90
Good	1.22	0.03
Fair	3.20	0.27
Poor	7.70	3.80

*The OHIP total scores are composites of the standardized subscale scores.

or dentures." The next level of consequence in this hierarchical model is disability, which is defined as a limitation or lack of ability in the performance of everyday activities. Differences in endorsements of items from the OHIP physical disability scale indicate that more African Americans suffered communicative problems (speech unclear, others misunderstood words, avoidance of smiling) and problems related to diet and nutrition (food avoidance, less flavor in food) than did white respondents. Item endorsements on the OHIP psychologic disability scale suggest that more African Americans felt depressed and embarrassed because of oral health conditions than did white respondents. Responses to items on the OHIP social disability scale, while consistent with previously noted patterns of disparities in impact, did not demonstrate statistically significant differences. The final level of consequence of oral disease is handicap, representing the experience of disadvantage. More African American than white respondents indicated that their general health had worsened and that they were unable to enjoy the company of others (see Table 12-4 for items on the OHIP handicap subscale).

The internal consistency of the seven subscales was similar in both racial groups using Cronbach's alphas, ranging from .73 to .86 in African Americans and from .69 to .87 in whites. Several methods have been described for combining item responses to obtain subscale scores.[20,21] Because the OHIP subscales have different numbers of items, a total OHIP score was computed by transforming each of the seven subscale scores into a standardized score and adding these standardized scores together.

Table 12-5 presents the relationship between the total OHIP score and self-ratings of oral health. Among both African American and white adults, there is a linear relationship between perceptions of oral health and perceived impact of oral conditions. Respondents who view their oral health as excellent indicate minimal impact on the OHIP, whereas those who rate their oral health as poor report the greatest impact of oral conditions in their daily lives. A similar pattern exists between perceptions of general health and total OHIP scores. Among African Americans, however, there is a more pronounced impact of oral conditions at each level of self-rated general health.

The analyses reported thus far describe striking differences in oral health and the impact of oral conditions between the two respondent groups. However, they provide little insight into possible reasons for these disparities. Racial or ethnic categories potentially represent a host of

Table 12-6 Regression model predicting OHIP total scores for dentate respondents*

Predictor variables	Unstandardized regression coefficients	P
Problems paying for dental care	2.8	< .001
No. of checkups in the past year	1.5	.002
Self-reported oral health status	1.8	< .001
Satisfied with the way mouth looks	1.4	< .001
Self-reported general health status	0.9	< .001
Decayed surfaces	0.2	< .001
Race (African American = 0)	−0.9	.100

*R^2 = 0.41 (ie, this model accounts for 41% of the variance in OHIP score).

differences in social conditions, health beliefs and behaviors, and health care. To determine whether consideration of some of these factors would attenuate the effect of racial grouping, a multivariate regression model was tested. Included in the model were predictor variables representing demographics, enabling resources, oral health behaviors, and need. The dependent variable was the OHIP total score. Table 12-6 presents a model that accounts for 41% of the variance in OHIP score. Controlling for factors such as problems with paying for dental care, number of checkups in the past year, satisfaction with the appearance of the mouth, self-rated oral and general health, and number of decayed surfaces, the effect of race on OHIP scores is substantially reduced.

Although the cross-sectional nature of these data precludes the identification of definitive causal linkages, one can see that many of the factors in this multivariate model are potentially modifiable. For example, the restoration of decayed surfaces as well as problems with paying for dental care are issues of access that could be addressed with changes in public health policies. The effect of checkup frequency on the impact of oral conditions is somewhat paradoxical. As the number of checkups increases, the OHIP score increases. It may be that treatment

or symptomatic visits are being captured in the checkup variable. Further analyses may clarify this relationship.

Summary

The results of this study confirm the existence of racial/ethnic oral health disparities. These results also show that these disparities have profound effects on the lives of individuals. The design of this study provides both advantages and challenges to understanding why these differences in oral health and OHRQOL exist. Health is determined in a complex manner that can change over time. Race or ethnic groupings serve as a proxy variable for a multitude of factors that contribute to health status. Rather than genetic variation, it has been proposed that a primary reason for the persistent effect of race is because income, education, and other factors representing societal structure are not equivalent across racial and ethnic groupings.[2,22–25] However, there is evidence that African Americans have higher mortality and morbidity rates than their white counterparts in similar income and education categories for several diseases and adverse health outcomes.[25–29] The mechanisms that cause these persistent racial and ethnic differences in the experience of health undoubtedly operate in this study as well.

The oversampling of higher-income African Americans in this study provides more precise estimates of variables associated with income. The population weights applied in the analyses result in the disproportionate representation of African Americans in the lower categories of income, which reflects current societal conditions. The breadth of data collected allows us to evaluate the role of clinical indicators of disease, factors representing societal conditions, and individual beliefs and behaviors as they influence the OHRQOL of the study participants.

However, this study cannot address potential causal linkages among these factors because of its cross-sectional design. Ultimately, the causal mechanisms must be identified to eliminate health disparities. Studies such as the one presented herein often deal with diseases or conditions that have developed over the course of several years, sometimes since childhood. An understanding of the factors that are related to preclinical or asymptomatic stages of disease and its progression and how these factors are influenced by race will be necessary. This understanding will ultimately come from well-designed prospective studies that evaluate patients, beginning at younger ages and continuing longitudinally over extended periods. These studies need to include both objective, clinical measures of oral health as well as more subjective beliefs, attitudes, values, behaviors, and experiences. The more descriptive, cross-sectional studies such as this one will provide information as to which variables need to be included in more costly designs that investigate causal linkages. Both kinds of studies will lead to a better understanding and an amelioration of processes that operate in the US ethnic and racial groupings that currently experience a greater burden of disease and consequent effects on well-being and QOL.

Acknowledgment

The study reported here, entitled "Predictors of Oral Health in African Americans," was supported by National Institute of Dental and Craniofacial Research grant DE10145 to Drs W. Paul Lang and David L. Ronis.

References

1. US Public Health Service, US Department of Health and Human Services. Oral Health in America: A Report of the Surgeon General—Executive Summary. Government Printing Office, 2000.
2. Locker D. Measuring oral health: A conceptual framework. Community Dent Health 1988;5:3–18.
3. Williams DR, Collins C. US socioeconomic and racial differences in health: Patterns and explanations. Ann Rev Sociol 1995;21:349–386.
4. Manton KG, Patrick CH, Johnson KW. Health differentials between blacks and whites: Recent trends in mortality and morbidity. Milbank Q 1987;65(suppl 1):129–199.
5. Cooper RS. Health and the social status of blacks in the United States. Ann Epidemiol 1993;3:137–144.
6. Hummer RA. Black-white differences in health and mortality: A review and conceptual model. Sociol Q 1996;37:105–125.
7. Lillie-Blanton M, Parsons PE, Gayle H, Dievler A. Racial differences in health: Not just black and white, but shades of gray. Ann Rev Public Health 1996;17:411–448.
8. Total tooth loss among persons age greater than or equal to 65 years: Selected states, 1995-1997. Mor Mortal Wkly Rep CDC Surveill Summ 1999;48:206–210.
9. Burt BA, Eklund SA. Dentistry, Dental Practice, and the Community. Philadelphia: Saunders, 1999.
10. Manski R, Moeller JF, Maas WR. Dental services. An analysis of utilization over 20 years. J Am Dent Assoc 2001;132:655–664.
11. Davidson PL, Anderson RM. Determinants of dental care utilization for diverse ethnic and age groups. Adv Dent Res 1997;11:254–262.
12. Mueller CD, Shur CL, Paramore LC. Access to dental care in the United States: Estimates from a 1994 survey. J Am Dent Assoc 1998;129:429–437.
13. Slade GD, Spencer AJ. Development and evaluation of the Oral Health Impact Profile. Community Dent Health 1994;11:3–11.
14. Hunt RJ, Slade GD, Strauss RP. Differences between racial groups in the impact of oral disorders among older adults in North Carolina. J Public Health Dent 1995;55:205–209.
15. Slade G, Spencer A, Locker D, Hunt R, Strauss R, Beck J. Variations in the social impact of oral conditions among older adults in South Australia, Ontario, and North Carolina. J Dent Res 1996;75:1439–1450.

16. Andersen R, Newman JF. Societal and individual determinants of medical care utilization in the United States. Milbank Mem Fund Q Health Soc 1973;51: 95–124.

17. Aday LA, Andersen R. A framework for the study of access to medical care. Health Serv Res 1974;9: 208–220.

18. Andersen RM. Revisiting the behavioral model and access to medical care: Does it matter? J Health Soc Behav 1995;36:1–10.

19. Miller AJ, Brunelle JA, Carlos JP, Brown LJ, Loe H. Oral Health of United States Adults: The National Survey of Oral Health in US Employed Adults and Seniors, 1985–1986—National Findings. Washington, DC: US Department of Health and Human Services, Public Health Services, National Institutes of Health, 1987.

20. Slade G. Derivation and validation of a short-form oral health impact profile. Community Dent Oral Epidemiol 1997;25:284–290.

21. Allen P, McMillan AS, Locker D. An assessment of change in the Oral Health Impact Profile in a clinical trial. Community Dent Oral Epidemiol 2001;29: 175–182.

22. Krieger N, Williams DR, Moss NE. Measuring social class in US public health research: Concepts, methodologies, and guidelines. Ann Rev Public Health 1997; 18:341–378.

23. Lynch JW, Kaplan GA. Socioeconomic position. In: Berkman LF, Kawachi I (eds). Social Epidemiology. New York: Oxford University Press, 2000:13–35.

24. Kaufman JS, Cooper RS, McGee DL. Socioeconomic status and health in blacks and whites: The problem of residual confounding and the resilience of race. Epidemiology 1997;8:621–628.

25. House JS, Williams DR. Understanding and reducing socioeconomic and racial/ethnic disparities in health. In: Smedley BD, Syme SL (eds). Promoting Health: Intervention Strategies from Social and Behavioral Research. Washington, DC: National Academy Press, 2000:81–124.

26. Keil JE, Sutherland SE, Knapp RG, Tyroler HA. Does equal socioeconomic status in black and white men mean equal risk of mortality? Am J Public Health 1992;82:1133–1139.

27. Schoendorf KC, Hogue CJR, Kleinman JC, Rowley D. Mortality among infants of black as compared to white college-educated parents. N Engl J Med 1992;326: 1522–1526.

28. Williams DR, Lavizzo-Mourey R, Warren RC. The concept of race and health status in America. Public Health Rep 1994;109:26–41.

29. Kaplan GA, Everson SA, Lynch JW. The contribution of social and behavioral research to an understanding of the distribution of disease: A multilevel approach. In: Smedley BD, Syme SL (eds). Promoting Health: Intervention Strategies from Social and Behavioral Research. Washington, DC: National Academy Press, 2000:37-80.

CHAPTER 13

Impact of Medical Conditions on Oral Health and Quality of Life

Guido Heydecke, DDS, Dr Med Dent

John P. Gobetti, DDS, MS

Most dental visits are for routine dental care such as cleanings or caries removal. Most dental patients are healthy and their health status does not interfere with their dental treatment. However, there are patients who suffer significantly from systemic health conditions that have an impact not only on their daily lives, but also on their dental care. A number of these general health conditions influence the patients' oral health and their oral health–related quality of life (OHRQOL).

The oral cavity enables individuals to perform two basic functions, speech and alimentation.[1] Eating and drinking are not only associated with nutrition, but they also satisfy the pleasures of taste and consumption. Furthermore, eating, drinking, and speaking, as well as kissing, are social functions that require a healthy oral cavity. Mastication and salivation depend on the health of the oral tissues, teeth, neural and muscular tissues, sensation, and saliva. Impairments on any level may interfere with swallowing and compromise the protec-

tion of the airway.[2] Systemic health and the health of all oral tissues is important in preparing food for proper digestion and also for protecting the respiratory tract against aspiration of food and fluids.

Teeth also contribute greatly to the esthetic appearance of the face. The presence or absence of teeth influences the appearance of the face and the patient's self-image and confidence. Appearance is an important aspect in social interactions, as is the clarity of speech, which depends on the presence and position of teeth.[3]

Disease conditions may cause functional impairments and discomfort or pain, which, in turn, affect a patient's quality of life (QOL). If parts of the stomatognathic system are damaged or missing, this is likely to have a strong impact on the individual, especially if essential functions like eating and communicating are impeded. Oral health can thus affect a person's QOL. Up to 75% of people believe that the impact of oral health is greatest in the areas of eating, comfort, and appearance.[4] General disease

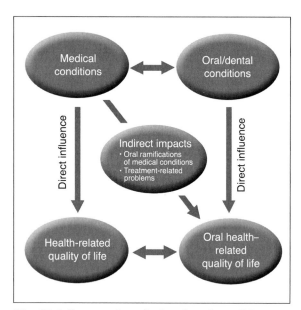

Fig 13-1 Impact of medical and oral conditions on quality of life.

conditions produce various oral sequelae[2,5,6] and thus affect oral health and OHRQOL. In dental conditions, the impact on oral health and OHRQOL is direct, while in medical conditions the impact on oral health is indirect and mediated through oral sequelae of the disease or through its treatment (Fig 13-1).

The most frequently occurring general health conditions that affect oral health will be described in this chapter. This information will be supplemented by a description of their ramifications for a patient's QOL.

Systemic Diseases and Oral Health

The most common causes of death in the United States are diseases of the heart, followed by malignant neoplasms, cerebrovascular diseases, chronic obstructive pulmonary disease, and dia-betes (Table 13-1).[7] Among chronic conditions excluding impairments, arthritis is most prevalent, followed by chronic sinusitis, hypertension, allergic rhinitis, and heart disease (Table 13-2). However, among persons aged 65 years and older, high blood pressure, heart disease, and diabetes are most prevalent.[8]

Many chronic and acute conditions are prevalent today in a medically compromised patient; however, only those conditions and their treatments that account for the most and worst oral sequelae will be described here. These include heart disease, cerebrovascular disease, hypertension, diabetes, arthritis, and cancer.

Heart Disease

Diseases of the heart are the most common cause of death in the United States. Ischemic heart disease, myocardial infarction, and hypertension account for most of the deaths related to heart disease (see Table 13-1).[7] Coronary heart disease has significant effects on the health and QOL of patients. Because the heart is often referred to as the center of the body and mind, an injury to the heart is perceived as a threat to the whole person. Cardiac pain is the immediate consequence of manifest heart disease and has a large impact on QOL, which is seen to be significantly affected in patients after a cardiac incident.[9] Therapeutic interventions improve the clinical condition of most patients markedly, but the defects and residual distress persist for long periods.[9,10] Cardiac patients score significantly lower than the population as a whole on scales measuring physical function, role function, bodily pain, and social function. Quality of life in cardiac patients is heavily impaired by their inability to work, angina pain, dyspnea, and coexistent lung disorders.[10] Because the relationship between QOL and clinical indicators of disease severity is nonlinear, QOL scores decrease rapidly with a higher severity score.[11] However, change and improvement in QOL in cardiac patients are difficult to quantify because of the insufficient sensitivity of generic instruments for measuring QOL changes in cardiac

Table 13-1 Most common diseases causing mortality in the United States*

Rank	Disease	No. of deaths (per 100,000 people in 1997)
1	Diseases of the heart	130.5
2	Malignant neoplasms	125.6
3	Cerebrovascular diseases	25.9
4	Chronic obstructive pulmonary diseases	21.1
5	Diabetes	13.5

*Data from the National Center for Health Statistics.[7]

Table 13-2 Reported chronic conditions in the United States*

Rank	Disease	Rate (per 1,000 people in 1996)
1	Arthritis	127.3
2	Chronic sinusitis	125.0
3	Hypertension	107.1
4	Allergic rhinitis	89.8
5	Heart disease	78.2
6	Asthma	55.2
7	Chronic bronchitis	53.5
8	Hemorrhoids	32.3
9	Dermatitis	31.2
10	Diabetes	28.9

*Data from Adams et al.[8]

conditions (eg, Short Form 36 Health Survey [SF-36], Schedule for Evaluation of Individual Quality of Life [SEIQoL], Quality of Life Index [QLI], Quality of Life After Marginal Infarction [QLMI]).[12]

Oral sequelae of heart disease are numerous. The most striking component is orofacial pain, originating as a projection from the heart area. Such cardiac pain is experienced in the neck, mandible, and clavicular area. The inability to chew and swallow can also be experienced as "false" symptoms originating from cardiac conditions.[13] Pain is known to influence OHRQOL and general QOL significantly.[14–17]

There is little evidence of the extent to which acute heart conditions have a direct influence on oral health. It has been suggested that patients with acute heart disease have poorer oral health than do healthy controls. However, because heart disease is often associated with a high degree of comorbidity,[18] other factors may contribute to a reduction in oral health.

Research shows that patients with heart disease have poor oral health and fewer teeth.[19] Several studies demonstrated that dental and periodontal conditions contribute to an increased risk of heart disease with the release of bacteria and bacterial products like lipopolysaccharides or antigens into the blood flow.[20,21] Individuals with a history of atherosclerotic disease, ischemic heart disease, and heart failure, on average, have fewer teeth present. Subjects with a history of heart disease are also more likely to be edentulous.[22] These compromised oral conditions contribute to a lower OHRQOL.

Other effects on oral health in patients with heart disease are mostly drug induced. Calcium channel blockers and angiotensin-converting enzyme inhibitors have been documented to cause gingival hyperplasia and gingival bleeding and to facilitate gingivitis.[23,24] Together with reduced oral hygiene, this condition facilitates plaque accumulation, which, in turn, leads to reduced gingival health and finally to more severe forms of periodontitis. Research shows that periodontal conditions reduce OHRQOL and general QOL.[15,25] The treatment of cardiac disease and hypertension with certain drugs often has the side effects of salivary gland dysfunction, xerostomia (calcium channel blockers, diuretics, beta-blockers), and alterations in taste.[5] Lowered saliva flow rates have a deleterious effect on OHRQOL.[26] Partially or completely edentulous cardiac patients are also likely to select a softer diet, which often has a high carbohydrate and fat content because it excludes healthier foods like vegetables or salad that are too difficult to chew.

Cerebrovascular Disease

Cerebrovascular disease is the third most common cause of death in the US general population (see Table 13-1). Cerebrovascular incidents or strokes generally cause significant neurologic deficits. They often result in physical, perceptual, and communication disorders that have an impact on activities of daily living. Only about 50% of patients who have had a stroke recover completely. Common consequences of neurologic deficits in the remainder of patients are ongoing problems with speech, memory, mood, and self-care.[27] The level of activity and QOL are the most important primary outcome measures in patients who have had a stroke.[28] Sur-vivors of strokes usually experience significant reductions in health-related QOL compared with the general population. The effects include impairment of social role functions, mobility restrictions, restrictions of personal and leisure time activity, and stress. Many long-term stroke survivors continuously suffer from depression.[29] Further impacts stem from related conditions like hypertension, which are often found in patients with cerebrovascular disease.[27,30]

Cerebrovascular disease also has a detrimental effect on oral health. Oral motor and sensory deficiencies result in impaired lip and tongue function. These deficits then impair oral functions, namely speaking, eating, and drinking, which ultimately interfere with social interaction.[4,15,16,31–33] Eating and speech impairment have been demonstrated to cause significant impacts on OHRQOL. Reduced sensory and motor capacity lead to poorer dental hygiene. Paralysis, limited to one side of the body, can hamper effective brushing of the teeth, followed by an increase in accumulation of plaque and oral microorganisms.[34,35] The increased number of bacteria triggers caries and periodontal disease. Further problems relate to dysphagia. Up to 85% of patients who have had a stroke show abnormalities of oral and pharyngeal function. Problems during swallowing can easily result in aspiration of foods and fluids.[36]

Hypertension

Hypertension was the third most common chronic condition in the United States in 1996 (see Table 13-2).[8] The prevalence in persons older than 65 years is even higher.[7] The treatment of hypertension has been demonstrated to lower the morbidity and mortality associated with cerebrovascular and coronary heart disease.[37] Although hypertension is generally regarded as a symptomless disease, a "silent killer," patients with this condition regularly report a lower health-related QOL than do healthy persons. Hypertensive individuals are affected more by bodily pain, reduced vitality, and impaired social function.[30] Hypertension can either be treated with medication or lifestyle changes like dietary adjustments, smoking cessation, exercise, and weight loss. Once patients diagnosed with hypertension receive medication, they are likely to require it for the rest of their lives.[38]

The treatment of high blood pressure with antihypertensive drugs usually has a positive effect on the patients' QOL.[39] Long-term improvements are greatest with combinations of beta-blockers (acebutolol) and a diuretic (chlorthalidone) over a period of up to 4 years. The impact of antihypertensive drug treatment is controversial. One study found no negative impact on general health-related QOL,[39] while others found that some β-blockers (carvedilol) and diuretics (trichlormethiazide) interfered with sexual function in men.[40, 41]

The influence of hypertension alone on oral health has not been clearly established. However, it has been demonstrated that salivary gland function is altered in hypertensive patients who do not take any medication.[42] Common side effects of antihypertensive drugs include xerostomia, gingival hyperplasia, and other mucosal side effects.[24] Thiazide diuretics can result in lichenoid reactions, erosions, and ulcerations of the buccal mucosa.[43] The resulting oral pain and discomfort have a significant negative effect on OHRQOL.[15,16,32,33] In addition, there is evidence that patients receiving antihypertensive drugs have lower salivary flow rates, and even the composition of the saliva may be affected.[44] Patients with dry mouth often experience significant oral discomfort, mucositis, microbial infections, taste impairment, and difficulties with chewing and swallowing. Research shows that the symptoms found in xerostomia have a large, negative impact on OHRQOL.[26] These patients may also be affected by the negative biologic consequences of reduced amounts of saliva such as increased plaque accumulation, root and generalized caries, and premature loss of teeth.[45] Individuals with higher decayed, missing, and filled (DMF) teeth scores clearly demonstrate a reduction of OHRQOL.[32,33]

Diabetes

Diabetes is the tenth most prevalent chronic condition in the US population (see Table 13-2).[8] It also is the fifth most common cause of death in the United States (see Table 13-1).[7] Diabetes mellitus is a metabolic disease that affects most of the human organ systems including oral tissues. Patients with diabetes often feel challenged by their disease; the demands of the daily management of diabetes are substantial. Patients with diabetes in general report a lower QOL than healthy individuals. Diabetes impedes physical functioning, role functioning, and general health perceptions.[46] The treatment of diabetes requires a continuous effort to stabilize the metabolic state. Patients with type 1 diabetes are generally more dissatisfied, more worried, and have a lower general QOL than do patients with type 2 diabetes.[47,48] Diabetes is associated with a significantly higher risk of being unable to perform mobility-related tasks, like walking a quarter mile, climbing stairs, or doing housework, all of which affect QOL.[49]

Several clinical studies have reported an increased incidence and severity of oral disease in patients with diabetes, especially when poorly controlled.[50] The most prevalent oral condition associated with diabetes mellitus is periodontal disease.[51] Ultimately, periodontal disease leads to loss of teeth. Diabetics exhibit a higher score of missing teeth that can be explained by periodontal attachment loss and alveolar bone loss.[52] Bone loss is significantly higher and also progresses at a higher rate in patients with type 2 diabetes than in healthy individuals.[53] Furthermore, the smell and taste functions seem to be negatively affected in diabetic patients because of the occurrence of peripheral neuropathy. This is a common long-term complication that is associated with poorer QOL.[48,54] The resulting poor control of diet is further complicated by the presence of a change in salivary production and chemistry in some diabetic patients. Controversial results have been reported on the reduced saliva production in diabetic patients, which might be modulated by medication for the treatment of other systemic conditions.[55,56] Diabetic thirst adds to this finding.

A higher caries incidence and reduced numbers of teeth are often found in diabetic populations, with all components of the DMF score being consistently higher than in the general population.[57] Lower numbers of teeth, periodontal conditions, and dry mouth contribute significantly to lower QOL in diabetics.[15,16,32,33]

Arthritis

Arthritis is the most common chronic debilitating disease in the United States today, affecting more than 43 million people (see Table 13-2).[8,58] Arthritis is prevalent in the form of osteoarthritis, for which the most powerful risk factor is age, and rheumatoid arthritis, which is an autoimmune disease.

People suffering from arthritis generally experience various symptoms that influence their functional status as well as their health-related QOL. Patients with arthritis have a poorer self-reported health status in all domains of living, including psychologic disability.[59] With increasing disease severity, higher impacts are recorded, particularly on the scales measuring mobility and physical function.[59,60] Limited dexterity is frequently reported, which interferes with essential tasks like eating, self-care activities such as oral hygiene, and leisure activities and makes some patients dependent on help from others. Many patients feel embarrassed by having to ask others for help and therefore try to tolerate their pain. Most of the problems reported by patients with arthritis are associated with pain. Many patients also suffer from the loss of social interactions triggered by activity restriction associated with depression.[60,61] While patients with osteoarthritis are more worried about their physical disability and crippling, patients with the autoimmune form are also concerned about the long-term prognosis of their disease, the future, and death.[62]

Osteoarthritis and rheumatoid arthritis both affect the temporomandibular joint.[63,64] Degen-erative joint disease of the temporomandibular joint often presents with various clinical symptoms, ranging from unilateral and bilateral pain to pain during mastication and limited range of motion. In the case of autoimmune rheumatoid arthritis, the onset of the disease occurs at an earlier age with similar symptoms, clicking, crepitation, and muscle pain. The joint pain during mastication leads to avoidance patterns during chewing, which in turn results in less effective mastication.[64]

Rheumatoid arthritis is often associated with other autoimmune diseases. Secondary Sjögren syndrome is often found in patients with rheumatoid arthritis. One serious oral consequence of Sjögren syndrome is damage to the salivary glands. The symptom most commonly reported is intense oral dryness because of significantly reduced amounts of saliva compared with healthy individuals. Other complaints are sensitivity to acids, difficulty eating dry foods, and dryness of lips and tongue.[65,66] The issue of susceptibility of patients with Sjögren syndrome to increased periodontal disease has been controversial.[65,67] However, these patients have higher DMF scores and a higher incidence of cervical caries and candidiasis than the general population.[65,68]

Medications for patients suffering from rheumatoid arthritis often have oral sequelae. The use of cytostatic drugs is effective. However, it causes oral mucositis, ulceration, xerostomia, infections, and pain. The reactions to other drugs used such as gold salts, cyclosporine, and nonsteroidal anti-inflammatory drugs are similar.[69,70] Xerostomia-related symptoms often have a detrimental effect on OHRQOL.[26]

In summary, many of the conditions associated with Sjögren syndrome and arthritis such as pain, xerostomia, oral discomforts because of ulcerations, caries, and tooth loss, are known to be strong predictors of a lower OHRQOL.[15,16,26,36]

Cancer

Cancer is second to heart disease as the leading cause of death in the United States.[7] Most cancers found in organs other than the oral cavity or the head and neck region do not affect oral health directly. The exceptions are leukemia and lymphomas. Patients with leukemia and lymphoma frequently display oral manifestations like gingival bleeding and hyperplasia or extranodal tumors.[23] All forms of cancer affect the general health and QOL of patients. Patients with cancer, especially in advanced stages, suffer from declining functional status, pain that is often poorly controlled, and severe symptoms of the disease.[71]

Pain is one of the most common problems in advanced stages of cancer. It can be somatic, visceral, or neuropathic. Each of the individual sources of pain is associated with a classic clinical presentation, which requires proper diagnosis and specific attention. Radiation and chemotherapy may cause damage to neural tissue and thereby induce pain. Appropriate pain control is necessary for these conditions.[72,73] Following is a clinical case describing the effect of cancer and its treatment on oral health and the subsequent QOL issues that arise.

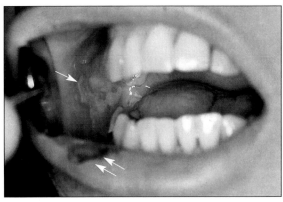

Fig 13-2 Mucosal *(arrow)* and lip *(double arrow)* ulcerations secondary to mucositis arising because of chemotherapy in a patient with breast cancer.

A 46-year old woman was referred to a tertiary care clinic for oral medicine. She had metastasizing breast cancer for which she was receiving chemotherapy with 5-fluorouracil. She had health insurance coverage through Medicaid.

The patient could not open her mouth wide or eat because of large mucosal ulcerations. Because of the eating problems and cancer cachexia, she had lost 39 pounds in weight. The patient was suffering from pseudomembranous and chronic erythematic *Candida* infections, angular cheilitis, and perioral herpes simplex. Because of her immunosuppressive medication, the normal organisms in the oral cavities had become pathogenic. The rubbing of her teeth against the mucosa caused irritation and erosions (Fig 13-2). She also had xerostomia secondary to the chemotherapy. Furthermore, she had alterations in taste due to her medications. Her light pink gingival tissue indicated that she was anemic and had pancytopenia due to the chemotherapy. She had difficulty with mastication; some of her teeth were missing and additional extractions were necessary.

The most urgent issues were to provide the patient with improved oral comfort and pain relief to allow for proper nutrition. She tolerated high-caloric foods like cheesecake, which were soft and cold. A partial denture was suggested but postponed because of financial limitations. Neosporin ointment was used for lip care. Hyperhydration was suggested through increased intake of fluids. Biotene products, mouthwash, and a mild toothpaste were used to support the symptomatic treatment of xerostomia. A soft brush and nontraumatic method of brushing facilitated oral hygiene. Frequent rinsing of the mouth to remove any leftover food was suggested.

As seen in the preceding case description, chemotherapy gives rise to the strongest side effects in cancer therapy. Immunosuppressive chemotherapeutic medications are stomatotoxic. They cause a multitude of oral impacts by disrupting the mucosal tissue barrier. Some of

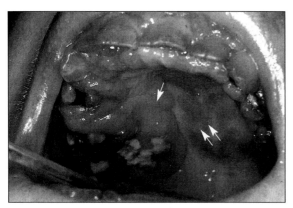

Fig 13-3 Leukemic gingival infiltrate *(arrow)* with superimposed *Candida* infection in a patient with monocytic leukemia. Note the hematoma on the palate arising because of thrombocytopenia *(double arrow)*.

the consequences of this treatment modality include severe oral mucositis, gingivitis, ulcerations, and secondary bacterial and viral infections in up to 40% of the patients who receive it (Fig 13-3).[74–76] Other effects include the alteration of chemosensory function, leading to impaired taste.[74] Taste problems, nausea, and vomiting contribute to a lack of appetite and lead to undernutrition in patients with cancer. Lack of appetite is a frequent complaint of patients with severe illness. The presence of cancer often has a direct effect on reducing appetite. Another cause yielding poor appetite is depression related to the cancer diagnosis or antitumor therapy.[77] The lack of appetite often causes a reduced intake of necessary foods and a change in diet, which detracts from QOL because favorite foods are no longer enjoyed. These changes contribute to an overall feeling of sickness and ultimately lead to severe weight loss.[78,79]

The severity of the effect of cancer on diet and nutrition also depends on the function of the salivary glands. Patients subjected to radiotherapy of the head and neck area consistently suffer from xerostomia, which requires changes in diet, saliva substitution, and meticulous oral health care. Other symptoms are alteration and loss of taste as well as trismus, limited jaw movement, and risk of osteoradionecrosis.[80] Patients treated with radiotherapy often report lower QOL than do patients who undergo surgical treatment alone.[81,82] In addition, dry mouth and alterations in taste persist, restricting food choices for patients with head and neck cancer, and thus producing long-term negative effects on their QOL. Patients receiving radiotherapy report pronounced negative effects related to the treatment.[82,83]

Leukemia and lymphoma often result in oral ulcers, which are prone to secondary infection. Gingivitis and spontaneous bleeding might be amplified by poor oral hygiene. Lymphomas present with extranodal tumors. Their symptoms include burning mouth syndrome.[23] Cancers of the head and neck region, including oral cancer, frequently have a permanent injurious effect on the patient. The direct effects on OHRQOL are pronounced in patients with oral cancer. Patients with oral and pharyngeal cancer suffer from considerable losses causing significant facial disfiguration and speech, mastication, eating, and swallowing problems. Impairments are the consequences of both the tumor itself as well as the treatment with surgery, chemotherapy, or radiotherapy. Patients with oral cancer have significantly lower functional status scores than healthy individuals, both before and after surgical therapy. Surgery also has been demonstrated to lower QOL with regard to the perception of emotional behavior, communication, and eating.[84,85]

Oral consequences of radiotherapy and chemotherapy also include increased incidence of dental caries, gingivitis, and periodontal disease, and difficulty swallowing. Frequent vomiting can lead to acidic erosion of enamel and dentin. All of these conditions require and are responsive to special care, like regular dental hygiene, application of topical fluoride products, and dietary adjustments.[79] It is therefore imperative to monitor these patients and address any sequelae. Even when compared with other cancer patient populations that are not disease-free, patients with head and neck cancer have a

Table 13-3 Effects on oral health related to damage to oral tissues

Oral tissue affected	Oral health outcomes
Teeth	Caries Periodontal disease Loss of teeth
Oral mucosa	Infections Mucositis Ulceration Neoplasms
Salivary glands	Infections Impaired function Neoplasms
Orofacial muscles	Trismus Neoplasms

significantly lower QOL.[82] Furthermore, symptoms often persist after the completion of therapy, delaying recovery and compromising QOL.[6] Patients with head and neck cancer do not return to a normal state of health,[86] and neither does their QOL.

Oral Health Care for Medically Compromised Patients

Research has shown that all of the aforementioned conditions have an impact on OHRQOL (Table 13-3). Many of these general health conditions and their treatments directly or indirectly involve the teeth and the periodontal attachment. Teeth can be affected by radiotherapy administered for cancer, which predisposes them to caries secondary to xerostomia. The damage of salivary gland tissue leads to a reduced salivary flow. This further increases the number of oral microorganisms that are often increased after ra-

diotherapy.[87,88] Unfortunately, patients with cancer often display poor oral hygiene.[89] Professional hygiene instruction is necessary for this group of patients to counteract the progression of caries and periodontitis. Additional benefits can be expected from fluoride products, antibacterial mouthrinses, salivary substitutes, or stimulating agents (pilocarpine HCL, Salagen, MGI Pharma, Bloomington, MN).[79,90] Similarly, professional oral health care is indicated for patients with limitations of lip and tongue movements after a stroke, because this limits the self-cleaning effects.[34,35] The situation of these patients may be further complicated by limitations of their manual dexterity. Professional oral hygiene has been demonstrated to significantly improve the OHRQOL of patients who have had a stroke. Patients with regular oral hygiene experience fewer effects from caries, lose fewer teeth, and have fewer chewing and eating problems.[91]

Reduced rates of caries and periodontal disease as well as fewer missing teeth have a beneficial effect on OHRQOL.[15,16,32,91] Therefore, oral health care is necessary to counteract the negative effect of general medical conditions and/or their treatment on oral health. The replacement of missing teeth using fixed and removable prosthodontic appliances has been demonstrated to improve OHRQOL significantly. This applies to both partial and complete edentulism.[92]

Salivary gland tissue is highly susceptible to radiation damage. A reduction in stimulated and resting salivary flow can persist for many years and produce complaints of dry mouth. Xerostomia is also associated with significant oral discomfort due to mucositis, increased oral infections, difficulty in chewing and swallowing, and impaired taste.[93,94] These symptoms significantly impair OHRQOL.[26] While minimizing the irradiation of glandular tissue is important, further management of xerostomia can include the use of salivary stimulants and substitutes or chewing gum for the stimulation of salivary output.[95,96] Increased salivary output and fewer dry-mouth symptoms facilitate eating, swallowing, and wearing dentures, and thus improve QOL.[26,97,98]

Mucositis is another severe complication of chemotherapy or radiotherapy. The pain associated with mucositis can be intense and affects mastication, eating, swallowing, and thus QOL.[98,99] A symptomatic treatment of mucositis is indicated because eventually the epithelium will regenerate. The suggested treatments include changing the diet to a soft and nonirritating one and the use of a chlorhexidine mouthrinse. Pain is the most common symptom in patients with cancer and has major impacts on OHRQOL in all patients.[15,16,25,32,33,98] Because pain has a major impact on QOL, appropriate pain control is mandatory, and can be achieved with topical anesthetic agents and mouthwashes containing diphenhydramine.

Eating and swallowing problems have been reported in association with several medical conditions and significantly affect QOL.[15,16,97–99] Eating problems may be linked to side effects of treatment like xerostomia, mucositis, taste and smell alterations, and dysphagia. Depending on the cause, adjustments in diet are recommended. This may include foods of a softer, more liquid consistency that also meet high caloric and protein requirements. In cases where sensitivity to food is a problem, the avoidance of highly seasoned, spiced, or acidic food and food with offensive smells is beneficial.[79] Eating problems are extremely distressing to the affected patient and to observers because the refusal to eat is associated with disease. Eating problems related to the condition or low numbers of teeth can be addressed with the appropriate dental care. Because eating and drinking are essential sources of pleasure, it is extremely important to restore the patient's ability to engage in these activities.

Patients with medical conditions frequently experience orofacial pain. In cases of referred pain such as that seen in heart disease, the primary condition needs to be addressed. Radiation therapy administered to the head and neck area can lead to fibrosis, and surgery may cause temporomandibular disorders. Physical therapy such as range of movement exercises may be helpful in maintaining or increasing the range of motion in such patients. Furthermore, appropriate pain control using nonsteroidal anti-inflammatory drugs may be of value. Research shows that temporomandibular pain has a large impact on QOL. Patients with pain associated with temporomandibular disorders are compromised in their social functions and activities of daily living. Intellectual functioning, rest and sleep are also compromised.[100] Compared with populations who experience pain, patients with orofacial pain experience significantly greater psychologic effects. Depressive symptoms as well as functional impacts on chewing are markedly increased in these patients.[17]

Conclusions

The number of people suffering from chronic medical conditions is enormous. Quality of life has become one of the important outcome measures of chronic diseases and other medical conditions, because it incorporates the patients' evaluation of the importance of functional, psychologic, and social outcomes.

In the current highly specialized health care system, each medical condition is treated separately. However, quite frequently, patients with severe and chronic diseases suffer from multiple conditions, which give rise to oral impacts in addition to the characteristic general health effects. These oral conditions usually have a negative impact on the patient's QOL, which makes it imperative that the patient get appropriate care. Speaking, eating, drinking, and social interactions are essential parts of life that can only be performed if the highly sensitive oral cavity is in adequate condition. Depending on the severity of symptoms, a team approach involving a dentist, dental hygienist, physician, psychologist, nutritionist, and physical therapist seems indicated. The overall goal of all oral health care should be that the patient has a good OHRQOL, that is, that he or she can perform daily activities involving the oral cavity with no pain, with good function, and without embarrassment. The key to achieving this goal lies in successful communication with the patient and the assessment of individual needs.

References

1. Papas AS, Niessen LC, Chauncey HH. Geriatric Dentistry: Aging and Oral Health. St Louis: Mosby, 1991.
2. Ship JA, Duffy V, Jones JA, Langmore S. Geriatric oral health and its impact on eating. J Am Geriatr Soc 1996;44:456–464.
3. Elias AC, Sheiham A. The relationship between satisfaction with mouth and number and position of teeth. J Oral Rehabil 1998;25:649–661.
4. McGrath CM, Bedi R, Gilthorpe MS. Oral health related quality of life: Views of the public in the United Kingdom. Community Dent Health 2000;17:3–7.
5. Ghezzi EM, Ship JA. Systemic diseases and their treatments in the elderly: Impact on oral health. J Public Health Dent 2000;60:289–296.
6. Robins Sadler G, Oberle-Edwards L, Farooqi A, Hryniuk WM. Oral sequelae of chemotherapy: An important teaching opportunity for oncology health care providers and their patients. Support Care Cancer 2000;8:209–214.
7. National Center for Health Statistics. Health, United States, 1999, with Health and Aging Chartbook. Hyattsville, MD: National Center for Health Statistics, 1999:142.
8. Adams PF, Hendershot GE, Marano MA. Current estimates from the National Health Interview Survey, 1996. Vital Health Stat 10 1999;(200):81–82.
9. Westin L, Carlsson R, Israelsson B, Willenheimer R, Cline C, McNeil TF. Quality of life in patients with ischaemic heart disease: A prospective controlled study. J Intern Med 1997;242:239–247.
10. Brown N, Melville M, Gray D, et al. Quality of life four years after acute myocardial infarction: Short Form 36 scores compared with a normal population. Heart 1999;81:352–358.
11. Ferrucci L, Baldasseroni S, Bandinelli S, et al. Disease severity and health-related quality of life across different chronic conditions. J Am Geriatr Soc 2000;48:1490–1495.
12. Smith HJ, Taylor R, Mitchell A. A comparison of four quality of life instruments in cardiac patients: SF-36, QLI, QLMI, and SEIQoL. Heart 2000;84:390–394.
13. Tzukert A, Hasin Y, Sharav Y. Orofacial pain of cardiac origin. Oral Surg Oral Med Oral Pathol 1981;51:484–486.
14. Hagen KB, Kvien TK, Bjorndal A. Musculoskeletal pain and quality of life in patients with noninflammatory joint pain compared to rheumatoid arthritis: A population survey. J Rheumatol 1997;24:1703–1709.
15. Locker D, Miller Y. Evaluation of subjective oral health status indicators. J Public Health Dent 1994;54:167–176.
16. Slade GD, Spencer AJ. Social impact of oral conditions among older adults. Aust Dent J 1994;39:358–364.
17. Murray H, Locker D, Mock D, Tenenbaum HC. Pain and the quality of life in patients referred to a craniofacial pain unit. J Orofac Pain 1996;10:316–323.
18. Riedinger MS, Dracup KA, Brecht ML, Padilla G, Sarna L, Ganz PA. Quality of life in patients with heart failure: Do gender differences exist? Heart Lung 2001;30:105–116.
19. Joshipura KJ, Rimm EB, Douglass CW, Trichopoulos D, Ascherio A, Willett WC. Poor oral health and coronary heart disease. J Dent Res 1996;75:1631–1636.
20. Loesche WJ, Schork A, Terpenning MS, Chen YM, Dominguez BL, Grossman N. Assessing the relationship between dental disease and coronary heart disease in elderly U.S. veterans. J Am Dent Assoc 1998;129:301–311.
21. Mattila KJ, Nieminen MS, Valtonen VV, et al. Association between dental health and acute myocardial infarction. Br Med J 1989;298:779–781.

22. Hamasha AA, Hand JS, Levy SM. Medical conditions associated with missing teeth and edentulism in the institutionalized elderly. Spec Care Dent 1998;18:123–127.

23. Little JW, Falace DA. Dental Management of the Medically Compromised Patient. St Louis: Mosby, 1993:170, 455–457.

24. Miller CS, Damm DD. Incidence of verapamil-induced gingival hyperplasia in a dental population. J Periodontol 1992;63:453–456.

25. Reisine ST. The effects of pain and oral health on the quality of life [review]. Community Dent Health 1988;5:63–68.

26. Henson BS, Inglehart MR, Eisbruch A, Ship JA. Preserved salivary output and xerostomia-related quality of life in head and neck cancer patients receiving parotid-sparing radiotherapy. Oral Oncol 2001;37:84–93.

27. Hackett ML, Anderson CS. Health outcomes 1 year after subarachnoid hemorrhage: An international population-based study—The Australian Cooperative Research on Subarachnoid Hemorrhage Study Group. Neurology 2000;55:658–662.

28. Duncan PW, Jorgensen HS, Wade DT. Outcome measures in acute stroke trials: A systematic review and some recommendations to improve practice. Stroke 2000;31:1429–1438.

29. Kim P, Warren S, Madill H, Hadley M. Quality of life of stroke survivors. Qual Life Res 1999;8:293–301.

30. Bardage C, Isacson DG. Hypertension and health-related quality of life: An epidemiological study in Sweden. J Clin Epidemiol 2001;54:172–181.

31. Ostuni E. Stroke and the dental patient. J Am Dent Assoc 1994;125:721–727.

32. Atchison KA, Dolan TA. Development of the Geriatric Oral Health Assessment Index. J Dent Educ 1990;54:680–687.

33. Slade GD, Spencer AJ. Development and evaluation of the Oral Health Impact Profile. Community Dent Health 1994;11:3–11.

34. Kamen S. Oral health care for the stroke survivor. J Calif Dent Assoc 1997;25:297–303.

35. Michishige F, Yoshinaga S, Harada E, et al. Relationships between activity of daily living, and oral cavity care and the number of oral cavity microorganisms in patients with cerebrovascular diseases. J Med Invest 1999;46:79–85.

36. Chen MY, Ott DJ, Peele VN, Gelfand DW. Oropharynx in patients with cerebrovascular disease: Evaluation with videofluoroscopy. Radiology 1990;176:641–643.

37. Collins R, Peto R, Godwin J, MacMahon S. Blood pressure and coronary heart disease. Lancet 1990;336:370–371.

38. Stamler R, Stamler J, Grimm R, et al. Nutritional therapy for high blood pressure: Final report of a four-year randomized controlled trial—the Hypertension Control Program. JAMA 1987;257:1484–1491.

39. Grimm RH Jr, Grandits GA, Cutler JA, et al. Relationships of quality-of-life measures to long-term lifestyle and drug treatment in the Treatment of Mild Hypertension Study. Arch Intern Med 1997;157:638–648.

40. Fogari R, Zoppi A, Poletti L, Marasi G, Mugellini A, Corradi L. Sexual activity in hypertensive men treated with valsartan or carvedilol: A crossover study. Am J Hypertens 2001;14:27–31.

41. Ogihara T, Kuramoto K. Effect of long-term treatment with antihypertensive drugs on quality of life of elderly patients with hypertension: A double-blind comparative study between a calcium antagonist and a diuretic—NICS-EH Study Group, National Intervention Cooperative Study in Elderly Hypertensives. Hypertens Res 2000;23:33–37.

42. Rahn KH, van Baak M, van Hooff M. Studies on salivary flow in borderline hypertension. J Hypertens 1982;1:77.

43. Wright JM. Oral manifestations of drug reactions. Dent Clin North Am 1984;28:529–543.

44. Streckfus CF, Welsh S, Strahl RC. Diminution of parotid IgA secretion in an elderly black population taking antihypertension medications. Oral Surg Oral Med Oral Pathol 1991;71:50–54.

45. Streckfus CF, Strahl RC, Fleek ME, Greene BG. Prevalence of root decay in inner city geriatric patients taking anti-hypertension medications. J Md State Dent Assoc 1985;28:80–81.

46. Stewart AL, Hays RD, Ware JE, Jr. The MOS short-form general health survey: Reliability and validity in a patient population. Med Care 1988;26:724–735.

47. Davis TM, Clifford RM, Davis WA. Effect of insulin therapy on quality of life in Type 2 diabetes mellitus: The Fremantle Diabetes Study. Diabetes Res Clin Pract 2001;52:63–71.

48. Hirsch A, Bartholomae C, Volmer T. Dimensions of quality of life in people with non–insulin-dependent diabetes. Qual Life Res 2000;9:207-218.

49. Gregg EW, Beckles GL, Williamson DF, et al. Diabetes and physical disability among older U.S. adults. Diabetes Care 2000;23:1272–1277.

50. Sastrowijoto SH, Abbas F, Abraham-Inpijn L, van der Velden U. Relationship between bleeding/plaque ratio, family history of diabetes mellitus and impaired glucose tolerance. J Clin Periodontol 1990;17:55–60.

51. Shlossman M, Knowler WC, Pettitt DJ, Genco RJ. Type 2 diabetes mellitus and periodontal disease. J Am Dent Assoc 1990;121:532–536.

52. Albrecht M, Banoczy J, Tamas G Jr. Dental and oral symptoms of diabetes mellitus. Community Dent Oral Epidemiol 1988;16:378–380.

53. Taylor GW, Burt BA, Becker MP, et al. Non-insulin dependent diabetes mellitus and alveolar bone loss progression over 2 years. J Periodontol 1998;69:76–83.

54. Schelling JL, Tetreault L, Lasagna L, Davis M. Abnormal taste threshold in diabetes. Lancet 1965;1: 508–512.

55. Lamey PJ, Fisher BM, Frier BM. The effects of diabetes and autonomic neuropathy on parotid salivary flow in man. Diabetes Med 1986;3:537–540.

56. Chavez EM, Borrell LN, Taylor GW, Ship JA. A longitudinal analysis of salivary flow in control subjects and older adults with type 2 diabetes. Oral Surg Oral Med Oral Pathol Oral Radiol Endod 2001;91:166–173.

57. Jones RB, McCallum RM, Kay EJ, Kirkin V, McDonald P. Oral health and oral health behaviour in a population of diabetic outpatient clinic attenders. Community Dent Oral Epidemiol 1992;20:204–207.

58. Brandt KD. Osteoarthritis. In: Stein JH, Eisenberg JM (eds). Internal Medicine, ed 5. St. Louis: Mosby, 1998:1264–1268.

59. Hopman-Rock M, Kraaimaat FW, Bijlsma JW. Quality of life in elderly subjects with pain in the hip or knee. Qual Life Res 1997;6:67–76.

60. Whalley D, McKenna SP, de Jong Z, van der Heijde D. Quality of life in rheumatoid arthritis. Br J Rheumatol 1997;36:884–888.

61. Liang MH, Rogers M, Larson M, et al. The psychosocial impact of systemic lupus erythematosus and rheumatoid arthritis. Arthritis Rheum 1984;27:13–19.

62. Archenholtz B, Burckhardt CS, Segesten K. Quality of life of women with systemic lupus erythematosus or rheumatoid arthritis: Domains of importance and dissatisfaction. Qual Life Res 1999;8:411–416.

63. Bibb CA, Atchison KA, Pullinger AG, Bittar GT. Jaw function status in an elderly community sample. Community Dent Oral Epidemiol 1995;23:303–308.

64. Harper RP, Brown CM, Triplett MM, Villasenor A, Gatchel RJ. Masticatory function in patients with juvenile rheumatoid arthritis. Pediatr Dent 2000;22:200-206.

65. Lundstrom IM, Lindstrom FD. Subjective and clinical oral symptoms in patients with primary Sjogren's syndrome. Clin Exp Rheumatol 1995;13:725–731.

66. Soto-Rojas AE, Villa AR, Sifuentes-Osornio J, Alarcon-Segovia D, Kraus A. Oral manifestations in patients with Sjogren's syndrome. J Rheumatol 1998;25: 906–910.

67. Laurell L, Hugoson A, Hakansson J, et al. General oral status in adults with rheumatoid arthritis. Community Dent Oral Epidemiol 1989;17:230–233.

68. Soto-Rojas AE, Villa AR, Sifuentes-Osornio J, Alarcon-Segovia D, Kraus A. Oral candidiasis and Sjogren's syndrome. J Rheumatol 1998;25:911–915.

69. Jolivet J, Cowan KH, Curt GA, Clendeninn NJ, Chabner BA. The pharmacology and clinical use of methotrexate. N Engl J Med 1983;309:1094–1104.

70. Treister N, Glick M. Rheumatoid arthritis: A review and suggested dental care considerations. J Am Dent Assoc 1999;130:689–698.

71. McCarthy EP, Phillips RS, Zhong Z, Drews RE, Lynn J. Dying with cancer: Patients' function, symptoms, and care preferences as death approaches. J Am Geriatr Soc 2000;48:S110–S121.

72. Foley KM. Cancer pain syndromes. J Pain Symptom Manage 1987;2:S13–S17.

73. Patt RB. Cancer Pain. Philadelphia: Lippincott, 1993.

74. Graham KM, Pecoraro DA, Ventura M, Meyer CC. Reducing the incidence of stomatitis using a quality assessment and improvement approach. Cancer Nurs 1993;16:117–122.

75. Nikoskelainen J. Oral infections related to radiation and immunosuppressive therapy. J Clin Periodontol 1990;17:504–507.

76. Peterson DE. Oral toxicity of chemotherapeutic agents. Semin Oncol 1992;19:478–491.

77. Feuz A, Rapin CH. An observational study of the role of pain control and food adaptation of elderly patients with terminal cancer. J Am Diet Assoc 1994;94: 767–770.

78. Puccio M, Nathanson L. The cancer cachexia syndrome. Semin Oncol 1997;24:277–287.

79. Minasian A, Dwyer JT. Nutritional implications of dental and swallowing issues in head and neck cancer. Oncology 1998;12:1155–1162 [discussion 62–69].

80. Scully C, Epstein JB. Oral health care for the cancer patient. Eur J Cancer B Oral Oncol 1996;32B:281–292.

81. Allal AS, Dulguerov P, Bieri S, Lehmann W, Kurtz JM. Assessment of quality of life in patients treated with accelerated radiotherapy for laryngeal and hypopharyngeal carcinomas. Head Neck 2000;22:288–293.

82. Gritz ER, Carmack CL, de Moor C, et al. First year after head and neck cancer: Quality of life. J Clin Oncol 1999;17:352–360.

83. Hammerlid E, Wirblad B, Sandin C, et al. Malnutrition and food intake in relation to quality of life in head and neck cancer patients. Head Neck 1998;20: 540–548.

84. Rogers SN, Lowe D, Brown JS, Vaughan ED. The University of Washington head and neck cancer measure as a predictor of outcome following primary surgery for oral cancer. Head Neck 1999;21:394–401.

85. Langius A, Bjorvell H, Lind MG. Functional status and coping in patients with oral and pharyngeal cancer before and after surgery. Head Neck 1994;16:559–568.

86. Schag CA, Ganz PA, Wing DS, Sim MS, Lee JJ. Quality of life in adult survivors of lung, colon and prostate cancer. Qual Life Res 1994;3:127–141.

87. Bucher JA, Fleming TJ, Fuller LM, Keene HJ. Preliminary observations on the effect of mantle field radiotherapy on salivary flow rates in patients with Hodgkin's disease. J Dent Res 1988;67:518–521.

88. Markitziu A, Zafiropoulos G, Tsalikis L, Cohen L. Gingival health and salivary function in head and neck-irradiated patients: A five-year follow-up. Oral Surg Oral Med Oral Pathol 1992;73:427–433.

89. Lockhart PB, Clark J. Pretherapy dental status of patients with malignant conditions of the head and neck. Oral Surg Oral Med Oral Pathol 1994;77:236–241.

90. Singh N, Scully C, Joyston-Bechal S. Oral complications of cancer therapies: Prevention and management. Clin Oncol 1996;8:15–24.

91. Gadbury-Amyot CC, Williams KB, Krust-Bray K, Manne D, Collins P. Validity and reliability of the oral health-related quality of life instrument for dental hygiene. J Dent Hyg 1999;73:126–134.

92. Awad MA, Locker D, Korner-Bitensky N, Feine JS. Measuring the effect of intra-oral implant rehabilitation on health-related quality of life in a randomized controlled clinical trial. J Dent Res 2000;79:1659–1663.

93. Thiel HJ, Fietkau R, Sauer R. Malnutrition and the role of nutritional support for radiation therapy patients: Recent results. Cancer Res 1988;108:205–226.

94. Al-Tikriti U, Martin MV, Bramley PA. A pilot study of the clinical effects of irradiation on the oral tissues. Br J Oral Maxillofac Surg 1984;22:77–86.

95. Bjornstrom M, Axell T, Birkhed D. Comparison between saliva stimulants and saliva substitutes in patients with symptoms related to dry mouth: A multicentre study. Swed Dent J 1990;14:153–161.

96. Aagaard A, Godiksen S, Teglers PT, Schiodt M, Glenert U. Comparison between new saliva stimulants in patients with dry mouth: A placebo-controlled double-blind crossover study. J Oral Pathol Med 1992;21:376–380.

97. Kressin N, Spiro A III, Bosse R, Garcia R, Kazis L. Assessing oral health-related quality of life: Findings from the normative aging study. Med Care 1996;34:416–427.

98. Baker C, Schuller DE. A functional status scale for measuring quality of life outcomes in head and neck cancer patients. Cancer Nurs 1995;18:452–457 [erratum 1996;19:79].

99. Bjordal K, Hammerlid E, Ahlner-Elmqvist M, et al. Quality of life in head and neck cancer patients: Validation of the European Organization for Research and Treatment of Cancer Quality of Life Questionnaire-H&N35. J Clin Oncol 1999;17:1008–1019.

100. Reisine ST, Weber J. The effects of temporomandibular joint disorders on patients' quality of life. Community Dent Health 1989;6:257–270.

Oral Health–Related Quality of Life in Patients with Oral Cancer

Jonathan A. Ship, DMD

Cancers of the oral cavity and oropharynx region have significant rates of morbidity and mortality associated with them. Treatment of these conditions often causes permanent esthetic, functional, and quality-of-life (QOL) problems. Although older adults are at greatest risk for developing oral cancer, they have a poor knowledge of its risk factors, signs, and symptoms.[1] A major impediment to treating oral cancer is that diagnosis is established late in the oncogenic process, which has morbid consequences for survival and QOL outcomes.

Epidemiology and Demographics

In 2000, there were an estimated 30,200 cases of cancer of the oral cavity and pharynx and 7,800 related deaths.[2] More cases of oropharyngeal cancer were diagnosed that year than were cancers of the liver, pancreas, cervix, ovary, testes, kidney, brain, and thyroid; Hodgkin disease; or leukemia. Despite considerable clinical and basic science research, mortality rates associated with oropharyngeal cancers remain high. From 1974 to 1995, there were no changes in the 5-year mortality rates for oropharyngeal cancers in the United States.[2] The overall 5-year survival rate of these cancers is only about 53%. This rate is significantly lower than that associated with many other cancers such as breast cancer (85%), prostate cancer (92%), Hodgkin disease (82%), and melanoma (88%).[2] Between 1989 and 1993, the median age at death of patients with oropharyngeal cancer was 67 years,[3] and 83.2% of deaths from these cancers occurred in patients 55 years and older. Therefore, there is considerable interest in developing treatment modalities that will be curative without causing long-term and permanent diminished QOL in these survivors.

Box 14-1 Etiopathogenesis of oropharyngeal cancer

I. Sociodemographic factors
   A. Age > 50 years
   B. Male gender
II. Chemical factors
   A. Alcohol
   B. Tobacco
   C. Smokeless tobacco
   D. Toxins
III. Physical factors
   A. Radiographs
   B. Ultraviolet light
IV. Biologic factors
   A. Viruses (eg, human papilloma virus, herpes simplex virus)
   B. Fungi
V. Genomic factors
   A. Genetic damage
   B. Activation of oncogenes
   C. Inactivation of tumor suppressor genes
VI. Possible contributory factors
   A. Lichen planus
   B. Trauma
   C. Dysplasia

Risk Factors and Etiopathogenesis

The greatest risk factor for the development of oral cancer is age.[4] From 1989 to 1993, the median age of patients at the time of diagnosis was 64 years.[3] Men are also more than twice as likely to develop oral cancers than are women. Black men and women have higher rates of oropharyngeal cancers than patients in any other racial group.[4] From 1973 to 1993, the incidence of oropharyngeal cancer decreased slightly (7.9%) for white patients, while it increased (26.3%) for black patients.[5]

Tobacco use is the second major risk factor for developing oral cancer, and its use is closely associated with survival rates. Approximately 25% of patients who were smoking at the time

of diagnosis and after treatment completion experienced a second occurrence of a primary oropharyngeal cancer (mean follow-up period, 5 years), compared with only 14.4% of those patients who were not smoking at the time of diagnosis.[4] Furthermore, 5-year survival rates for nonsmokers are considerably better (43%) than those for smokers (27%).[4] The third major risk factor for oral cancer is alcohol consumption. Both alcohol and tobacco use have a strong positive correlation with oral cancer,[6–8] and when combined, the risks are compounded and the survival rate is considerably lower.

The etiologic factors involved in the pathogenesis of oral cancer may be categorized as chemical, physical, biologic, and genetic (Box 14-1). The three most common factors are age (older than 50 years), alcohol consumption, and tobacco use. The outcomes of these three factors as well as of other factors shown in Box 14-1 are probably direct or indirect genetic alterations, which accumulate over time and eventually cause neoplastic transformation. Most likely, no single factor is solely responsible for cancer development. Rather, a combination of multiple factors acting synergistically causes premalignant and malignant tumors to develop over time in the oral cavity.

Early Detection

Early detection of oral cancer is critical because patients with early-stage tumors have considerably better survival rates than patients with late-stage cancers that have already spread to regional tissues and lymphatics. For example, the 5-year survival rate for small and localized tongue cancers (stage I and II) is 67%, while for patients with tongue cancers with lymph node involvement and possible metastasis (stage III and IV), it is 30%.[4] Late diagnosis of oral cancer is attributable to numerous factors, including lack of patient knowledge regarding the signs and symptoms of oral cancer, insufficient oral cancer screening examinations, patient procrastination, and improper diagnosis of oral lesions.

Therefore, to improve oral cancer–associated morbidity and mortality, early detection and therapy must be more strongly emphasized.

Characterization of Oral Cancers

The majority (90%) of oral and oropharyngeal cancers are squamous cell carcinomas, with the remaining being mixed cell and salivary gland tumors.[9] Lymphomas frequently are found in the lymph nodes of the neck region. Occasionally malignancies in distant sites (eg, breast, lung, bone, or brain) will metastasize to the oral cavity. Therefore head and neck examinations are required on an annual basis in all older persons. Importantly, one of the national health objectives for the year 2000 was to increase the percentage of people over 50 years of age who receive oral cancer screenings from their primary care providers to 40%.[10]

Signs and Symptoms of Oral Cancer

Most oral cancers can be found during routine clinical examinations.[11] The most prevalent premalignant oral lesion is leukoplakia. Pain is a common complaint, and the typical sign is a nonhealing, erosive, ulcerative, or exophytic mass of at least 4 weeks' duration.[4] Early tumors may be asymptomatic, with an innocuous-appearing oral mucosal lesion. Other signs and symptoms include erythroplakia; mixed leukoplakia and erythroplakia; pigmented lesions; indurated ulcers; a lump or mass felt inside the mouth; wartlike masses (verrucous carcinomas); pain or difficulty swallowing, speaking, or chewing; bleeding; and paresthesias in the orofacial region.[4,12] Lesions that are fixed to underlying mucosal and muscular tissues tend to have a worse prognosis compared with lesions that are freely movable on palpation. Finally, re-

gional lymphadenopathy may be a sign of local metastasis.[4]

The most common lesion sites are the ventrolateral border of the tongue, the lip, the floor of the mouth, and the retromolar trigone.[4,12] Lesions located in the anterior oral cavity region are more likely to be localized at the time of diagnosis, and therefore are associated with a better prognosis than those located in the posterior oropharynx.[4] Cancers of the lower lip are much more prevalent than lesions of the upper lip, and their prognosis tends to be better.

Diagnosis of Oral Cancer

Diagnosis begins with a careful review of the chief complaint; medical, dental, and psychosocial history; and a comprehensive clinical examination of the head, neck, and oral cavity.[13] This review can help identify risk factors for oropharyngeal cancers (eg, alcohol and tobacco utilization) and also reveal suspicious oral lesions and enlarged neck lymph nodes. The next step is to eliminate any potential factors that may contribute to the development of an intraoral lesion (eg, removal of a denture for several days). If the lesion has failed to heal in approximately 4 weeks, a biopsy is required to establish a definitive diagnosis.[4,14]

A computer-assisted method of analysis of the oral brush biopsy (OralCDx; OralScan Laboratories Inc, Suffern, NY) is now available for detecting precancerous and cancerous lesions of the oral mucosa.[15] Using a novel brush, a transepithelial specimen can be obtained quickly, without local anesthesia, and with a minimally invasive technique. This method has a sensitivity and specificity of over 95% for detecting dysplastic and cancerous lesions.[15] Importantly, it does not replace the need for an incisional or excisional tissue biopsy to establish a histopathologic diagnosis. Rather, it is designed to assist clinicians in determining the nature of clinically ambiguous oral epithelial lesions. After an oral cancer has been confirmed with histopathologic specimens, various imaging techniques (eg, magnetic resonance imaging, computed tomography) are used to define the borders of the neoplasm and to determine if the lymph nodes are involved. This information is essential to plan for surgery, radiotherapy, and/or chemotherapy.

Treatment and Its Influence on QOL

Various methods are used in the treatment of oral cancer, all of which cause significant side effects (Table 14-1). The QOL of these patients with oral cancer therefore is generally poor,[16] and long-term survivors of head and neck cancer report a high level of disease- and treatment-related symptoms.[17]

Treatment methods

The most common therapy for oral cancer is surgery, which is designed to remove neoplastic tissue with a margin of adjacent normal tissue. There are numerous factors that must be considered, including cancer stage, concurrent medical problems and medications, plans for radiotherapy or chemotherapy, tumor site and lymph node involvement, and reconstruction options to restore esthetics, as well as motor and sensory function. Combined surgery and radiation treatment are widely advocated for advanced-stage cancers to improve survival and decrease the likelihood of local or regional tumor recurrence.[4] The use of surgical flaps, reconstruction of craniofacial bones, bone grafts, micro-reinnervation techniques, dental implants, and maxillofacial prostheses have significantly improved the QOL of patients after surgery.

Radiotherapy is frequently used in combination with surgery for curative purposes.[18] Small tumors may only require therapeutic doses of radiotherapy without surgical intervention, while larger and more disseminated tumors will probably require multimodal therapy. Unilateral head and neck radiotherapy is selected when a unilateral primary lesion does not cross the mid-

line and is considered to be at low risk for contralateral neck node involvement. Where the tumor and lymph node spread is more extensive and the risk for contralateral neck node involvement is considered to be high, bilateral neck radiation is used. Radiation dosages are typically 45 to 50 Gy for clinically negative areas at risk for macroscopic disease, 57 to 63 Gy for excised tumor beds in which no macroscopic tumor remains, and 66 to 70 Gy for macroscopic tumors.

Several regimens of chemotherapy have been evaluated for the definitive treatment of head and neck cancers, as have cotreatment modalities with surgery and/or radiotherapy. Treatment with cisplatin, fluorouracil, L-leucovorin, interferon alpha, methotrexate, and others for certain tumors of the head and neck region has been successful.[19,20] In addition, there has been considerable interest in identifying chemoprevention strategies that may prevent, reduce, or eradicate premalignant tumors. Retinoids have received the most research attention[21,22] and advances in the understanding of the role of the p53 gene, nuclear retinoid receptors, and other cellular and molecular biomarkers of oral cancers will help identify additional effective and safe chemoprevention techniques.[23]

Effects of Treatment on QOL

The oral, pharyngeal, and systemic effects of surgery, radiotherapy, and chemotherapy can be devastating for the patient. While some of these adverse sequelae are of short duration, others can persist for the patient's lifetime.

Several questionnaires have been developed to assess the QOL of patients with oral cancer (Table 14-2). These surveys were used in clinical investigations to examine the influence of the cancer-related treatment on a patient's QOL. Recent data from clinical trials suggest that QOL measurements may independently predict survival.[38] Furthermore, patient-oriented QOL evaluation has become a useful adjunct to more traditional measures used to assess the effectiveness of new therapies.[39] Valid QOL information will help the team of care providers to better under-

Table 14-1 Treatment methods for oral cancers

Treatment method	Description	Indications	Side effects
Chemoprevention	Diet supplements, drugs, or antioxidants (retinoids)	High-risk groups Prevention of recurrence Prevention of dysplasia	Dermatologic changes Triglyceridemia
Chemotherapy	5-fluorouracil, cisplatin, leucovorin, interferon alpha, methotrexate	Nonresectable tumor Palliative treatment Adjunctive treatment	Nausea, vomiting Malaise Immunosuppression Leukopenia, anemia
Radiation therapy	Unilateral or bilateral high-energy external beam radiation for the destruction of tumor tissue and potential lymph node involvement	Positive or suspect surgical margins Alternative to surgical treatment Unilateral neck radiation: tumors that do not cross the midline with low risk for contralateral neck node involvement Bilateral neck radiation: tumors that are more extensive with a high risk for contralateral neck node involvement	Salivary dysfunction Mucositis Candidiasis Xerostomia Dental caries Dermatitis Osteoradionecrosis Dysphagia Dysgeusia Trismus Neck fibrosis
Surgery	Surgical excision of tumor and suspected/positive lymph nodes of ipsilateral and/or contralateral neck; may include resection of bone	Management of primary lesions Recurrences Lymph node metastasis Bone invasion Perineural invasion Trismus	Disfiguration Loss of motor function Dysesthesia Paresthesia Dysphagia Salivary dysfunction
Combination therapy	Use of two or more treatment modalities simultaneously or consecutively	Used when added benefits exceed that of a single modality (ie, surgically resected lesion with one positive margin) and the overall outcome is the best by clinical judgment	See above

Table 14-2 QOL questionnaires for oral cancer–associated therapies

Condition evaluated	Name of questionnaire
Xerostomia	Xerostomia-Related Quality of Life Scale[24] Xerostomia Questionnaire[24] NIDCR Xerostomia Questionnaire[25] SOMA scale[26]
Mucositis/stomatitis	SOMA scale[26] World Health Organization Stomatitis[27] Byfield Stomatitis[28] Mucositis Study Group Oral Mucositis Scoring System[29]
General	Subjective Performance Status Scale[30] EORTC Quality of Life Questionnaire[31] Head and Neck Radiotherapy Questionnaire[32] Quality of Life–Radiation Therapy Instrument (QOL-RTI): Head and Neck Companion Module[33] Performance Status Scale for Head and Neck Cancer Patients (PSS-HN)[34] Functional Assessment of Cancer Therapy (FACT)—Head and Neck[35] Common Toxicity Criteria (version 2.0)[36] The Head and Neck Quality of Life Questionnaire[37]

stand patients' physical and emotional problems. Ultimately, this can allow clinicians to improve the assessment, treatment, and rehabilitation of patients with head and neck cancer.[39]

Surgery

Surgical complications of oral surgery depend on the extent of tissue removal from head, neck, oral, and pharyngeal regions. The appearance of the head and neck region can be permanently affected, which can cause severe emotional disturbances. If the surgical margins are inadequate, recurrences may result, necessitating additional surgery, radiotherapy, and/or chemotherapy. Motor nerve paresthesias, which can impair face, eye, neck, mandibular, tongue, and pharyngeal movements can occur. Sensory dysesthesias will diminish feeling in the face and oral regions, and can alter taste, salivation, chewing, swallowing, and denture retention. Radiation treatment can also cause diminished jaw opening because of sclerosed skeletal muscles.[40] These conditions

are frequently permanent, and have long-term consequences for a patient's QOL.

One study reported that patients' emotional functioning was still adversely affected 7 to 11 years after the completion of surgery and radiotherapy.[17] Significant oral-functional deficits were also reported in patients who were disease free after surgery and radiotherapy for advanced oral cavity cancers.[30] With increasing T stage, functional results (ability to eat in public, clarity of speech, normalcy of diet) deteriorated. Furthermore, patients with lesions at the base of the tongue had a worse functional outcome for both early T stage (T1/T2) and advanced T stage (T3/T4) compared with patients with cancers at other sites.

Radiation therapy

Radiation therapy has myriad detrimental side effects to the oral cavity.[18,41] Therapeutic dosages to the tumor typically exceed 60 Gy; whereas oral mucositis and salivary dysfunction can occur after only 2 to 3 days of radiation treatment (typically 4 to 6 Gy). An upper limit of 24 to 26 Gy has been demonstrated to cause permanent salivary dysfunction.[42] Patients receiving radiation therapy often experience oral discomfort, mucositis, difficulty in chewing and swallowing, taste changes, an increased incidence of dental caries, oral microbial changes, chronic esophagitis, an inability to wear dentures, and a diminished QOL.[43] The neck area is involved as well. One study demonstrated the presence of persistent complications after neck radiation, which included limitation of neck movement, diminished thyroid function, accelerated carotid artery narrowing, and skin changes.[44]

Salivary gland dysfunction and associated complaints of a dry mouth (xerostomia) are permanent after therapeutic dosages of radiation are administered to major salivary glands, resulting in various oral and pharyngeal complications. Because these complications are associated with swallowing, tasting, chewing, sensory and motor function, and pain, the patients' QOL is adversely affected. Recent investigations have demonstrated impaired xerostomia-related QOL assessments up to 2 years after head and neck radiotherapy using standard three-beam techniques.[24,45,46] Other studies have demonstrated high prevalence of xerostomic complaints many years after the completion of head and neck radiotherapy.[16,17,41,44,47–49]

A final long-term consequence of head and neck radiotherapy is osteoradionecrosis.[50] Although the risk of developing osteoradionecrosis is low during and immediately after radiotherapy, the risk increases over time.[51] Subjects at risk are those who receive radiation of more than 60 Gy to the mandible, undergo surgical procedures in irradiated bone, and are wearing prostheses.

Chemotherapy

Chemotherapy causes short-term oropharyngeal problems, such as mucositis and oral ulcerations, salivary gland dysfunction, xerostomia, dysphagia, dysgeusia, recurrent fungal infections, and pain.[52,53] Chemotherapy-induced mucositis can be so severe as to limit the number and duration of medication dosages administered to patients with head and neck cancer. Many of these oral changes occur during and immediately after chemotherapy, but some sequelae persist for longer periods. One study demonstrated that chemotherapy-induced taste aberrations contributed to the development of food avoidance and aversion,[54] which can cause significant malnutrition. Another investigation that evaluated QOL outcomes in patients with head and neck cancer treated with chemotherapy and radiotherapy found that 1 year after the completion of cancer therapy, 50% of the patients were only able to ingest soft foods or liquids.[55] This specific functional deficit was not related to global QOL, nor to specific QOL dimensions. Residual pain was present in 15% of patients, which appeared to influence both functioning and QOL parameters. Further, decreased QOL and increased depressive symptoms were related to the total number and severity of residual effects.

Preserving QOL in Patients with Oral Cancer

General Reduction of Toxicity

Prevention and management of oral cancer therapy–related injury is a multiphase and continuous process that provides multiple opportunities to improve a patient's QOL. The process starts with multidisciplinary collaboration among all health care workers involved in the patient's therapy from initial diagnosis to posttreatment routine follow-up. It also requires continuous and effective communication among the patient and care providers. Numerous therapeutic modalities, including pharmaceutical agents (referred to as toxicity antagonists), that modulate normal tissue response or interfere with mechanisms of toxicity are currently under development.[56] It is hoped that discovery of more effective agents will allow treatment of high-risk disease to be intensified, and

Table 14-3 Therapies to enhance QOL in patients with oral cancer

Problem	Description and characteristics	Prevention and management
Xerostomia Dry mouth	Decreased salivary output Increased complaints of dry mouth Increased susceptibility to microbial infections and dental caries Poorly fitting dentures Impaired chewing and swallowing	Salivary gland–sparing radiotherapy techniques Rx: Pilocarpine 5 mg; one tablet 3 times a day and at night to stimulate saliva for > 3 months Rx: Cevimeline 15 mg; two tablets 3 times a day to stimulate saliva for > 3 months Rx: Fluoride treatments (see below) NonRx: Artificial saliva solutions Take frequent sips of water Use sugarless candies and sugarless gums Avoid high-sugar-content foods
Mucositis/stomatitis Sore mouth	Painful erythemic and ulcerative lesions of oral mucosa Superinfection of these lesions is common	Rx: 2% xylocaine or benadryl 12.5 mg/5 mL elixir mixed with Maalox, Kaopectate, or sucralfate; 5 mL rinse and spit 3 times a day NonRx: Biotene products for oral comfort Use popsicles and ice cream for comfort Maintain carbohydrate, protein, and fluid intake to protect nutritional health
Candidiasis Yeast infection	Opportunistic organism that grows when normal oral flora is disrupted Raised white or cottage cheese–like patches that can be scraped off	Rx: Analgesic rinses (see mucositis section) Rx: Nystatin 100,000 units/mL rinse and swallow 5 mL 3 times a day × 10 days; clotrimazole 10 mg troches 4 times a day × 10 days Rx: Ketaconazole 200 mg every day or fluconazole 100 mg 2 tablets stat then 1 tablet every day for 10 days or until condition is cleared
Herpes simplex lesions Cold sores	Appear on lips and possibly on oral mucosal surfaces Primary infections or recurrent episodes can occur	Rx: Acyclovir 200 mg or valacyclovir HCl 500 mg 4 times a day × 10 days Rx: Acyclovir ointment 5% or penciclovir cream 1% every 2 hours at prodrome × 5 days
Dysgeusia Altered taste	Loss of or altered taste Abnormal sensitivity (frequently bitter) to one or more stimulants Poor nutrition can result	Enhance flavor of foods Avoid acidic foods and beverages Stress nutritional concerns and weight management, consult nutritionist
Trismus Decreased jaw mobility	Fibrosis of the chewing muscles, common in treatment of lesions of the nasopharynx, maxillary sinus, palate	Mechanical stretching of the muscles of mastication with wooden tongue blades. Start with 2 blades, each day adding 1–2 blades, ending with 7 blades stacked on each other by end of the first week. Then add according to pain and opening ability. Exercise jaw 20 repetitions, 3 times daily Use a mechanical device (Therabite) to aid in stretching

Table 14-3 (cont) Therapies to enhance QOL in patients with oral cancer

Problem	Description and characteristics	Prevention and management
Radiation Caries Dental cavities	Rapid progression of new and recurrent cavities Caused by decrease in salivary output and increase in cariogenic bacteria	Rx: Lifetime daily brushing with 1.0% NaFl or 0.4 SnF$_2$ toothpaste Rx: Construction of customized fluoride trays for teeth Frequent dental examinations and dental cleanings (every 3–6 months) Follow guidelines for xerostomia Restore decayed teeth as quickly as possible
Osteoradionecrosis Devitalized and/or infected bone	Bone loses its vascularity after radiotherapy and becomes necrotic Bone loses ability to withstand trauma, regenerate, or fight infection Mandible more susceptible than maxilla	Prevention by preradiotherapy extraction of teeth with extensive caries and periodontal bone loss Avoid ill-fitting dentures Conservative soft tissue curettage and irrigation Restore decayed teeth as quickly as possible so that infection does not spread into the bone Rx: Clindamycin 300 mg 4 times a day for 10 days or similar antimicrobial with good bone absorption for management of dental/alveolar infections Rx: 20 dives hyperbaric oxygen before surgery and 10 dives after surgery

ultimately allow clinicians to substantially reduce treatment-related morbidity and mortality (Table 14-3).

Salivary Gland–Sparing Radiotherapy Techniques

The deleterious effects of head and neck radiation on salivary glands can be severe and permanent.[57] Preservation of salivary function in patients with oral cancer could play a vital role in restoring essential activities of daily life (eg, eating, swallowing, and speaking) and maintaining a person's QOL. Recently developed salivary gland–sparing radiotherapy techniques minimize radiation dosages to radiation-sensitive structures at low risk for cancer spread while providing therapeutic dosages to tumors and regional lymph nodes.[42,58,59] These parotid gland–sparing techniques can protect contralateral parotid function for up to 2 years after completion of radiotherapy.[60] At the same time, tumors and lymph nodes at risk for cancer spread are treated appropriately, without an increase in the incidence of locoregional tumor recurrence.[42,61] Importantly, these salivary gland–sparing techniques also have resulted in the improvement of xerostomia-related QOL.[24,45,46]

Another technique currently undergoing investigation to preserve salivary function during chemotherapy and radiotherapy is daily intravenous use of a cytoprotectant, amifostine.[62] Xerostomia and mucositis were significantly diminished in patients receiving head and neck radiotherapy when amifostine was administered intravenously just before each daily dose of radiation.[63,64] Furthermore, one study reported a lower incidence of xerostomia and taste loss 1 year after radiotherapy in patients treated with amifostine compared with subjects treated with radiotherapy alone, with no differences in survival rates.[64] Amifostine causes significant side effects; therefore, its use is limited. However, it represents the emergence of novel cytoprotective agents that may reduce the incidence and severity of radiotherapy-associated acute and late toxicities while preserving its antitumor activity.

Salivary Hypofunction and Xerostomia Therapies

There are numerous therapeutic modalities for salivary hypofunction and symptoms of xerostomia. However, few of these modalities have demonstrated consistent benefits and complete patient compliance.[65] The principal goal of therapy is to increase salivary output in patients who have remaining viable salivary tissue with the use of gustatory, mechanical, or pharmaceutical agents. For example, muscarinic agonists, such as pilocarpine[66–69] or cevimeline,[70] can increase salivary output in patients after radiotherapy and diminish symptoms of xerostomia. Sugarless chewing gums and mints will also help increase salivary output in xerostomic patients.[71]

If remaining viable salivary tissue has been destroyed by tumors, surgery, and/or radiotherapy, exogenous agents, such as the artificial saliva compounds found in rinses, sprays, and gels, are required to alleviate complaints of a dry mouth. Creation of a biocompatible and patient-acceptable type of artificial saliva has so far evaded scientific discovery. This is in part because of difficulties in assembling artificial mucins.[72] One study investigated the use of topical Oral Balance gel and Biotene toothpaste (Laclede Professional Products, Gardena, CA) in comparison with carboxymethylcellulose gel and commercial toothpaste applications, and reported superior palliative effects of the test products compared with the placebo.[73] Further in-

vestigation is required to identify and evaluate new products that will increase salivary output and diminish xerostomia in patients who have undergone radiotherapy.

Mucositis Therapies

Radiation and chemotherapy cause severe oral mucositis, which can limit further oncologic therapy and contribute to morbidity and mortality.[74] Therefore much effort has been dedicated toward preventing and treating mucositis.[75–77] Sucralfate,[78,79] granulocyte-macrophage colony-stimulating factor,[80] transforming growth factor–beta3,[81] benzydamine hydrochloride,[82] antibiotic pastilles containing amphotericin, polymyxin and tobramycin,[83] and low-energy helium/neon laser[84] have all demonstrated some efficacy; however, more investigations are required to identify agents that will substantially prevent mucositis.

Fluoride Therapies

Patients undergoing head and neck radiotherapy are susceptible to new and recurrent dental caries because of salivary hypofunction. These patients need an effective prophylactic regimen for the rest of their lives to preserve their teeth.[85] Fluoride therapy is an essential part of this regimen. Daily topical neutral sodium fluoride gel placed in custom vinyl trays was found to suppress changes in cariogenic flora with reduced Streptococcus mutans counts.[86,87] Preservation of teeth is particularly important in patients who have undergone maxillofacial surgery to support intraoral prostheses, facilitate chewing and swallowing, and help preserve facial esthetics.

Replacement of Teeth with Prostheses

Preservation of teeth is important to assist in esthetics, mastication, speech, and deglutition. The patient with cancer who has experienced acute and long-term treatment-related toxicities may be particularly vulnerable to diminished QOL in the absence of teeth and/or replacement prostheses. A recent study reported that dental status had an important posttherapeutic effect on QOL in patients with upper aerodigestive tract cancer.[88] Subjects who were partially dentate without any dental prostheses reported significantly more dental problems and difficulty eating and enjoying their meals compared with patients who were partially dentate and wore prostheses.[88]

If surgery has involved removal of critical soft and hard tissue structures in the oral cavity and face, then close coordination among oncologists, general dentists, oral and maxillofacial surgeons, and prosthodontists is required for adequate patient rehabilitation.[52,89] In the last decade, endosseous implants have proven to be successful replacements for fixed and removable prostheses in healthy and even medically compromised patients. Therefore, in the patient with cancer, implant-supported prostheses can enhance chewing, swallowing, and facial esthetics, and should be considered in the treatment plan for any patient who has undergone cancer therapy.[90]

Obturators are frequently necessary in patients who have undergone maxillary resections. One study reported that a well-functioning obturator in patients who underwent a resection of the maxilla for maxillary antrum and/or hard palate cancers restored speech and eating function and contributed to improved QOL.[91] Patients who were satisfied with their obturators reported less difficulty in pronouncing words, improved chewing and swallowing of food, and less change in voice quality after surgery. Importantly, these factors were found to improve psychologic, vocational, family, social, and sexual adjustment after cancer surgery.[91]

Prevention and Treatment of Osteoradionecrosis

Although osteoradionecrosis after radiotherapy has a low prevalence, when it occurs it can cause a lifetime of compromised facial esthetics, impaired oral and pharyngeal function, and pain.[50] Prevention of osteoradionecrosis requires a partnership between patients and health care providers. Careful eating and use of removable prostheses is required to protect mucosal tissues from trauma. Daily oral hygiene is necessary to prevent caries and periodontal diseases, and frequent oral evaluations by dental professionals are critical to identify oral conditions that would predispose the patient to developing osteoradionecrosis. Hyperbaric oxygen has been recommended by many institutions to treat osteoradionecrosis and to prevent osteoradionecrosis when surgery is required in the irradiated mandible or maxilla.[92–98] Other investigators have suggested that postradiotherapy extractions can be performed without hyperbaric oxygen.[99] Further research is required to develop sensitive markers and efficacious therapies for postirradiation osteoradionecrosis.

Surgery-Sparing Cancer Therapy

New multimodal techniques are being developed and tested to determine if surgery can be avoided in patients with head and neck cancer for organ preservation. A recent investigation reported that in comparison with control subjects, a combination of induction chemotherapy and sequential radiotherapy in patients with potentially resectable head and neck cancer did not compromise survival.[100] These and other regimens may be particularly useful in patients for whom surgery could be functionally debilitating.

Prevention of New Cancers

The ultimate goal of cancer therapy is to prevent the occurrence of new tumors. Research has therefore focused on identifying compounds that can reverse premalignant lesions and prevent the initiation of second primary tumors (ie, chemoprevention). For example, retinoids have demonstrated some success for chemoprevention.[21–23,101] It soon may be possible to use biomarkers to identify patients who are most at risk for developing head and neck cancer and who are most likely to benefit from chemopreventive interventions.[22]

Conclusions

Cancers of the oral cavity and oropharynx region have significant morbidity and mortality, and treatment causes permanent esthetic, functional, and QOL problems. Current research is aimed at investigating methods to reduce salivary toxicity and improve salivation, prevent and treat mucositis and osteoradionecrosis, preserve teeth and replace them with prostheses, spare organs without surgery, and ultimately prevent the occurrence of new tumors. Collaboration is required among basic, clinical, behavioral, and epidemiologic scientists, as well as patients and their team of caregivers to advance the early detection and management of the disease and the rehabilitation of these patients. Ultimately, these efforts will play a significant role in improving the morbidity and mortality rates associated with oral cancer, and in enhancing the QOL of these patients.

References

1. Horowitz AM, Nourjah P, Gift HC. U.S. adult knowledge of risk factors and signs of oral cancers: 1990. J Am Dent Assoc 1995;126:39–45.

2. Greenlee RT, Murray T, Bolden S, Wingo PA. Cancer Statistics, 2000. CA Cancer J Clin 2000;50:7–33.

3. Cancer Facts and Figures: 1996. Atlanta: American Cancer Society, 1996.

4. Silverman SJ. Oral Cancer, ed 4. Hamilton, Ontario: B.C. Decker, 1998.

5. Ries LAG, Kosary CL, Hankey BF, Harras A, Miller BA, Edwards BK. SEER Cancer Statistics Review, 1973-1993: Tables and Graphs. Bethesda, MD: National Cancer Institute, 1996.

6. Hoffmann D, Djordjevic MV. Chemical composition and carcinogenicity of smokeless tobacco. Adv Dent Res 1997;11:322–329.

7. Xu J, Gimenez-Conti IB, Cunningham JE, et al. Alterations of p53, cyclin D1, Rb, and H-ras in human oral carcinomas related to tobacco use. Cancer 1998;83:204–212.

8. Lewin F, Norell SE, Johansson H, et al. Smoking tobacco, oral snuff, and alcohol in the etiology of squamous cell carcinoma of the head and neck: A population-based case-referent study in Sweden. Cancer 1998;82:1367–1375.

9. Silverman S Jr. Precancerous lesions and oral cancer in the elderly. Clin Geriatr Med 1992;8:529–541.

10. Healthy People 2000. DHHS publication PHS 91-50212. Washington, DC: US Department of Health and Human Services, Public Health Service, 1991.

11. Ship JA, Chavez EM, Gould KL, Henson BS, Sarmadi M. Evaluation and management of oral cancer. Home Health Care Consult 1999;6:2–12.

12. Regezzi J, Sciubba J. Clinical-pathological correlations. In: Regezzi J, Sciubba J (eds). Oral Pathology. Philadelphia: Saunders, 1989:68–77.

13. Ship JA, Mohammad AR. Clinician's Guide to Oral Health in Geriatric Patients. Baltimore, MD: American Academy of Oral Medicine, 1999.

14. Golden DP, Hooley JR. Oral mucosal biopsy procedures: Excisional and incisional. Dent Clin North Am 1994;38:279–300.

15. Sciubba JJ. Improving detection of precancerous and cancerous oral lesions: Computer-assisted analysis of the oral brush biopsy—US Collaborative OralCDx Study Group. J Am Dent Assoc 1999;130:1445–1457.

16. Epstein JB, Emerton S, Kolbinson DA, et al. Quality of life and oral function following radiotherapy for head and neck cancer. Head Neck 1999;21:1–11.

17. Bjordal K, Kaasa S, Mastekaasa A. Quality of life in patients treated for head and neck cancer: A follow-up study 7 to 11 years after radiotherapy. Int J Radiat Oncol Biol Phys 1994;28:847–856.

18. Million RR, Cassisi NJ. Management of Head and Neck Cancer, ed 2. Philadelphia: Lippincott, 1994.

19. Shin DM, Glisson BS, Khuri FR, Hong WK, Lippman SM. Role of paclitaxel, ifosfamide, and cisplatin in patients with recurrent or metastatic squamous cell carcinoma of the head and neck. Semin Oncol 1998;25 (2, suppl 4):40–44.

20. Asaumi J, Nishijima K. Low dose sequential methotrexate and 5-fluorouracil administration is effective and safe as neo-adjuvant chemotherapy in oral cancer. In Vivo 1996;10:559–562.

21. Lippman SM, Batsakis JG, Toth BB, et al. Comparison of low-dose isotretinoin with beta carotene to prevent oral carcinogenesis. N Engl J Med 1993;328:15–20.

22. Khuri FR, Lippman SM, Spitz MR, Lotan R, Hong WK. Molecular epidemiology and retinoid chemoprevention of head and neck cancer. J Natl Cancer Inst 1997;89:199–211.

23. Lippman SM, Spitz MR, Huber MH, Hong WK. Strategies for chemoprevention study of premalignancy and second primary tumors in the head and neck. Curr Opin Oncol 1995;7:234–241.

24. Henson BS, Inglehart MR, Eisbruch A, Ship JA. Preserved salivary output and xerostomia-related quality of life in head and neck cancer patients receiving parotid-sparing radiotherapy. Oral Oncol 2001;37:84–93.

25. Fox PC, Busch KA, Baum BJ. Subjective reports of xerostomia and objective measures of salivary gland performance. J Am Dent Assoc 1987;115:581–584.

26. LENT SOMA Tables. Radiother Oncol 1995;35:17–60.

27. Miller AB, Hoogstraten B, Staquet M, Winkler A. Reporting results of cancer treatment. Cancer 1981;47:207–214.

28. Byfield JE, Frankel SS, Sharp TR, Hornbeck CL, Callipari FB. Phase I and pharmacologic study of 72-hour infused 5-fluorouracil and hyperfractionated cyclical radiation. Int J Radiat Oncol Biol Phys 1985;11:791–800.

29. Sonis ST, Eilers JP, Epstein JB, et al. Validation of a new scoring system for the assessment of clinical trial research of oral mucositis induced by radiation or chemotherapy: Mucositis Study Group. Cancer 1999;85:2103–2113.

30. Zelefsky MJ, Gaynor J, Kraus D, Strong EW, Shah JP, Harrison LB. Long-term subjective functional outcome of surgery plus postoperative radiotherapy for advanced stage oral cavity and oropharyngeal carcinoma. Am J Surg 1996;171:258–261.

31. Bjordal K, Ahlner-Elmqvist M, Tollesson E, et al. Development of a European Organization for Research and Treatment of Cancer (EORTC) questionnaire module to be used in quality of life assessments in head and neck cancer patients. EORTC Quality of Life Study Group. Acta Oncol 1994;33:879–885.

32. Browman GP, Levine MN, Hodson DI, et al. The Head and Neck Radiotherapy Questionnaire: A morbidity/quality-of-life instrument for clinical trials of radiation therapy in locally advanced head and neck cancer. J Clin Oncol 1993;11:863–872.

33. Trotti A, Johnson DJ, Gwede C, et al. Development of a head and neck companion module for the quality of life-radiation therapy instrument (QOL-RTI). Int J Radiat Oncol Biol Phys 1998;42:257–261.

34. List MA, Ritter-Sterr C, Lansky SB. A performance status scale for head and neck cancer patients. Cancer 1990;66:564–569.

35. Cella DF, Tulsky DS, Gray G, et al. The Functional Assessment of Cancer Therapy scale: Development and validation of the general measure. J Clin Oncol 1993;11:570–579.

36. Trotti A, Byhardt R, Stetz J, et al. Common toxicity criteria, version 2.0: An improved reference for grading the acute effects of cancer treatment: Impact on radiotherapy. Int J Radiat Oncol Biol Phys 2000;47:13–47.

37. Terrell JE, Nanavati KA, Esclamado RM, Bishop JK, Bradford CR, Wolf GT. Head and neck cancer—Specific quality of life: Instrument validation. Arch Otolaryngol Head Neck Surg 1997;123:1125–1132.

38. Chang VT, Thaler HT, Polyak TA, Kornblith AB, Lepore JM, Portenoy RK. Quality of life and survival: The role of multidimensional symptom assessment. Cancer 1998;83:173–179.

39. Terrell JE. Quality of life assessment in head and neck cancer patients. Hematol Oncol Clin North Am 1999;13:849–865.

40. Goldstein M, Maxymiw WG, Cummings BJ, Wood RE. The effects of antitumor irradiation on mandibular opening and mobility: A prospective study of 58 patients. Oral Surg Oral Med Oral Pathol Oral Radiol Endod 1999;88:365–373.

41. Valdez IH, Atkinson JC, Ship JA, Fox PC. Major salivary gland function in patients with radiation-induced xerostomia: Flow rates and sialochemistry. Int J Radiat Oncol Biol Phys 1993;25:41–47.

42. Eisbruch A, Ten Haken RK, Kim HM, Marsh LH, Ship JA. Dose, volume, and function relationships in parotid salivary glands following conformal and intensity modulated irradiation of head and neck cancer. Int J Radiat Oncol Biol Phys 1999;45:577–587.

43. Parsons JT. The effect of radiation on normal tissues of the head and neck. In: Million RR, Cassisi NJ (eds). Management of Head and Neck Cancer: A Multidisciplinary Approach, ed 2. Philadelphia: Lippincott, 1994:245–289.

44. August M, Wang J, Plante D, Wang CC. Complications associated with therapeutic neck radiation. J Oral Maxillofac Surg 1996;54:1409–1416.

45. Eisbruch A, Kim HM, Terrell JE, Marsh LH, Dawson LA, Ship JA. Xerostomia and its predictors following parotid-sparing irradiation of head-and-neck cancer. Int J Radiat Oncol Biol Phys 2001;50:695–704.

46. Malouf JG, Aragon C, Henson BS, Eisbruch A, Ship JA. Influence of parotid-sparing radiotherapy on xerostomia in head and neck cancer patients. Cancer Detect Prev (in press).

47. Harrison LB, Zelefsky MJ, Pfister DG, et al. Detailed quality of life assessment in patients treated with primary radiotherapy for squamous cell cancer of the base of the tongue. Head Neck 1997;19:169–175.

48. List MA, Siston A, Haraf D, et al. Quality of life and performance in advanced head and neck cancer patients on concomitant chemoradiotherapy: A prospective examination. J Clin Oncol 1999;17:1020–1028.

49. Jensen AB, Hansen O, Jorgensen K, Bastholt L. Influence of late side-effects upon daily life after radiotherapy for laryngeal and pharyngeal cancer. Acta Oncol 1994;33:487–491.

50. Marx RE, Johnson RP. Studies in the radiobiology of osteoradionecrosis and their clinical significance. Oral Surg Oral Med Oral Pathol 1987;64:379–390.

51. Silverman S Jr. Oral cancer: Complications of therapy. Oral Surg Oral Med Oral Pathol Oral Radiol Endod 1999;88:122–126.

52. Scully C, Epstein JB. Oral health care for the cancer patient. Oral Oncol 1996;32B:281–292.

53. Lockhart PB, Clark JR. Oral complications following neoadjuvant chemotherapy in patients with head and neck cancer. NCI Monogr 1990;9:99–101.

54. Holmes S. Food avoidance in patients undergoing cancer chemotherapy. Support Care Cancer 1993;1:326–330.

55. List MA, Mumby P, Haraf D, et al. Performance and quality of life outcome in patients completing concomitant chemoradiotherapy protocols for head and neck cancer. Qual Life Res 1997;6:274–284.

56. Trotti A. Toxicity antagonists in cancer therapy. Curr Opin Oncol 1997;9:569–578.

57. Greenspan D. Oral complications of cancer therapies: Management of salivary dysfunction. NCI Monogr 1990;9:159–161.

58. Eisbruch A, Marsh LH, Martel MK, et al. Comprehensive irradiation of head and neck cancer using conformal multisegmental fields: Assessment of target coverage and noninvolved tissue sparing. Int J Radiat Oncol Biol Phys 1998;41:559–568.

59. Eisbruch A, Ship JA, Martel MK, et al. Parotid gland sparing in patients undergoing bilateral head and neck irradiation: Techniques and early results. Int J Radiat Oncol Biol Phys 1996;36:469–480.

60. Henson BS, Eisbruch A, D'Hondt E, Ship JA. Two-year longitudinal study of parotid salivary flow rates in head and neck cancer patients receiving unilateral neck parotid-sparing radiotherapy treatment. Oral Oncol 1999;35:234–241.

61. Dawson LA, Anzai Y, Marsh L, et al. Patterns of local-regional recurrence following parotid-sparing conformal and segmental intensity-modulated radiotherapy for head and neck cancer. Int J Radiat Oncol Biol Phys 2000;46:1117–1126.

62. Capizzi RL, Oster W. Chemoprotective and radioprotective effects of amifostine: An update of clinical trials. Int J Hematol 2000;72:425–435.

63. Wagner W, Prott FJ, Schonekas KG. Amifostine: A radioprotector in locally advanced head and neck tumors. Oncol Rep 1998;5:1255–1257.

64. Buntzel J, Kuttner K, Frohlich D, Glatzel M. Selective cytoprotection with amifostine in concurrent radiochemotherapy for head and neck cancer. Ann Oncol 1998;9:505–509.

65. Atkinson JC, Wu A. Salivary gland dysfunction: Causes, symptoms, treatment. J Am Dent Assoc 1994; 125:409–416.

66. Johnson JT, Ferretti GA, Nethery WJ, et al. Oral pilocarpine for post-irradiation xerostomia in patients with head and neck cancer. N Engl J Med 1993;329: 390–395.

67. LeVeque FG, Montgomery M, Potter D, et al. A multicenter, randomized, double-blind, placebo-controlled, dose-titration study of oral pilocarpine for treatment of radiation-induced xerostomia in head and neck cancer patients. J Clin Oncol 1993;11:1124–1131.

68. Rieke JW, Hafermann MD, Johnson JT, et al. Oral pilocarpine for radiation-induced xerostomia: Integrated efficacy and safety results from two prospective randomized clinical trials. Int J Radiat Oncol Biol Phys 1995;31:661–669.

69. Niedermeier W, Matthaeus C, Meyer C, Staar S, Muller RP, Schulze HJ. Radiation-induced hyposalivation and its treatment with oral pilocarpine. Oral Surg Oral Med Oral Pathol Oral Radiol Endod 1998;86: 541–549.

70. Cevimeline (Evoxac) for dry mouth. Med Lett Drugs Ther 2000;42(1084):70.

71. Dawes C. Physiological factors affecting salivary flow rate, oral sugar clearance, and the sensation of dry mouth in man. J Dent Res 1987;66(special issue): 648–653.

72. Tabak LA. In defense of the oral cavity: Structure, biosynthesis, and function of salivary mucins. Ann Rev Physiol 1995;57:547–564.

73. Epstein JB, Emerton S, Le ND, Stevenson-Moore P. A double-blind crossover trial of Oral Balance gel and Biotene toothpaste versus placebo in patients with xerostomia following radiation therapy. Oral Oncol 1999;35:132–137.

74. Epstein JB, Chow AW. Oral complications associated with immunosuppression and cancer therapies. Infect Dis Clin North Am 1999;13:901–923.

75. Knox JJ, Puodziunas AL, Feld R. Chemotherapy-induced oral mucositis: Prevention and management. Drugs Aging 2000;17:257–267.

76. Herrstedt J. Prevention and management of mucositis in patients with cancer. Int J Antimicrob Agents 2000; 16:161–163.

77. Plevova P. Prevention and treatment of chemotherapy- and radiotherapy-induced oral mucositis: A review. Oral Oncol 1999;35:453–470.

78. Cengiz M, Ozyar E, Ozturk D, Akyol F, Atahan IL, Hayran M. Sucralfate in the prevention of radiation-induced oral mucositis. J Clin Gastroenterol 1999;28: 40–43.

79. Etiz D, Erkal HS, Serin M, et al. Clinical and histopathological evaluation of sucralfate in prevention of oral mucositis induced by radiation therapy in patients with head and neck malignancies. Oral Oncol 2000;36: 116–120.

80. Rosso M, Blasi G, Gherlone E, Rosso R. Effect of granulocyte-macrophage colony-stimulating factor on prevention of mucositis in head and neck cancer patients treated with chemo-radiotherapy. J Chemother 1997;9:382–385.

81. Wymenga AN, van der Graaf WT, Hofstra LS, et al. Phase I study of transforming growth factor-beta3 mouthwashes for prevention of chemotherapy-induced mucositis. Clin Cancer Res 1999;5:1363–1368.

82. Epstein JB, Stevenson-Moore P, Jackson S, Mohamed JH, Spinelli JJ. Prevention of oral mucositis in radiation therapy: A controlled study with benzydamine hydrochloride rinse. Int J Radiat Oncol Biol Phys 1989; 16:1571–1575.

83. Symonds RP, McIlroy P, Khorrami J, et al. The reduction of radiation mucositis by selective decontamination antibiotic pastilles: A placebo-controlled double-blind trial. Br J Cancer 1996;74:312–317.

84. Bensadoun RJ, Franquin JC, Ciais G, et al. Low-energy He/Ne laser in the prevention of radiation-induced mucositis: A multicenter phase III randomized study in patients with head and neck cancer. Support Care Cancer 1999;7:244–252.

85. Makkonen TA, Nordman E. Estimation of long-term salivary gland damage induced by radiotherapy. Acta Oncol 1987;26:307–312.

86. Epstein JB, Chin EA, Jacobson JJ, Rishiraj B, Le N. The relationships among fluoride, cariogenic oral flora, and salivary flow rate during radiation therapy. Oral Surg Oral Med Oral Pathol Oral Radiol Endod 1998;86:286–292.

87. Epstein JB, van der Meij EH, Lunn R, Stevenson-Moore P. Effects of compliance with fluoride gel application on caries and caries risk in patients after radiation therapy for head and neck cancer. Oral Surg Oral Med Oral Pathol Oral Radiol Endod 1996;82:268–275.

88. Allison PJ, Locker D, Feine JS. The relationship between dental status and health-related quality of life in upper aerodigestive tract cancer patients. Oral Oncol 1999;35:138–143.

89. Maxymiw WG, Wood RE, Anderson JD. The immediate role of the dentist in the maxillectomy patient. J Otolaryngol 1989;18:303–305.

90. Marx RE, Morales MJ. The use of implants in the reconstruction of oral cancer patients. Dent Clin North Am 1998;42:177–202.

91. Kornblith AB, Zlotolow IM, Gooen J, et al. Quality of life of maxillectomy patients using an obturator prosthesis. Head Neck 1996;18:323–334.

92. Nemeth Z, Somogyi A, Takacsi-Nagy Z, Barabas J, Nemeth G, Szabo G. Possibilities of preventing osteoradionecrosis during complex therapy of tumors of the oral cavity. Pathol Oncol Res 2000;6:53–58.

93. Vudiniabola S, Pirone C, Williamson J, Goss AN. Hyperbaric oxygen in the prevention of osteoradionecrosis of the jaws. Aust Dent J 1999;44:243–247.

94. Cronje FJ. A review of the Marx protocols: Prevention and management of osteoradionecrosis by combining surgery and hyperbaric oxygen therapy. SADJ 1998;53:469–471.

95. Shaha AR, Cordeiro PG, Hidalgo DA, et al. Resection and immediate microvascular reconstruction in the management of osteoradionecrosis of the mandible. Head Neck 1997;19:406–411.

96. Zbar RI, Funk GF, McCulloch TM, Graham SM, Hoffman HT. Pectoralis major myofascial flap: A valuable tool in contemporary head and neck reconstruction. Head Neck 1997;19:412–418.

97. Friedman RB. Osteoradionecrosis: Causes and prevention. NCI Monogr 1990;(9):145–149.

98. Marx RE, Johnson RP, Kline SN. Prevention of osteoradionecrosis: A randomized prospective clinical trial of hyperbaric oxygen versus penicillin. J Am Dent Assoc 1985;111:49–54.

99. Maxymiw WG, Wood RE, Liu FF. Postradiation dental extractions without hyperbaric oxygen. Oral Surg Oral Med Oral Pathol 1991;72:270–274.

100. Urba SG, Wolf GT, Bradford CR, et al. Neoadjuvant therapy for organ preservation in head and neck cancer. Laryngoscope 2000;110:2074–2080.

101. Park SH, Gray WC, Hernandez I, et al. Phase I trial of all-trans retinoic acid in patients with treated head and neck squamous carcinoma. Clin Cancer Res 2000;6:847–854.

Quality of Life and Pain: Methodology in Theory and Practice

Charles J. Kowalski, PhD

Christian S. Stohler, DMD, Dr Med Dent

"The art of life is the avoiding of pain." —Thomas Jefferson

The following eight themes are developed in this chapter.

1. Health-related quality of life (HRQOL) is an important outcome variable in clinical trials involving chronic conditions such as persistent pain.
2. The quality of clinical trials can be substantially enhanced by following the Consolidated Standards of Reporting Trials (CONSORT) guidelines.
3. Certain expansions and refinements of the CONSORT guidelines will prove useful in HRQOL research and will result in a more open, efficient, and self-contained research environment.
4. Often, if not always, pain will be included in the assessment of HRQOL.
5. HRQOL instruments should include personal, subjective judgments about what HRQOL means to the individual.
6. The relationship between satisfaction with treatment and HRQOL is examined.

7. The use of the "smallest detectable difference" (SDD) to facilitate decisions about the significance of individual changes in HRQOL scores is discussed.
8. HRQOL outcomes are considered from the perspective of ethically responsible research.

Clinical Trials and Chronic Conditions

There seems to be general agreement that HRQOL should be used more often as an outcome measure in clinical trials research. Indeed, for patients with a chronic condition for which a cure is not probable, HRQOL may be the only relevant outcome.[1] New treatments that increase survival time may do so at the expense of unwanted side effects; therefore, *quality* as well as *quantity* of life must be considered. The National Cancer Institute and other funding agencies and professional organizations now strongly encourage or require researchers to include HRQOL as the primary, or at least one of the secondary, outcome measures in such situations.[2] Still, implementation has been slow. A study conducted in 1998 found that less than 5% of all trials listed in the Cochrane Controlled Trials Register reported on QOL, and this percentage was less than 10% for cancer trials.[3] One might expect, because of the very nature of the disease, that HRQOL would be used much more often in cancer trials. Reasons for and voiced support in favor of this notion have been given by clinical trial groups in North America and Europe, national and international cancer institutes and societies, regulatory agencies responsible for the approval of new anticancer agents, and the pharmaceutical industry. Many of these reasons are directly applicable to other chronic conditions.[4]

HRQOL measures are unique among all outcomes that might be used in a given clinical trial because change in these measures can occur upon admission to the trial, before any treatment is even delivered. Patients with chronic conditions might hope for a cure, but management is the more realistic goal, which begins with caring, listening, explaining, and working together. HRQOL is not just an outcome, it is a treatment target for patients with chronic conditions, and the effects can often be seen even before formal treatment is begun.

However, there are problems beyond merely the quantity of HRQOL reports. The *quality* of the reporting of QOL outcomes has been problematic as well. A plethora of instruments have been used without apparent regard for properties such as validity, reliability, and responsiveness. In addition, it has not always been clearly defined which aspect of HRQOL has been studied. Quite frequently, it is even unclear if the patient, the health care provider, or a relative made the assessment. In a review of 75 articles with "quality of life" in their titles, only 15% defined this term, only 36% gave reasons for their choice of instrument, and only 13% invited patients to contribute personal assessments.[5] The following outcomes were all referred to as QOL

outcomes in recent clinical trials[6]: psychiatric morbidity, number and severity of symptoms, cognitive ability, social contact, ability to work, physical capacity, and diarrheal frequency.

Problems such as these resulted in a call to employ and expand the CONSORT guidelines to include recommendations regarding which HRQOL instruments should be used in different situations.[7] In particular, as evidence accumulates concerning the quality of studies and which instrument should be used when studying a specific intervention to be used for a certain condition in a particular population (age, ethnicity, culture), this evidence would need to be catalogued and made readily available. For example, recommendations might be made as to what instrument is viewed as being most useful to assess the efficacy of coronary bypass grafts in European cardiac patients, or one might ask how to best compare prosthetic devices in edentulous middle-aged Canadians. Thus, a CONSORT expansion could include guidelines both for (prospective) use of instruments and for reporting results. Every research report should include the rationale for using the instrument in the population of patients studied and with respect to the interventions being compared (eg, costs, side effects).

The CONSORT Guidelines

In 1994, guidelines for reporting clinical trials were proposed by two groups and were subsequently combined in a unified statement.[8] This CONSORT statement lists 21 items that, along with a flowchart, describe the patients' progress through the trial. The intent is to ensure that authors provide enough information about how a clinical trial was performed to enable readers to judge the credibility of the results. The guidelines specify what should be included under each of six major headings (Title, Abstract, Methods, etc) by listing several subheadings under each heading. For example, under the "Methods" heading, the subheadings are "Protocol" and "Patient Assignment"; under the "Results" heading, the subheadings are "Participant Flow" and "Analysis."

The subheading "Participant Flow and Follow-up" is accompanied by a flowchart that summarizes all participant activities, including numbers and timing of randomized assignment, interventions, and measurements for each group. Guidelines for the five items expected to be covered under the subheading "Analysis" are as follows:

1. State the estimated effect of the intervention on primary and secondary outcome measures in terms of confidence intervals, whenever feasible.
2. State the results in absolute numbers (10/20, not 50%).
3. Provide summary data and descriptive and inferential statistics in sufficient detail to permit alternative analyses and replication.
4. Describe prognostic variables (covariates) by treatment group as well as any attempt to adjust for them.
5. Describe protocol deviations, giving reasons for them.

These guidelines are meant to ensure that all statistical methods used in the analyses are specified. A final requirement of CONSORT is the provision of the number of eligible patients not recruited, that is, subjects who refused participation. This is the level of detail required of the proposal and necessitates the inclusion of (useful) information not usually provided.

Staquet and colleagues[9] describe all of the information that should be included under each heading/subheading and occasionally ask for even more detail than the CONSORT guidelines. For example, they suggest that the numbers of patients in each of the following categories should be specified:

1. Eligible and entered into the trial
2. Excluded from the analysis because of inadequate data
3. Excluded because of missing data
4. Adequately followed up
5. Unavailable for follow-up
6. Died during the trial
7. Adequately treated according to protocol
8. Failed to complete the treatment according to protocol
9. Received treatments not specified in the protocol

It should be reiterated that differing contexts do indeed require the use of different tools for the measurement of HRQOL. At the most basic level, there is the distinction between "disease-specific" and "generic" instruments. Disease-specific measures focus on those problems specific to, or most closely associated with, a particular condition; generic measures are intended to be broadly applicable, valid across patients presenting with varied diseases or disorders and/or symptom profiles. Each type of instrument has its own advantages and disadvantages. Generic instruments allow cross-condition and cross-intervention comparisons; specific measures are likely to be more responsive to changes in a specific disease entity. As research evidence and experience accumulate, decision rules could be developed. To aid this process, the CONSORT guidelines require expansion.

Symptoms, side effects, and QOL issues are likely to vary in different subsets of patients. For patients with cancer, they may depend on disease site (such as oral cavity, lung, prostate, bone, or breast), stage of disease (advanced or early), treatment modality (chemotherapy or surgery), and patients' age, gender, ethnicity, and cultural background. The one constant factor that characterizes responses to both health challenges and to interventions designed to minimize their harmful effects is variability. Different individuals presented with a common stimulus react differently. The same individual presented with the same stimulus at different times, or under different conditions, might respond differently.

Beyond the CONSORT Guidelines

Adopting the CONSORT guidelines will produce high-quality, informative reports of a clinical trial's structure and outcomes. In the context of trials concerned with HRQOL, certain refinements of these guidelines may further enhance information exchange. It has been suggested that each trial include details concerning the psychometrics of the instrument(s) used in populations of subjects like those being studied. When applicable, the data should also provide an indication of which scores on the scales/dimensions of HRQOL went up, down, or stayed the same. This information would be more useful than merely reporting the results of an omnibus test of significance. The authors should also describe those items or scales for which missing data were encountered, and how these items were treated. These expanded CONSORT guidelines would facilitate the use of well-validated HRQOL instruments in a given, specified situation.[7] Moreover, as suggested by Spilker,[10] HRQOL trials comparing medications should be required to evaluate all of the HRQOL domains (physical, psychologic, social, economic), as well as multiple components of each domain. Researchers should not be permitted to select for their study only those dimensions that show the good side of a medication. QOL is a multidimensional phenomenon, and patients need to know how interventions will affect movement in the biopsychosocial health space within which their lives are lived.

In summary, CONSORT and the suggested enhancements are a positive development. Recent initiatives to establish an international registry of (all) clinical trials, of which HRQOL trials would constitute a subset, clearly should be supported.[11,12] In such a registry, all trials would be registered in advance, and information would be provided about trial structure and outcomes, whether the outcome was positive or negative, or even if the trial was halted before its scheduled conclusion. Suggested information includes the following[11]:

1. Title of the trial
2. Research questions/hypotheses
3. Study population and interventions
4. Lead investigator and/or institution
5. Source of funding
6. Unique identifiers to prevent repeat registrations

7. Status of the trial (eg, ongoing or completed, whether trial is still open to accrual)
8. Other details of the methodology used, such as design, power calculation, outcomes, and types of analysis (for HRQOL trials, a summary statement would be included describing how the measurement instrument worked in the population studied)
9. Ethical aspects such as the type of consent used, the information given to participants, and the approval by institutional review boards/ethics committees
10. Results and whether they are published or unpublished, whether abstracts are presented, as well as references of the best account of the results
11. Full protocol

The exact structure of all of this information would need to be negotiated to accommodate differences in international laws and traditions. Such a registry promises a number of advantages. As described by Tonks,[11] it would reduce publication biases such as the underreporting of trials with disappointing, negative, or inconclusive results. Not reporting these results might mislead researchers conducting systematic reviews and clinicians practicing evidence-based medicine. It would also prevent unnecessary duplication of research, while encouraging appropriate replication and confirmation of results. It would alert researchers to gaps in the knowledge base, foster international collaboration among researchers, and stimulate recruitment to clinical trials. It would provide information about ongoing trials that will help funding bodies target their money where it is most needed, aid recruitment to trials by direct appeal to the public, and enable further research. Such a registry also would improve accessibility and therefore credibility of research performed by the pharmaceutical industry, which has been accused of attempting to suppress negative trial results, an accusation with important ethical and practical implications.[13] A registry might help satisfy the public demand for unbiased evidence on the effectiveness of treatments and promote the public accountability of medical research. Although a good start at a trial registry has been made, much remains to be done.[14]

Once the basic information on trials is made available, the next logical step would be to consider the open sharing of data. As part of the registry of a trial, the data should be made publicly available once it is completed and the results published. Because of modern electronic communication, constraints on space no longer exist, and open access to data (rendered anonymous) can be realized. A number of advantages would result.[15] The use of existing data to answer questions not directly addressed by the primary researchers would be an efficient use of resources. Replicating findings from one study within other data sets increases their robustness. In addition, when planning a study, data from earlier studies can help to refine the research question, select measurement instruments, and calculate sample sizes. Ultimately, new merged data sets can be created through linkage of different sets of records on the same people (if feasible, while providing appropriate confidentiality protection). Providing data will facilitate meta-analyses and offer opportunities for other researchers to check conclusions that would make fraud more difficult. Finally, in addition to having access to basic information on all trials, including the possibility of downloading copies of the raw data, a final step might ensure the openness that should characterize the scientific enterprise: Harold Varmus' proposed PubMed Central (PMC), a repository for literature in the life sciences, while still very much in its infancy, provides a freely accessible comprehensive electronic archive of all of the peer-reviewed biomedical literature.[16]

The question of how to encourage participation in these activities arises. One is struck by the fact that PMC is a grassroots effort. All scientists, from students to professors, are being asked to publish in, edit, review for, and personally subscribe to only those journals that grant unrestricted distribution rights to PMC within 6 months of publication. Perhaps this sort of voluntary approach is best. But more formal, compelling, and mandatory routes are also

available. The National Bioethics Advisory Commission recently recommended that Congress create a new, independent office to oversee all research involving human subjects. This National Office of Human Research Oversight (NOHRO) would develop and enforce new rules for such research. These rules would cover all research involving human participants, even research sponsored by corporations without federal funds. There would be no reason why NOHRO could not require that all clinical trials be registered, that their results be published in journals subscribing to PMC, and that the data be shared with other researchers within a reasonable time.

Pain As a Dimension of HRQOL

When considering the relationship between HRQOL and pain, two questions arise, namely (1) whether pain is a bona fide dimension of HRQOL that should be assessed in most, if not all, QOL studies, and (2) whether HRQOL is a useful descriptor/comparator in groups of patients with chronic pain and/or a useful outcome measure in clinical trials. In framing an answer to the first question, the definition of HRQOL needs to be considered, followed by considerations of the history of humans' fight against pain, and some statistical evidence showing that pain is in fact often included in HRQOL instruments. The second question can be approached by appealing to the special set of problems suffered by patients with chronic pain and by arguing that patients' satisfaction with treatment is closely related to HRQOL improvements.

There is little debate on the multidimensionality of HRQOL. However, there is little agreement about which dimensions should be included. Some HRQOL instruments include pain items, but others, such as the Sickness Impact Profile (SIP), one of the best known and widely used HRQOL instruments, do not. The SIP consists of 136 items divided into 12 categories, which are in turn clustered into three groups: independent living, physical, and psychosocial domains. The categories in the independent living group are "sleep and rest," "eating," "work," "home management," and "recreation." The categories under the physical domain include "ambulation," "mobility," "body care," and "movement." The categories in the psychosocial group are "social interaction," "alertness behavior," "emotional behavior," and "communication." The SIP has proved useful in various settings, including health surveys, program planning, policy formation, and monitoring patient progress,[17] thus testifying to the fact that explicit inclusion of pain may not be necessary in all studies involving HRQOL. However, in most clinical trials, the aim is to obtain unbiased, unconfounded estimates of the effect of the intervention. This makes it important to measure and correct for all relevant covariates, among which pain will often be counted. Whether or not one uses language that includes or excludes pain from the first-order dimensions of HRQOL, it is prudent to measure and account for the effects of pain. As stated by Berzon,[1] pain, "while not a specific HRQOL domain per se, will influence perceptions of functional status and overall life quality; therefore it may be appropriate to measure it within specific study designs."

The authors believe that it is important to include pain in most, if not all, studies focusing on HRQOL. The consideration of pain as a primary dimension of HRQOL is a function of nomenclature, not of intrinsic importance. Whether pain is considered a "specific HRQOL domain per se" will depend on the definition of HRQOL that is used. A definition[18] of HRQOL as "patients' appraisals of their current level of functioning and satisfaction with it compared to what they perceive to be ideal" may not explicitly include pain. However, other definitions certainly do. Indeed, pain measures have been equated to HRQOL in many studies. For example, recently, the Brief Pain Inventory (BPI) was used to evaluate QOL in patients with breast cancer who had undergone two different regimens of adjuvant irradiation.[19] Historical and statistical evidence in favor of including pain in studies focusing on HRQOL are presented next.

The first recorded reference to remedies for pain goes back to Ancient Egypt (circa 1550 BC), when Isis prescribed opium for Ra's headache.[20] This account goes on to describe other early approaches to pain relief which included purging, vomiting, poisoning, puncturing, cutting, cupping, blistering, leeching, heating, freezing, sweating, placing trephines, and administering shocks. Patients chewed, imbibed, or supped treatment with crocodile dung, teeth of swine, hooves of asses, spermatic fluid of frogs, eunuch fat, fly specks, lozenges of dried vipers, powder of precious stones, oils derived from ants, earthworms and spiders, feathers, hair, human perspiration, and moss scraped from the skull of a victim of a violent death. It seems obvious that people would not suffer such indignities if they were not truly suffering. The extent to which people will go to alleviate their pain speaks volumes about the importance of pain for a person's QOL.

Like HRQOL itself, pain is multidimensional. Each of the dimensions of pain might interact with other determinants of HRQOL. Chronic pain is not just a pain in the head, back, or neck. It is pain in the head, back, or neck along with fear, anxiety, disturbed sleep, loss of appetite, altered libido, depression, or loss of a job. It often brings hopelessness, helplessness, despair, bitterness, desperation, bewilderment, anger, resentment, or hostility. An important kind of pain is that accompanying temporomandibular disorders (TMD). However, TMD is not just joint pain; it often indicates a painful joint and recurring headaches, earaches, ringing in the ears, toothache, difficulty in swallowing, or painful neck spasms. Patients who suffer from TMD frequently hear a clicking or popping sound when they open or close their mouth. These symptoms often intensify while chewing, thereby affecting a person's diet. The muscle close to the ear may be painful and tender, and jaw movements are frequently limited and/or erratic. The experience of pain is compounded when caretakers, spouses, friends, and relatives suggest that the pain is psychosomatic in origin.

Box 15-1 HRQOL instruments including pain as an aspect of QOL*

Arthritis Impact Measurement Scales (AIMS)[†]
Physical and Mental Impairment-of-Function Evaluation (PAMIE)
Functional Assessment Inventory (FAI)
Functional Living Index—Cancer (FLIC)[†]
European Organization for Research and Treatment of Cancer (EORTC) Quality of Life Questionnaire (QLQ)[†]
Quality of Life Index (QL Index)
Dartmouth Primary Care Cooperative Information Project (COOP) Charts for Primary Care Practice[†]
Functional Status Questionnaire (FSQ)
Duke Health Profile (DUKE)[†]
McMaster Health Index Questionnaire (MHIQ)
Sickness Impact Profile (SIP)
Nottingham Health Profile (NHP)[†]
Short Form-36 Health Survey (SF-36)[†]
Short Form-20 Health Survey (SF-20)[†]
Self-Evaluation of Life Function (SELF) Scale[†]
Multilevel Assessment Instrument (MAI)
Older Americans Resources and Services (OARS) Multidimensional Functional Assessment Questionnaire (OMFAQ)
Comprehensive Assessment and Referral Evaluation (CARE)
Disability and Distress Scale[†]
EuroQol Quality of Life Scale[†]
Quality of Well-Being (QWB) Scale[†]

*Data from McDowell and Newell.[17]
[†]Instrument explicitly asks about pain.

The statistical evidence in favor of including pain in HRQOL assessment is substantial. As shown in Box 15-1, McDowell and Newell[17] found 21 different HRQOL instruments that include pain as an aspect of QOL. Spilker[21] also described a number of HRQOL instruments, including the Functional Assessment of Cancer Therapy (FACT), the Functional Assessment of HIV Infection (FAHI), the Health Utilities Index (HUI), Quality of Life—Cancer (QOL-CA), and the World Health Organization Quality of Life (WHOQOL) Assessment Instrument.

Instruments purporting to measure pain often include other HRQOL dimensions. The International Association for the Study of Pain defines pain as "an unpleasant sensory and emotional experience associated with actual or potential tissue damage, or described in terms of such damage." Pain is not only a painful stimulus. It also includes a person's emotional reaction to it, and how the person integrates these reactions to form

an experience. The following pain measurement instruments were evaluated by McDowell and Newell[17]: visual analog scales (VAS), McGill Pain Questionnaire (MPQ), BPI, Medical Outcomes Study Pain Measures, Oswestry Low Back Pain Disability Questionnaire, Back Pain Classification Scale, Pain and Distress Scale, Illness Behavior Questionnaire, and Pain Perception Profile.

Visual analog scales are often used to measure the unpleasantness as well as the intensity of a painful experience. The MPQ was constructed to include the sensory, affective, and evaluative domains. The BPI and the Medical Outcomes Study Pain Measures both ask patients to rate how much the pain has interfered with their enjoyment of life. The Oswestry Low Back Pain Disability Questionnaire asks about how pain interferes with sex life, social life, and traveling. The Back Pain Classification Scale contains many of the descriptors comprising the MPQ, including "cruel," "annoying," "exhausting," "agonizing," "terrifying," "torturing," and "fearful." The Pain and Distress Scale assesses mood and behavior changes that are the result of pain, but does not ask about the pain per se. Similarly, the Illness Behavior Questionnaire asks more about reactions to pain (along seven dimensions) than the pain itself. The Pain Perception Profile, the most focused of the instruments listed, assesses more than just the feeling and the intensity of the painful stimulus, it also measures unpleasantness. It is clear that to understand pain, one must assess not only the strength of the signal, but also the patient's reaction to it. To assess the degree to which pain has an effect on the person's life, mood, functionality, or spirit, one needs to assess HRQOL. This is especially true when working with patients with chronic pain. Long-lasting and recurring pain acts as a severe stressor that has a profound impact on a patient's psychologic state and social well-being.

The inclusion of pain in a HRQOL measure is mandatory when the subjects of inquiry are patients with chronic pain. This is because management strategies based on the application of pathophysiologic theories to carefully recorded physical symptoms are often inadequate to produce relief.[22] When the pain becomes chronic, it often points to the difficulty in establishing a definite diagnosis and the failure of conservative treatment. The level of pain reported is often considered to be out of proportion and patients with chronic pain have a greater likelihood of developing psychologic problems. As stated by Lee and Rowlington,[22] "Faced with a condition that cannot be satisfactorily diagnosed and for which little or no relief can be found, unable to function in his or her normal day-to-day existence because of preoccupation with that pain and its unanswered questions, the chronic pain patient is beset with dissatisfaction and a deteriorating QOL." If researchers or clinicians study chronic pain and its impact, they must study not only the pain itself, but also the context within which it occurs and the patient's reactions to it.

It is now well established that the intensity and unpleasantness of a painful experience respond differently to, among other things, (1) narcotics,

(2) information concerning the pain challenge, and (3) hypnotic suggestion. Fentanyl (a short-acting narcotic) reduces sensory intensity without reducing the unpleasantness of painful electric stimulation of tooth pulp, whereas diazepam (a minor tranquilizer) reduces unpleasantness but not the intensity of cutaneous electric stimulation. Expectations can also shape reactions in experiments on pain. When noxious stimuli were preceded by a warning, the resulting unpleasantness ratings were reduced. However, the intensity ratings did not change. It seems as if the subjects would rather know that the next stimulus will be painful than to be taken by surprise. In a study of hypnotic suggestion and heat pain, directing hypnosis toward unpleasantness reduces unpleasantness, but not intensity. However, when the hypnosis is directed at intensity, both the intensity and unpleasantness ratings are attenuated. This finding suggests that the sensation may be the cause of unpleasantness, but not vice versa. All of the aforementioned clearly points to the fact that there are at least two distinct and separate dimensions to painful experiences, and that studies of pain that fail to include both of these dimensions can be misleading.

Subjectivity of HRQOL

When studying HRQOL instruments, the questions asked, the response format provided, and the relative weights (if any) applied to the answers have all been predetermined. The patient does not provide any input into shaping the questionnaire. The respondent may not find any of the survey questions interesting or even applicable in the context of his or her condition. The instrument may be psychometrically flawless, but reliability does not imply relevance. The Schedule for Evaluation of Individual Quality of Life (SEIQOL) is an explicit attempt to measure QOL on a more personal level. It is based on the premise that a person's QOL is what he or she states it to be. It is important to note that an individual's conception of what constitutes QOL need not be limited to aspects

Table 15-1 Results of a study illustrating problems with interpreting research results*

Dimension	Treatment 1 (n = 181)	Treatment 2 (n = 143)	Treatment 3 (n = 162)
General well-being	Improved	Stable	Stable
Physical symptoms	Stable	Improved	Worsened
Sexual function	Stable	Worsened	Worsened
Work performance	Improved	Worsened	Stable
Sleep dysfunction	Stable	Stable	Stable
Cognitive function	Worsened	Improved	Improved
Life satisfaction	Stable	Worsened	Worsened
Social participation	Worsened	Stable	Improved

*Data from Croog et al.[23]

of health. Gill and Feinstein[5] argue in favor of letting respondents rate the importance of each dimension of their QOL and choose the dimensions to be included. It is not merely the symptoms or limitations in functioning that affect QOL that are important, but also the meaning and significance of these symptoms to the individual patient. Patients with identical health status may have experiences ranging from despair to happiness.[6] The SEIQOL consists of three relatively simple steps. First, respondents determine five areas of life they consider to be most important to their QOL. Second, on a VAS, respondents rate their current status/functioning of each area (V_i). Third, respondents then assign weights (w_i, all positive with a sum of 1) to each of the five areas. SEIQOL scores are then the weighted average of the five VAS scores:

$$Score = w_1 V_1 + w_2 V_2 + w_3 V_3 + w_4 V_4 + w_5 V_5$$

In addition to providing a QOL score that is determined by an individual, the very process of obtaining a baseline value might well facilitate the diagnostic process. It is likely to enable clinicians to better formulate and monitor therapeutic strategies. It will heighten the subject's awareness, thus facilitating communication and joint decision making. It should increase compliance and ultimately affect the patient's satisfaction with treatment. In the context of clinical trials,

the SEIQOL has the further advantage of producing a single (univariate) value representing QOL, which will simplify analyses. One of the major problems with multivariate outcomes involves the interpretation of results that indicate that the patients in one arm of a trial improve along several dimensions, while the patients in another improve along other dimensions. With some changes made for emphasis, Table 15-1 shows the effects of three modes of antihypertensive therapy on QOL.[23]

Different people might prefer different treatments depending on what they think about the relative importance of each dimension. Is maintenance of sexual function worth some loss in cognitive function? Why does reduction in physical symptoms not result in more life satisfaction? Are the mental and social aspects of one's life more important than the physical? Again, the importance of the weights assigned to the dimensions is apparent. Weights will be assigned, either explicitly as part of the analysis or implicitly in interpretation, discussion, or application. The clinical relevance of the results is at stake here—what does it mean if two or three among the eight or nine domains of the QOL instrument improve, when patterns of improvement/deterioration differ among the arms, and/or if differences between them are slight? Recent examples of these phenomena are not hard to find.[24]

Whether one uses an existing instrument (implicit weights) or the SEIQOL (explicit weights), weighing outcomes by importance is not a trivial task. The sets of weights assigned in most situations will exhibit high interindividual variability. It is difficult to get people to agree about which weights to assign. For example, in May 1989, the state of Oregon unveiled a draft of a priority list for medical interventions, which was withdrawn almost immediately. This list was the result of careful analyses including the definitions of appropriate health outcomes, their costs, and effects on QOL, but it had set various counterintuitive priorities. For example, dental caps to relieve the discomfort of pulp exposure had been assigned a higher priority than surgery for life-threatening ectopic pregnancy; splints for joints with TMD outranked emergency appendectomies, and treatments for thumb-sucking, crooked teeth, and acute headaches all scored higher than therapies for cystic fibrosis and acquired immunodeficiency syndrome (AIDS).[25] In addition to attesting to the strength of the dental lobby in Oregon, this experience clearly indicates that assigning priorities is difficult and highly subjective. It points to the fact that the SEIQOL's individual assignation of weights to reflect a person's values is a considerable advantage.

A recent study[26] found that patients who acquired AIDS through intravenous drug use differed from homosexual patients. For drug users, most frequently family was nominated the most important QOL domain, followed by health, drugs, and drug-related issues, including money for purchasing drugs. For the homosexual group, health, friends and social life, and psychologic issues like self-acceptance and sense of control were selected equally often. These profiles differ enough to suggest that different management strategies might be appropriate for these two groups.

Individual weights of HRQOL dimensions are incorporated into the FACT scale. The FACT family (eg, FACT-G, general; FACT-C, patients with colorectal cancer; FACT-H&N, patients with head and neck cancer) assesses the impact of cancer on five dimensions: the physical, social, emotional, and functional domains, and the relationship with the physician. Each domain is scored on a 5-point scale, with 0 indicating "not at all," 1 indicating "a little bit," 2 indicating "somewhat," 3 indicating "quite a bit," and 4 indicating "very much." In addition, the patient is asked for each dimension, "How much does (this dimension) affect your QOL?" The answer to this question is scored on a scale of 0 to 10, with 0 corresponding to "not at all" and 10 to "very much so." Use of these weights is still in the experimental stage.

Satisfaction with Treatment and HRQOL

QOL cannot be evaluated without a reference to satisfaction.[22] A number of definitions of QOL are based on this connection, some of which were discussed by King and colleagues.[2] QOL is defined in the literature as:

1. The degree of satisfaction with perceived present life circumstances.[27]
2. An individual's perceptions of well-being that stem from satisfaction or dissatisfaction with dimensions of life that are important to the individual.[28]
3. Patients' appraisal of and satisfaction with their current level of functioning compared with what they perceive to be possible or ideal.[18]
4. Personal opinions reflecting satisfaction with current circumstances, participation in activities and relations, and the opportunity to have control over one's life and choices.[29]
5. The way in which individuals view their own health and the degree to which they are satisfied with it.[30]

Patient satisfaction is determined more by QOL issues than by moving clinical measurements closer to normative values. In the context of oral health, satisfaction with pain management is only moderately correlated with a reduction in pain intensity, and patients' satisfaction with dental prostheses is more determined by comfort, ability to chew and speak, and ease of cleaning than by occlusal measurements. Fiske et al[31] found that oral handicaps; compromised diet; altered meals; unsatisfactory appearance; embarrassment about dentition; restricted smiling, laughing, or talking because of dental conditions; and mouth pain were common in more than 80% of older, mostly edentulous adults. These measures provided considerably more understanding of oral dysfunction than did traditional measures of denture stability, retention, fit, occlusion, and use.

At the most fundamental level, satisfaction is associated with pain relief. In addition, however, other dimensions of satisfaction must be assessed in patients with chronic pain.[22] Deyo and Diehl[32] studied patients with back pain and found that their satisfaction was largely determined by the quality of the information provided about the origin of the problem. Ware et al[33] suggested that satisfaction with treatment depended on a number of factors, only one of which was concerned with efficacy. The other factors listed were interpersonal manner, technical quality, accessibility/convenience, finances, efficacy/outcomes, continuity, and physical environment and availability.

From this perspective, satisfaction may be defined as "an attitudinal response to value judgments that patients make about their clinical encounter."[34] The whole encounter is important, not only its outcome. It may be useful to distinguish between affective and cognitive components of HRQOL.[35] Affect refers to the emotions or pleasantness of experiences, whereas cognition refers to rational appraisal as demonstrated by reason, thought, and satisfaction. Just as pain has its sensory, affective, and evaluative components, HRQOL has an immediate and a more reflective, evaluative side. Satisfaction with one's condition defines HRQOL. Satisfaction with treatment is related not only with positive changes in the condition, but also to comfort with the process.

A 1994 review of 195 satisfaction studies showed that 80% of the studies produced a new satisfaction measure because of the belief that existing instruments were unsatisfactory in some way.[36] Sixty percent of these studies did not report on reliability and/or validity.

Smallest Detectable Difference

Although HRQOL is a subjective variable, it is often measured with a precision equal to that of many objective clinical measures. Most HRQOL measures are easy to administer and quantify. However, their results are not so easy to interpret. The clinical significance of HRQOL scores or changes in HRQOL scores are sometimes difficult to assess. In these instances, it may be useful to measure the SDD.

The SDD of an outcome variable describes the level of improvement necessary to provide convincing evidence that an intervention has been successful.[37,38] If a measure has imperfect reliability, repeating the measure can produce a different value even if no change has actually occurred. The SDD provides a numeric cutoff point that allows us to judge whether an observed change is because of a real change in the measure or simply the result of inconsistency of measurement. The SDD is a simple function of the standard error of measurement (SEM), where $SEM = SD \times (1 - R)^{1/2}$. The SD is a reflection of the amount of variability in the measure expected among subjects from the same population as the subject to be assessed, and R is the reliability (intraclass correlation coefficient) of the measure. The SEM is found to be useful when constructing confidence intervals for the true value of a finding in an individual. If the observed value is X, then the true value of X would fall with approximately 95% confidence into the interval of $X \pm 2SEM$. The SDD is found using the equation $SDD = 2SEM \times 2^{1/2}$. The usefulness of this quantity is illustrated below.

Studies have provided details, further references, and dental examples involving VAS and the Mandibular Function Impairment Questionnaire in patients with TMDs.[37,38] For example, McDowell and Newell[17] describe the Arthritis Impact Measurement Scales (AIMS) instrument, an HRQOL measure. The AIMS instrument consists of 67 items that have been thoroughly studied for validity and reliability. It is self-administered and can be completed in 15 minutes. The instrument assesses three components of HRQOL: physical functioning (mobility, physical activity, dexterity, household activities, and activities of daily living), psychologic status (depression and anxiety), and pain. All AIMS component scores are standardized to cover a range of 0 to 10, in which higher numbers represent poorer HRQOL. The reliability coefficients range from 0.7 to 0.9. Each component typically shows an SD of 2. Assuming R = 0.7 and SD = 2, the SEM is approximately 1 and the SDD is approximately 2.8. Based on this, if a subject had an initial value of 6 on one of the scales, an approximate 95% confidence interval for the true value would be 6 ± 2 or (4, 8). A later score would have to change by at least 2.8 (> 8.8 or < 3.2) to signal real change (either deterioration or improvement). If R were 0.8, SDD would be approximately 2.5 and the interval would be (4.2, 7.8). For R = 0.9, SDD would be approximately 1.8 and the confidence interval (4.8, 7.2). To further illustrate the usefulness of this methodology, Kropmans et al[38] considered a patient with an initial score of 40 on the Mandibular Function Impairment Questionnaire (range, 0 to 68). After 4 weeks of therapy, the score was 34, a reduction of 6 points. A comparison with SDD of 14 indicates that this difference is not a real improvement.

Clinical Trials, HRQOL Outcomes, and Ethics

A responsible conduct of research with human subjects is guided by the principles of autonomy, beneficence, and justice. Autonomy, or respect for persons, incorporates the ideas that individuals should be treated as autonomous agents and that persons with diminished autonomy are entitled to increased protection. In research using human subjects, autonomy is readily associated with obtaining the potential subject's informed consent to participate. Informed consent involves three elements: capacity, information, and voluntariness. The person must be able to understand, be given all the information necessary to reach an informed decision, and be free to choose. When one considers the informational component of this process, subjects will most likely have concerns about their feelings about the drug and their ability to perform tasks after taking it, and the consequences of not taking it. These questions are related to how an intervention is expected to influence QOL. Answers to questions such as these often require the patient to make a reasoned judgment about the situation and to choose wisely. Answers can only be obtained from clinical studies that include QOL as an outcome variable. Research that fails to provide information upon which answers to such questions may be based, provided only that the relevance of such questions can be foreseen, may be viewed as unethical.[39] That is, the responsible conduct of research requires that the research be capable of answering questions about how interventions affect lives.

Beneficence is described in terms of two complimentary rules: *(1)* do not harm and *(2)* maximize potential benefits while minimizing risks. The principle demands that study participation be associated with a favorable balance of benefits and risks if one is to have the information necessary to make a truly informed choice. Again, the only way to generate this information is to include QOL measures as outcomes in trials.

Finally, the principle of justice requires fairness in the burdens and benefits of research. Among other things, it requires the inclusion of diverse populations to gain any benefit from research findings. These groups may be found within a given culture, eg, rich and poor Americans, or they may cross over cultural boundaries. A fundamental cross-cultural issue concerns the very meaning of the QOL construct. QOL is a cultural construct conceived and developed by social scientists in the United States.[6]

The success of the construct in Western civilization is, by itself, not convincing evidence that QOL is a universally valid construct; it cannot be assumed to have universal meaning.[6] Even if such meaning were to be found, measurement problems would persist. Satisfaction with one's lot in life has much to do with what is normal and/or possible in one's environment. Identical response patterns to a questionnaire need not signal equality of anything other than the total score. For example, among the issues that must be faced when QOL instruments are to be used cross-culturally, the two most important ones are language and cultural differences in the meanings of words. It is therefore important that individual-specific HRQOL dimensions and attendant weights be developed.

These last considerations point to the fact that QOL concerns are integral to most health-related research. They also stress the significance of continuing to reflect on how to design and conduct studies and collect data that will allow researchers to adequately assess QOL and investigate its significance for healthy and sick patients.

References

1. Berzon RA. Understanding and using health-related quality of life instruments within clinical research studies. In: Staquet MJ, Hays RD, Fayers PM (eds). Quality of Life Assessment in Clinical Trials. Oxford: Oxford Univ Press, 1998:3–15.
2. King CR, Haberman M, Berry DL, et al. Quality of life and the cancer experience: The state-of-the-knowledge. Oncol Nurs Forum 1997;24:27–41.
3. Sanders C, Egger M, Donovan J, Tallon D, Frankel S. Reporting on quality of life in randomised controlled trials: Bibliographic study. BMJ 1998;317:1191–1194.
4. Aaronson NK, Cull AM, Kaasa S, Sprangers MAG. The European Organization for Research and Treatment of Cancer (EORTC) modular approach to quality of life assessment in oncology: An update. In: Spilker B (ed). Quality of Life and Pharmacoeconomics in Clinical Trials, ed 2. Philadelphia: Lippincott-Raven, 1996: 179–189.
5. Gill TM, Feinstein AR. A critical appraisal of the quality of quality-of-life measurements. JAMA 1994;272: 619–626.
6. Hunt SM. Cross-cultural issues in the use of quality of life measures in randomized controlled trials. In: Staquet MJ, Hays RD, Fayers PM (eds). Quality of Life Assessment in Clinical Trials. Oxford: Oxford Univ Press, 1998:51–67.
7. Wright SP. Reporting on quality of life in RCTs. CONSORT guidelines should be expanded. BMJ 1999;318: 1142.
8. Begg C, Cho M, Eastwood S, et al. Improving the quality of reporting of randomized controlled trials: The CONSORT statement. JAMA 1996;276:637–639.
9. Staquet MJ, Berzon RA, Osaba D, Machin D. Guidelines for reporting results of quality of life assessments in clinical trials. In: Staquet MJ, Hays RD, Fayers PM (eds). Quality of Life Assessment in Clinical Trials. Oxford: Oxford Univ Press, 1998:337–347.
10. Spilker B. Adopting higher standards for quality of life trials. In: Spilker B (ed). Quality of Life and Pharmacoeconomics in Clinical Trials, ed 2. Philadelphia: Lippincott-Raven, 1996:57–58.
11. Tonks A. Registering clinical trials. BMJ 1999;319: 1565–1568.
12. Simes RJ. Publication bias: The case for an international registry of clinical trials. J Clin Oncol 1986;4: 1529–1541.
13. Yamey G. Scientists who do not publish trial results are 'unethical.' BMJ 1999;319:939A.
14. Available at: http://www.controlledtrials.com. Accessed April 9, 2002.
15. Delamothe T. Whose data are they anyway? BMJ 1996;312:1241–1242.
16. Available at: http://www.pubmedcentral.nih.gov. Accessed April 9, 2002.
17. McDowell I, Newell C. Measuring Health, ed 2. Oxford: Oxford Univ Press, 1996.
18. Cella DF, Tulsky DS. Measuring quality of life today: Methodological aspects. Oncology 1990;5:29–38.
19. Kongsgaard UE, Erikstein B, Kvinnsland S. Late sequelae of post-mastectomy radiotherapy. In: Devor M, Rowbotham MC, Wiesenfeld-Hallin Z (eds). Proceedings of the 9th World Congress on Pain. Seattle: IASP Press, 2000:639–643.
20. Turk DC, Meichenbaum D, Genest M. Pain and Behavioral Medicine: A Cognitive-Behavioral Perspective. New York: Guilford, 1983.
21. Spilker B, ed. Quality of Life and Pharmacoeconomics in Clinical Trials, ed 2. Philadelphia: Lippincott-Raven, 1996.
22. Lee VC, Rowlington JC. Defining quality of life in chronic pain. In: Spilker B (ed). Quality of Life and Pharmacoeconomics in Clinical Trials, ed 2. Philadelphia: Lippincott-Raven, 1996:853–864.
23. Croog SH, Levine S, Testa MA, et al. The effects of antihypertensive therapy on the quality of life. N Engl J Med 1986;314:1657–1664.

24. Rush DR, Stelmach WJ, Young TL, et al. Clinical effectiveness and quality of life with ranitidine vs placebo in gastroesophageal reflux disease patients: A clinical experience network (CEN) study. J Fam Pract 1995;41:126–136.

25. Paltiel AD, Stinnett AA. Making health policy decisions: Is human instinct rational? Is rational choice human? Chance 1996;9:34–39.

26. Hickey AM, Bury G, O'Boyle CA, Bradley F, O'Kelly FD, Shannon W. A new short form quality of life measure (SEIQoL-DW): Application in a cohort of individuals with HIV/AIDS. BMJ 1996;313:29–33.

27. Young KJ, Longman AJ. Quality of life and persons with melanoma: A pilot study. Cancer Nurs 1983;6:219–225.

28. Ferrans CE, Powers MJ. Quality of life index: Development and psychometric properties. ANS Adv Nurs Sci 1985;8:15–24.

29. Keith K, Schalock R. The measurement of quality of life in adolescence: The quality of student life questionnaire. Am J Fam Ther 1994;22:83–87.

30. Vivier PM, Bernier JA, Starfield B. Current approaches to measuring health outcomes in pediatric research. Curr Opin Pediatr 1994;6:530–537.

31. Fiske J, Gelbier S, Watson RM. The benefit of dental care to an elderly population assessed using a sociodental measure of oral handicap. Br Dent J 1990;168:153–156.

32. Deyo RA, Diehl AK. Patient satisfaction with medical care for low-back pain. Spine 1986;11:28–30.

33. Ware JE Jr, Snyder MK, Wright WR, Davies AR. Defining and measuring patient satisfaction with medical care. Eval Program Plann 1983;6:247–263.

34. Maciejewski M, Kawiecki J, Rockwood T. Satisfaction. In: Kane RL (ed). Understanding Healthcare Outcomes Research. Gaithersburg, MD: Aspen, 1997:67–89.

35. de Haes CJM, de Ruiter JH, Temperlaar R, Pennink JW. The distinction between affect and cognition in the quality of life of cancer patients: Sensitivity and stability. Qual Life Res 1992;1:315–322.

36. Sitzia J. How valid and reliable are patient satisfaction data? An analysis of 195 studies. Int J Qual Health Care 1999;11:319–328.

37. Kropmans TJB, Dijkstra PU, Stegenga B, Stewart R, de Bont LGM. Smallest detectable difference in outcome variables related to painful restriction of the temporomandibular joint. J Dent Res 1999;78:784–789.

38. Kropmans TJB, Dijkstra PU, van Veen A, Stegenga B, de Bont LGM. The smallest detectable difference of mandibular function impairment in patients with painfully restricted temporomandibular joint. J Dent Res 1999;78:1445–1459.

39. Levine RJ. Quality of life assessment in clinical trials: An ethical perspective. In: Spilker B (ed). Quality of Life and Pharmacoeconomics in Clinical Trials, ed 2. Philadelphia: Lippincott-Raven, 1996:489–495.

Using Oral Health–Related Quality of Life to Refocus Dental Education

Marita Rohr Inglehart, Dr phil habil

Lisa A. Tedesco, PhD

Richard W. Valachovic, DMD

Oral health–related quality of life (OHRQOL) considerations play a central role in the future of dental education. Considering the structural factors that will shape dental health care in the future,[1] the challenges that oral health care providers face currently,[2,3] and the recommendations for the future of dental education,[4–6] the dental education community must begin to evaluate whether it is preparing future health care providers to be *(1)* truly patient-centered, *(2)* culturally competent, and *(3)* able to work from an interdisciplinary perspective that places oral health in the context of a patient's overall health. OHRQOL considerations are useful in refocusing the content of educational efforts on these three goals.

Current Trends in Dentistry

In June 2001, the American Dental Education Association (ADEA) published an association report on trends among dental patients and practitioners and in dental education in the US.[1] An analysis of population growth and life expectancy data showed that the number of future dental patients is increasing in the US. Additionally, the number of teeth requiring care per patient is growing because of the decline in edentulism. Between 1971 and 1994, the number of edentulous patients in the US decreased from 14.7% to 7.7% overall, and from 45.6% to 28.6% in the 65- to 74-year-old age group. At the same time, the percentage of patients receiving selected dental services such as oral examinations, prophylaxis, and fluoride treatments from private practitioners increased. Population demographics show a projected growth in the percentage of patients over 65 years of age as well as a substantial decrease in the white population from 73% in 1997 to a projected 52.8% in the year 2050.[1]

Given this projection of a growing demand for dental health care services in the future, it is interesting to note the trends among dental practitioners. While there was an increase in the ratio of dentists per 100,000 people in the US from 51.5 in 1950 to 59.5 in 1990, this number has been declining ever since. It is projected that there will be 52.7 dentists per 100,000 people in the US by the year 2020. Trends in dental education show that the number of graduating dentists from US dental schools is not likely to replace the number of dentists retiring over the next few decades.[1] Even more critical than the projected change in this ratio is the fact that certain areas in the country and particular segments of the US population are underserved.[2] The projections presented in this report, namely that in the US fewer dentists are likely to treat more patients, will have a profound effect on the future of dental education. Future dentists will have to be taught to be culturally competent and able to interact effectively with an increasingly diverse patient population.

Current State of Oral Health Care

The current situation in the oral health care field is another parameter affecting the future of dental education. The surgeon general's report on oral health in the US from the year 2000 provides an excellent overview for this purpose. This report was the first surgeon general's report on oral health in US history and gave unprecedented visibility to oral health concerns.[3] It addressed five oral health concerns that are crucially important for the future of dental education. First, the report addresses the definition of oral health, pointing out the crucial role oral health plays in a person's general health and quality of life (QOL). In doing so, the report suggests that the focus of oral health care should be on the patient as a whole person.

The second key area the report addresses is the status of oral health and oral health care in the US. The report shows that although a large segment of the US population enjoys a positive OHRQOL, there are many oral health care issues that need to be addressed. For example,

childhood caries, although a preventable disease, is still the most common childhood disease. Moreover, there are new challenges that will have to be met as the number of patients with complex health conditions and multiple medications increases in the future.[3] The report also documents striking health disparities between ethnic/racial groups and between patients with and without special needs. It is important for dental education to train professionals to be able and willing to provide services for the large segment of the population who are currently underserved, live with oral pain, and have difficulties with activities such as eating or speaking because of oral health problems.

The third area of oral health issues the report focuses on is the inextricable link between oral health and general health. This demonstrates the importance of preparing future oral health care providers to become part of an interdisciplinary team in order to assure optimal care for patients. To create such a team, it is important that oral health care professionals communicate with professionals from other health care disciplines regarding not only the relationship between oral and physical health, but even more importantly the effects of impaired oral health on a patient's QOL.

The fourth concern the report addresses is the way in which oral health is promoted and maintained and how oral diseases are prevented. The report stresses the advantage that dentistry has in comparison to many other areas of health care in that it has effective ways to prevent oral disease and promote good oral health and QOL. However, it also points to the importance of optimally utilizing these opportunities and preparing students with such a perspective in mind.

Finally, the report addresses the many factors that play a role in the need and opportunities for enhancing oral health for all Americans. In summary, this report offers a framework for action. It implies that dental education must teach future dental health care providers to provide truly patient-centered care, put oral health care in the context of a general health care model, and assure access to care for all patients.

Recommendations for the Future of Dental Education

The underlying tone of the surgeon general's report on oral health[2,3] was foreshadowed in the Institute of Medicine report about the future of dental education in 1995.[4-6] This important document on "Dental Education at the Crossroads—Challenges and Change" discusses the status of dental education in the US and outlines future goals for dental education. It lists 22 recommendations for the future of dental education; several of these recommendations directly relate to the themes of the surgeon general's report on oral health.[2,3] For example, some recommendations point to the significance of adopting a truly patient-centered approach, while others stress the importance of access to care for all population segments and the provision of such care by culturally competent health care providers. Still others focus on connecting dentistry administratively—in its research, teaching, and patient care efforts—with other units and disciplines.[4,5]

In January 1996, the American Association of Dental Schools (AADS; now the ADEA) conducted a survey to gain a better understanding of the attitudes of the professional dental community toward the 22 recommendations in the Institute of Medicine report. This survey was mailed out to dental school faculty (n = 4,927) and directors in hospital (n = 412), dental hygiene (n = 212), dental assistant (n = 229), and lab technician (n = 17) programs. The questionnaire asked respondents to rate each of the 22 recommendations on a 5-point scale, ranging from 1 = not at all to 5 = very, concerning *(1)* how important the recommendation is, *(2)* how positive the influence of the recommendation on dental education will be, and *(3)* how likely the respondent is to act on this recommendation. Responses were received from 1,864 persons by May 1, 1996 (response rate, 32.04%). This data is helpful in exploring how educators in the oral health field relate to the goals of educating future providers to be patient centered, culturally competent, and able to work on an interdisciplinary team.

As can be seen in Table 16-1, the responses show that educating students to provide truly patient-centered care (recommendation 6) is seen as most important (mean, 4.41), as being most influential in future educational activities (mean, 4.27), and as the most likely recommendation to be acted on (mean, 3.92). Educating students to be culturally competent (recommendation 22), however, received the lowest importance rating (mean, 3.37) as well as the lowest positive influence rating (mean, 3.24) and one of the lowest ratings concerning planned action (mean, 3.02). Recommendation 22 was most frequently named when respondents were asked additional questions concerning which of the recommendations would have the lowest priority in the respondents' own work right now (28.2%), in the future (24.8%), and in dental education in general (24.9%). It is apparent that cultural competency is not seen as very important; it is not perceived as having a positive impact on the future of dentistry or as a topic that requires action. Recommendation 5, which describes the relationship between medicine and dentistry, received intermediate ratings of importance (mean, 3.95), predicted positive influence (mean, 3.80), and planned actions (mean, 3.41). These data could be interpreted as partial support for including interdisciplinary considerations in future dental education efforts.

The cohort of respondents who were 40 years or younger in 1996 is likely to gain increasing influence in dental education and to shape dental education for the next two to three decades. It is interesting to note that these younger respondents are even more supportive of patient-centered education and interdisciplinary work than are older respondents (Table 16-2). However, it is discouraging that younger and older respondents do not differ significantly in their ratings of the importance, future influence, and likelihood to act on the recommendation concerned with diversity issues.

Recent data show that the number of female dental faculty is increasing.[1] It might therefore

Table 16-1 Average responses of dental professionals to questions concerning the Institute of Medicine recommendations*

Recommendation	Importance	Positive influence	Planned actions
1. Oral health services	3.89	3.63	3.08
2. Access to care and underserved populations	3.91	3.68	3.18
3. Financial assistance to students who work with underserved populations	3.89	3.69	2.72
4. Major curriculum reform	4.30	4.17	3.90
5. Medicine and dentistry	3.95	3.80	3.41
6. Efficient, effective, patient-centered care	4.41	4.27	3.92
7. Availability of postdoctoral education	3.66	3.59	2.83
8. Terms of employment	3.93	3.75	3.09
9. Research diversity	3.64	3.50	3.06
10. Collaborative research	3.92	3.76	3.25
11. Strengthening research	3.90	3.73	2.87
12. Patient care mission	4.20	4.08	3.66
13. Coordinated strategic planning	4.13	3.97	3.35
14. Accreditation of clinical facilities and services	3.52	3.40	2.82
15. Dental school value to the university	4.04	3.84	3.24
16. Financial management data	4.22	3.98	3.33
17. Cost reduction strategies	3.82	3.56	3.17
18. Accreditation	4.08	3.87	3.25
19. Licensure	4.27	4.14	3.25
20. Dental workforce	3.68	3.56	2.80
21. Workforce productivity	3.80	3.63	2.99
22. Diversity	3.37	3.24	3.02

*Based on a 5-point scale, ranging from 1 = not at all to 5 = very.

Table 16-2 Average responses of participants to questions concerning specific Institute of Medicine recommendations, based on age*

Recommendation	Question	≤ 40 years	> 40 years	P
5. Medicine and dentistry	Importance	4.19	3.90	< .001
	Influence	4.14	3.73	< .001
	Action	3.75	3.32	< .001
6. Patient-centered care	Importance	4.55	4.39	.01
	Influence	4.44	4.24	.004
	Action	4.16	3.86	.001
22. Diversity	Importance	3.46	3.32	.10
	Influence	3.32	3.19	.14
	Action	3.00	2.98	.87

*Based on a 5-point scale, ranging from 1 = not at all to 5 = very.

Table 16-3 Average responses of participants to questions concerning specific Institute of Medicine recommendations, based on gender*

Recommendation	Question	Male	Female	P
5. Medicine and dentistry	Importance	3.87	4.18	< .001
	Influence	3.69	4.09	< .001
	Action	3.35	3.51	.05
6. Patient-centered care	Importance	4.38	4.51	.02
	Influence	4.19	4.50	< .001
	Action	3.81	4.20	< .001
22. Diversity	Importance	3.23	3.71	< .001
	Influence	3.09	3.60	< .001
	Action	2.88	3.32	< .001

*Based on a 5-point scale, ranging from 1 = not at all to 5 = very.

be interesting to point out that female respondents differed significantly from male respondents in their ratings of the importance, influence, and likelihood to act on recommendations concerning patient-centered care, diversity, and interdisciplinary collaborations (Table 16-3). This finding implies increasing support for an inclusion of and focus on these three topics in dental education in the future.

With support from the surgeon general's report on oral health[2] and the Institute of Medicine's report on the future of dental education,[4] it seems justified to stress that future dental education needs to train patient-centered and culturally competent providers who are able to work from an interdisciplinary perspective. OHRQOL considerations can serve as a portal to dental education that focuses on these three goals.

Implementing Changes in Dental Education

From a patient's perspective, dentistry is all about QOL concerns. Pain and discomfort, the desire to be better able to function while eating or speaking, or the desire to show healthy teeth and not toothless gums when smiling are QOL concerns. A patient does not want to have caries because it might hurt. He or she does not want to have bleeding gingiva or bone loss because it might mean not being able to bite into a Granny Smith apple, or having to wear dentures in the future. For many centuries, providing emergency care was central to a dental care providers' work. Emergency care was and is driven by a patient's acutely impaired QOL. Even as the percentage of maintenance care has increased and dental health care providers' focus shifted to providing preventive care, QOL is central. Patients engage in oral health promotion activities because they want to have healthy teeth and gums that allow them to have a positive OHRQOL. If dental care providers are trained to embrace the concept of OHRQOL as the ultimate outcome of oral health care, it will allow them to understand their patients' motivations and communicate more effectively with their patients. It would make providers truly patient centered, motivate them to realize the significance of understanding and serving culturally diverse patients, and to cooperate closely with providers from other health care disciplines. Therefore, the question remains:

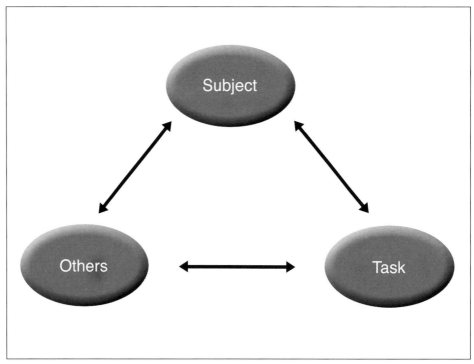

Fig 16-1 A biopsychosocial model for approaching oral health–related tasks.

How can dental education be refocused to train professionals that embrace this perspective?

Process and Content

Most publications on dental education focus either on evaluating programs and program outcomes or on rethinking the process of learning and teaching. A current example is the discussion of the benefits of problem-based versus traditional curricula.[7] It seems as if the process of dental education, ie, *how* to educate, receives more attention than the content of dental education, ie, *what* students need to know. There is no doubt that discussions of the process of dental education are crucial; however, such discussions only make sense if a clear vision of the content exists and the ultimate outcomes of dental education are clearly defined. Process considera-

tions need to serve the ultimate goal of helping students achieve defined educational outcomes.

One starting point for reflecting on the content of dental education is to consider a biopsychosocial model as a replacement for a purely biomedical/biodental model.[8] Such a model shifts the focus from considering only biologic and dental health factors to a more wholistic approach. Figure 16-1 attempts to capture this approach. In a biodental model, the focus would be on the oral cavity and how biologic factors affect it. A biopsychosocial perspective considers instead the task at hand. This task could range from providing health care to one patient to developing community programs that create access to care or making policy decisions that concern oral health issues. In each instance, the task is seen as influenced by the subject (eg, a patient, a community, or a population segment) and by rel-

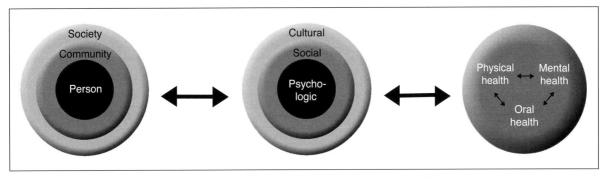

Fig 16-2 Interrelationship of factors involved in a biopsychosocial approach to oral heath care.

evant others (eg, significant others such as family and friends, dental care professionals, employers who may or may not provide dental insurance, or policy makers). Ultimately, considerations of the task, the subject involved, and relevant others will shape all efforts and outcomes.

Patient-Centered Focus

A biopsychosocial model involves all three of the goals identified above as crucial for the future of dental education. It is a patient-centered approach involving factors that range from cultural to biologic considerations and thus puts oral health in the context of general health. As illustrated in Fig 16-2, dental education is approached from a patient-centered perspective when oral health, OHRQOL, and access to oral health care are seen as a function of the person, the community the person lives in, and the societal regulations such as laws and social policies that determine whether a patient has access to oral health care. Patient-centered care also considers psychologic, social, and cultural factors as antecedents and a positive OHRQOL as the ultimate outcome of oral health care. Psychologic factors consist of affective, behavioral, and cognitive aspects that shape a person's cooperation with health care recommendations and oral health promotion efforts.[9] Relevant social factors

begin with messages about oral health promotion that the patient receives in the family.[10] Cultural factors shape a patient's expectations about oral health promotion and oral health care, how patients express pain, and how they communicate with providers.[11] Therefore, providers need to be aware of psychologic, social, and cultural factors in addition to biologic factors when providing care and educating patients about oral health promotion. Once such a biopsychosocial model is accepted, it becomes clear that oral health is intricately intertwined with general and mental health. As a result, the provider should be motivated to collaborate with providers from other disciplines.

Cultural Competency

A lot of progress has been made over the past decades in understanding the social and cultural dimensions of health.[12] Yet, a relatively low importance has been placed on these issues in dental education thus far (see Table 16-1). There is hope, however, that the findings of the surgeon general's report on oral health,[2] which points to the striking discrepancies in oral health and access to care for patients from different socioeconomic and ethnic/racial groups and for patients with and without special needs or disabilities, might contribute to a change.

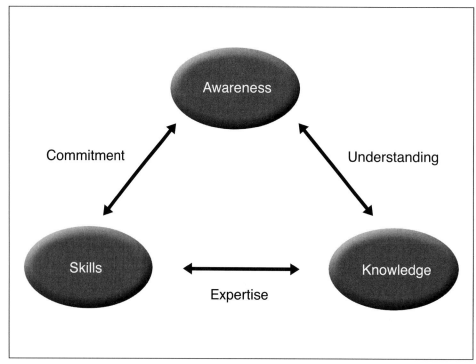

Fig 16-3 Outcomes of teaching cultural competency.

Further motivation may be provided by the Institute of Medicine report,[4] which stresses the importance of educating future providers to be culturally competent in its final recommendation. However, there are two main concerns that must be addressed if this recommendation is to be implemented.

The first concern is how to initiate the lifelong process of becoming culturally competent. The model in Fig 16-3 illustrates the components involved in this process, namely raising students' awareness about diversity issues, giving them the skills to function in a multicultural setting, and increasing their knowledge about cultural diversity. The model further shows how becoming aware of and having background knowledge about cultural differences and similarities will lead to a true understanding of the role that cultural factors play in patients' health and their uti-lization of health care services. Moreover, it demonstrates that having good cross-cultural communication skills and a solid background of cultural knowledge will increase providers' expertise in treating patients who might not conform to the provider's most familiar model of behavior or who have special health care needs. Finally, the model shows that with an increased awareness of the needs of certain patient populations and the level of comfort that comes with having good cross-cultural communication skills, commitment to treating diverse groups of patients will ultimately increase. The striking discrepancies that exist today in the health status and access to care for different groups of US patients[2] can only be reduced if dental education raises providers' awareness about these issues and provides them with the knowledge and skills they need to optimally treat all patients. A commitment to provide care will result if providers understand the needs and feel they have the expertise to act on these needs.

The second concern is how to initiate change to the dental education model so that considerations of the role of cultural factors are infused throughout the curriculum and not just dutifully covered in a 50-minute lecture. OHRQOL considerations can contribute to addressing this concern. As the shift occurs from educating students to concentrate on teeth, gums, and the oral cavity to considering patients in all their complexity, cultural factors automatically become salient. Any discussion of a patient's "case" then includes a discussion of cultural factors. Considerations focus on how this patient's background shapes expectations concerning oral health and oral health care, how treatment has to be provided to optimally suit the patient's needs, and how oral health education has to be structured to motivate the patient for the best possible oral health promotion.

At this point, it is important to stress the significance of preparing dental faculty to take on this charge of educating future providers to be culturally competent. Faculty development activities are crucial to the preparation of dental educators for this task. Additionally, resources need to be developed that will provide educators with materials they can learn from and then use in their instructional activities. The richness of the resource materials available in the medical field should guide efforts to create resources of equal quality for dental educators and clinicians.[13]

Interdisciplinary Collaboration

The third objective of future dental education is to educate providers to understand the relationship between oral health and general health and to be motivated to collaborate and consult with other health care professionals. These collaborations are two-way streets: It is crucial both to educate future dental health care providers about the significance of interdisciplinary collaborations and to educate providers from other health care fields about the role that oral health plays in a patient's general health and QOL. OHRQOL considerations can serve as a communication tool to raise awareness in providers from other fields. Early childhood caries (ECC) can serve as an example (see chapter 8 for more details). Pediatricians and pediatric nurses could be allies in preventing and combating this disease. However, in order to forge an alliance, these providers need to understand more than merely how common this disease is or how it is defined. If they realize the consequences of ECC for a child's health and QOL, they might be much more motivated to include ECC as a potential diagnosis. School nurses who understand the consequences of oral disease might consider that a child who is inattentive in the classroom or has impulse control problems might not have attention deficit hyperactivity disorder (ADHD), but instead might be plagued by a chronic toothache that keeps the child from sleeping through the night and causes significant pain. Close interdisciplinary collaborations need to be based on mutual understanding of each discipline's work. Oral health–related quality-of-life considerations do not only focus dental care providers on the patient and thus draw their attention to the patient's general health needs. They are also a communication tool that alerts providers from other health care fields to the significant role that oral health plays in a patient's general health.

Conclusion

Research on trends in dentistry and dental education show that in the future fewer dentists will take care of increasing numbers of patients.[1] Educating these patients about good oral health promotion and preventive care will therefore be crucial. Research also shows that certain population segments are drastically underserved.[2] Dental education has to make a contribution if this situation is to change. Finally, with the rapidly changing knowledge base and technology in all health care fields, interdisciplinary considerations and collaborations become increasingly important.[4] Structural factors,[1] status quo assessments,[2] and recommendations for the future of dental education[4] all converge to advocate the education of future providers to be patient-centered, culturally competent, and able to closely collaborate with providers from other health care fields. OHRQOL considerations can serve as a tool for bringing about these changes in the perspective of future clinicians.

Dental education aims at training future clinicians, researchers, and administrators as well as future dental educators. OHRQOL is a crucial concept in the professional lives of all these groups. It provides researchers with a chance to consider the larger perspective of how their research will ultimately serve patients. It focuses clinicians on providing truly patient-centered care. It can contribute to prioritizing the work of administrators, and it can motivate dental educators by showing them the tremendous difference that their students can make in the lives of patients.

References

1. Valachovic RW, Weaver RG, Sinkford JC, Haden K. Trends in dentistry and dental education. J Dent Educ 2001;65:539–561.
2. United States Public Health Service, Office of the Surgeon General, National Institute of Dental and Craniofacial Research. Oral Health in America: A report of the surgeon general: Executive summary. Rockville, MD: National Institute of Dental and Craniofacial Research, 2000.
3. Evans CA, Kleinman DV. The Surgeon General's report on America's oral health: Opportunities for the dental profession. J Am Dent Assoc 2000;131:1721–1728.
4. Field MJ (ed.). Dental Education at the Crossroads—Challenges and Change. Washington, DC: National Academy Press, 1995.
5. Dental education at the crossroads—Summary. J Dent Educ 1995;95:7–15.
6. Tedesco LA. Issues in dental curriculum development and change. J Dent Educ 1995;95:97–148.
7. Fincham AG, Shuler CF. The changing face of dental education: The impact of PBL. J Dent Educ 2001;65: 406–421.
8. Engel GL. The need for a new medical model: A challenge for biomedicine. Science 1977;196:129–136.
9. Inglehart M, Tedesco LA. Behavioral research related to oral hygiene practices: A new century model of oral health promotion. Periodontol 2000 1995;8:15–23.
10. Inglehart M, Tedesco LA. The role of the family in preventing oral diseases. In: Cohen LK, Gift HC (eds). Disease Prevention and Oral Health Promotion: Sociodental Sciences in Action. Copenhagen: Munksgaard, 1995:271–307.
11. Inglehart M, Tedesco LA. Increasing orthodontic patient cooperation in the 21st century: The role of cross-cultural communication issues. In: McNamara JA, Trotman CA (eds). Creating the Compliant Patient, Craniofacial Growth Series. Ann Arbor: Univ of Michigan, 1997:181–193.
12. Office of Behavioral and Social Sciences Research. Towards higher levels of analysis: Progress and promise in research on social and cultural dimensions of health. Executive summary. NIH publication 01-5020. Bethesda, MD: National Institute of Health, 2001.
13. American Medical Association. Cultural Competence Compendium. Chicago: American Medical Association, 1999.

CHAPTER 17

Research on Oral Health–Related Quality of Life: Current Status and Future Directions

Patricia S. Bryant, PhD

Dushanka V. Kleinman, DDS, PhD

Research on quality of life (QOL) has gained interest and visibility in recent decades both in the United States and internationally. "How" we live and not just "how long" we live has increasingly become recognized as a central issue in health care and health research. How we live includes a wide range of issues such as daily functioning, self-image and self-esteem, and the capacity to work with others and to participate in and contribute to society. The definition of health initially proposed by the World Health Organization (WHO) in 1948 anticipated this concept: "Health is a state of complete physical, mental, and social well-being and not merely the absence of disease or infirmity."[1] Now, more than 50 years later, we can see that this concept has helped encourage scientists and clinicians to explore, measure, and better understand the many interrelated aspects of health.

This chapter provides an overview of oral health–related quality of life (OHRQOL) research with a particular emphasis on research funded by the National Institute of Dental and Craniofacial Research (NIDCR), one of the institutes within the National Institutes of Health (NIH), the major federal source of funding for biomedical and behavioral research in the United States. The mission of the NIDCR is to improve oral, dental, and craniofacial health through research and research training. The majority of NIDCR-funded studies are conducted in the United States. However, many of the scientists receiving support from NIDCR are actively collaborating with scientists elsewhere in the world. For example, measures such as the Oral Health Impact Profile (OHIP) are being used in independent large-scale population surveys in Australia, Finland, and the United Kingdom. These studies allow for comparative analyses among US-based research studies on QOL and those conducted elsewhere in the world. In addition, investigators from 10 countries are currently collaborating in an NIDCR-funded planning grant establishing the foundation for developing a culturally sensitive measure of QOL in children. As measures are being developed and tested, we expect new opportunities for accelerating progress in QOL research through international collaborations.

Research Projects, Workshops, and Publications

In the United States, QOL assessment received heightened visibility with the release of the Healthy People 2010 health promotion and disease prevention initiative.[2,3] The first Healthy People initiative was started in 1979 and focused mainly on changes in disease measures. Current objectives of this initiative are organized around two overarching goals: *(1)* to increase quality and years of healthy life and *(2)* to eliminate health disparities.

The Healthy People 2010 initiative defines, assesses, and monitors specific health objectives for the overall US population as well as for specific population subgroups based on racial, ethnic, and age- or income level–related differences. Specific oral health and oral health–related objectives are among those being monitored.[4]

Quantitative Indicators of Research Support Trends

The Computer Retrieval of Information on Scientific Projects (CRISP) data system of the NIH uses scientific content coding of abstracts provided by all investigators with funded research grants.[5] The system's citations for projects active as of April 10, 2000, showed that 1,211 (3%) of approximately 41,570 NIH research projects active in May 2000 were coded to reflect a primary scientific emphasis on QOL measures or assessment. A much larger number of projects had been coded as showing a secondary or tertiary emphasis on QOL assessments. Clinical trials assessing the effects of various drugs or health care interventions were included, for example, in this latter group.

Published NIH announcements requesting research grant proposals in areas designated as being of particular scientific interest or need provide an additional indicator of gradually broadening interest in QOL assessments. Such announcements are published as requests for applications (RFAs) or program announcements (PAs) in the NIH's Guide to Grants and Contracts.[6] Between January 1992 and August 2001, almost 14% of these announcements included some reference to QOL (351 "hits" for QOL out of 4,884 documents captured in archived records for NIH's Guide to Grants and Contracts). Almost one fifth of these QOL hits appeared in announcements issued in 2000–2001 (66 of 351, or 18.8% of the total references to QOL across a 10-year interval of archived NIH research solicitations). RFAs and PAs have brought attention to QOL assessments in studies on genetics, aging, and child health, as well as in studies involving diseases such as cancer, arthritis, diabetes, neurologic disorders, visual disorders, oral diseases, mental illnesses, and cardiovascular disease.

Overall, both of the NIH databases described here indicate that there is sustained and even expanding scientific interest in QOL assessments. They also indicate that this topic contributes to the overall biomedical, clinical, and behavioral research enterprise.

NIDCR Support for Research on QOL

The NIDCR's investments in QOL research has more than tripled from 1997 to 2000. Table 17-1 summarizes 10 research projects receiving NIDCR support as of September 30, 2001.

Eight of ten grants with active funding on September 30, 2001 were newer projects, initially funded in 1998 or later. Several recently funded projects focus on developing improved measures for health-related quality of life (HRQOL), particularly measures applicable to assessing OHRQOL in children. This was a research gap, as noted earlier.[7] The summaries presented in Table 17-1 are based on information regarding study objectives and methods presented by the investigators in their grant proposals. Active NIDCR-supported projects are grouped into three categories, namely *(1)* development of

Table 17-1 QOL-related projects funded by the National Institute of Dental and Craniofacial Research as of September 2000*

Investigator/ Institution	Project title	Abstract
Development of QOL measures		
Broder, H. University of Medicine/Dentistry of New Jersey[†] (grant No. R21DE013721)	Measuring child OHRQOL	The goal is to use a planning strategy to develop a culturally sensitive measure of OHRQOL in children for use in international collaborative research. The measure would help explore variations in children's oral health in different cultures and delivery systems. The planning process will include the development of a coalition of OHRQOL expert investigators who will work together to complete and pretest measures in their own countries and in diverse populations.
Broder, H. University of Medicine/Dentistry of New Jersey[†] (grant No. R01DE013722)	Child oral health QOL questionnaire	Treatment of children with oral and orofacial conditions is based on broadly accepted standards tied to the evaluation of clinical parameters. However, little is known about treatment success—whether the desired clinical outcomes related to treatment are achieved or whether patients are satisfied with their treatment outcomes. Research in this area is limited by a lack of valid, reliable, and culturally sensitive instruments to assess perceived outcomes of care for children and their families. To address this deficiency, this study will develop a culturally sensitive instrument to assess the OHRQOL in children with various oral and orofacial conditions. To address age-appropriate developmental tasks, age-specific questionnaires are necessary for children to accommodate age-related changes in children's emotional and cognitive development. This study is the initial phase of a multistage effort to create two age-appropriate questionnaires for children aged 3–5 and 6–9 years.
Patrick, D. University of Washington[†] (grant No. R01DE013546)	QOL among adolescents with CFCs[‡]	The goal of this project is to explore the impacts of congenital and acquired CFCs on adolescents to develop QOL outcome measures to evaluate effectiveness of treatments. Both CFCs present at birth or those acquired up to age 18 years will be included. Measures will comprise a generic QOL instrument containing "verifiable" items that can be reported or observed as reliable by others and "subjective" items assessing feelings known only to the adolescent. The study will develop a module containing measures specific to adolescents with CFCs containing both verifiable and subjective items and measures specific to the individual.

Table 17-1 (cont) QOL-related projects funded by the National Institute of Dental and Craniofacial Research as of September 2000*

Investigator/ Institution	Project title	Abstract
Slade, G. University of North Carolina[†] (grant No. R29DE012366)	QOL outcomes for oral health care	The objective of this project is to develop and validate a modular instrument measuring QOL outcomes from oral health care. The need for such an instrument has emerged from oral health surveys that have demonstrated poorer QOL among people with untreated oral disease and inadequate dental care. However, recent findings suggest that instruments used to measure OHRQOL in such surveys are unsuited for use in outcomes research, in part because they appear to capture aspects of OHRQOL that are unresponsive to short-term change. This project aims to synthesize core questions from five existing OHRQOL instruments, then develop and evaluate the reliability and validity of the core instrument for assessing effects of oral health care.
Spiro, A. Boston University[†] (subproject in grant No. U54DE014264)	OHRQOL in children and adolescents	Although measures of OHRQOL exist for adults, there are no comparable measures for children. This project will develop a set of measures of pediatric OHRQOL, suitable for use with children and adolescents, which assess the impact of oral health on both children and their families. The following aims are proposed: *(1)* develop, refine, and validate a pediatric measure of OHRQOL for use with children and adolescents; *(2)* develop a comparable Spanish-language version; *(3)* conduct validation to assess sensitivity to change over time and responsiveness to interventions; *(4)* combine the OHRQOL assessment with other clinical, demographic, and psychosocial measures to explore potential sources of disparities in oral health; and *(5)* create a short version of the OHRQOL measures for screening purposes.
Workshops		
Bagramian, R. University of Michigan, Ann Arbor[†] (grant No. R25DE013839)	Interdisciplinary workshop on OHRQOL	This workshop introduced graduate students, postdoctoral students, and junior faculty to cross-disciplinary aspects of health and QOL research, especially in the area of oral and craniofacial health. The primary audience included students and faculty from oral epidemiology, oral clinical sciences, oral basic sciences, nursing research, and psychology, with a limited number of places for investigators at this level from other institutions. The workshop was preceded by an assessment of the needs of potential participants.

Table 17-1 (cont) QOL-related projects funded by the National Institute of Dental and Craniofacial Research as of September 2000*

Investigator/ Institution	Project title	Abstract
Use of QOL measures in research		
Atchison, K. University of California, Los Angeles[†] (grant No. R01DE013839)	Patient preferences for treatment of mandibular fractures	Mandibular fracture is one of the most common orofacial injuries for minority individuals. Patient involvement in treatment decisions may increase satisfaction with outcomes, and ultimately promote adherence to medical instructions. This has been especially important for treatments that produce side effects that significantly reduce the QOL of patients. Patient choice is not an option for management of some mandibular fractures in which the severity of the injury dictates the most applicable treatment modality; however, for many fractures either surgical (rigid internal fixation) or nonsurgical treatment (maxillomandibular fixation) is possible. The objective of this investigation is to advance the health profession's understanding of patient preferences for surgical vs nonsurgical treatment and how knowledge of potential pain-related suffering and functional limitations associated with treatment may affect patients' treatment preferences.
Gilbert, G. University of Alabama, Birmingham (grant No. R01DE011020)	Longitudinal oral health outcomes in high-risk adults	This research will identify benefits derived from the use of specific dental services (linked with benefits or lack thereof) as perceived by high-risk groups. It also will assess how these perceptions affect the use of dental care. Clinical, self-reported dimensions of oral health, use of specific dental services, and patient characteristic data will be analyzed to determine why these populations use dental care and what role dental care plays in people's QOL.
Gilbert, G. University of Alabama, Birmingham[†] (grant No. R01DE012457)	Dental care effect on outcomes important to patients	This research addresses a fundamental question: What is the effectiveness of dental care on dimensions of oral health that are most important to the patient? These dimensions include self-reported oral pain and discomfort, functional limitation, disease and tissue damage, and self-rated oral health. This research will investigate associations among regular dental attendance, problem-oriented dental attendance, cost of dental services, and use of specific types of dental care, with differences in each of these self-reported dimensions of oral health as well as with differences in clinical status.
Phillips, C. University of North Carolina[†] (grant No. R01DE013967)	Sensory retraining following orthognathic surgery	Abnormal facial sensation has a negative impact on patient's oral behaviors and may adversely affect a patient's QOL. The goal of this project is to evaluate sensory retraining, a rehabilitative therapy that offers significant potential for patients who experience impaired sensory function. A primary outcome assessment will be the patient's perception of the negative impact of altered sensation on daily life.

*Data from the National Institutes of Health.[4]
[†]Project received initial funding on or after January 1, 1998.
[‡]CFCs, Craniofacial conditions.

197

Box 17-1 Health outcomes methods symposia/conferences with published proceedings

Quality of Life and Oral and Craniofacial Issues, May 2000 (results published in this book)
Health Outcomes Assessment Symposium, September 1999[8]
International Workshop on Assessing Health-Related Quality of Life in Children with Cancer, June 1998[9]
Measuring Oral Health and Quality of Life, June 1995[10]
Health and Quality of Life Outcomes in Dialysis, December 1994[11]
Conference on Measuring the Effects of Medical Treatments, April 1994[12]
3rd Conference on Advances in Health Status Assessment, September 1991[13]
Quality of Life Assessment: Practice, Problems, and Promise, October 1990[14]
International Conference on the Measurement of Quality of Life as an Outcome in Clinical Trials, June 1989[15]
2nd Conference on Advances in Health Status Assessment, July 1988[16]
1st Conference on Advances in Health Status Assessment, February 1986[17]
Measuring QOL and Functional Status in Clinical and Epidemiological Research, June 1986[18]
Workshop on Assessment of Quality of Life in Clinical Trials of Cardiovascular Therapies, June 1983[19]
Conference on a Health Status Index, October 1972[20]

QOL measures, *(2)* workshops, and *(3)* use of QOL measures in research.

Workshops on QOL Outcomes Assessment

A number of workshops, conferences, and seminars focusing on QOL assessments have been held in the past several decades. Box 17-1 lists major workshops with published proceedings. Two of these workshops focused specifically on oral health and QOL.

The workshop "Measuring Oral Health and Quality of Life," held in 1995 at the University of North Carolina, was funded by NIDCR and the organization then known as the Agency for Health Care Policy and Research.[10] The meeting included presentations and discussions of recent findings of studies that used QOL instruments. The instruments considered were *(1)* the OHIP, *(2)* the Oral Health–Related Quality of Life Measures (OHRQOL), *(3)* Oral Impacts on Daily Performances (OIDP), *(4)* General Oral Health Assessment Index (GOHAI), *(5)* dental health questions from the Rand Health Insurance Study, and *(6)* the Geriatric Oral Health Assessment Index. Other instruments and indicators used to assess subjective oral health or the social impact of dental disease were also included. This seminal workshop provided opportunities to evaluate concepts underlying OHRQOL measurements and to examine strengths and deficiencies of existing instruments.

Major research recommendations that arose from this meeting include the following:

1. Oral health needs to be defined and conceptualized, and appropriate operational measures need to be brought into systematic use.
2. More research needs to be conducted to conceptualize and measure oral health as a system contributing to total health.
3. Mediating and independent variables influencing oral health outcomes need to be thoughtfully considered. The values of a specific indicator in representing risk and outcome need to be understood.
4. An assessment of "outcomes for whom" needs to be made to determine the nature and extent of indicators.

5. Methodological issues such as the following need to be addressed: development of outcome measures for longitudinal studies; appropriateness of measures as influenced by passage of time; sensitivity, specificity, reliability, and validity as addressed in studies with different subpopulations; and the application of methods from the broader field of HRQOL to oral health outcomes research.

A second meeting, held in Ann Arbor, MI, in May 2000 and entitled "Quality of Life and Oral and Craniofacial Issues," focused on fostering cross-disciplinary communication and research collaborations around issues of QOL and health. This meeting was supported jointly by NIDCR and the NIH's Office of Behavioral and Social Science Research. Chapters appearing in this volume originated from presentations at this workshop. This meeting provided QOL experts, as well as a select group of US and foreign clinical, public health, and behavioral science graduate students and faculty not previously involved in QOL research, with opportunities to discuss key conceptual and methodological issues in OHRQOL measurement and research.

In addition, in 1997, the NIDCR convened a meeting, entitled "Oral Health Promotion Research: Targeting a Research Agenda and Potential Research Collaborations," that was organized around four central research themes. One of these themes was outcomes/QOL assessment. Among the research opportunities identified at that meeting were the following:

1. Develop and validate measurement approaches and methodologies, particularly those fostering integration of information for general and oral health.
2. Modify or revalidate outcome measures for use with diverse population subgroups.
3. Evaluate the extent and characteristics of associations between clinical indicators of disease or responses to interventions and qualitative or patient-generated indicators reflecting functional or psychosocial impacts of diseases or interventions.

4. In assessing new technologies or interventions, include both patient-generated qualitative indicators of outcome as well as clinical outcome measures.
5. Validate measures and indicators within populations of various ages to determine whether the measure is sensitive to the impact of oral conditions at different stages in the life cycle.

NIDCR-Initiated Publications

In 1994, the NIDCR commissioned state-of-the-science reviews that were published in 1995 in a volume entitled *Disease Prevention and Oral Health Promotion*.[21] Each chapter includes a set of specific research recommendations that focus on social, psychologic, and economic impacts of oral conditions and treatments,[7] including the following:

1. Testing the sensitivity of generic health status indicators for persons with oral conditions and disorders
2. Exploring whether generic instruments such as the Sickness Illness Profile could be modified for use in patients with oral conditions
3. Addressing methodological problems, as well as comparing responses to various subjective oral health indicators in the same populations or patient groups
4. Investigating relationships between clinical indicators of disease and subjective indicators measuring disease impact
5. Assessing the value of subjective indicators in clinical trials of existing or new interventions or technologies
6. Testing measures and indicators in populations of all ages (noting the lack of measures applicable to children or adolescents)

Effects of oral health on well-being and QOL were key topics reviewed in a report developed by many agencies led by the NIDCR.[22] This document discusses the cultural, functional, and psychosocial dimensions of OHRQOL and provides specific examples of oral conditions influencing

Table 17-2 Studies of multidimensional OHRQOL measures*

Study	Population studied	No. of individuals	Assessment tool	Description of assessment tool
Gooch et al[23]	US insured aged 18–61 y	902 female, 756 male	Rand Dental Health Index	Three dental questions designed to represent factors contributing to adverse effects of dental disease
Atchison and Dolan[24]	California Medicare recipients aged > 65 y	1,000 female, 755 male	Geriatric Oral Health Assessment Index	A series of 12 questions measuring patient-reported dysfunction
Hunt et al[25]	North Carolina elderly (aged > 70 y)	440	Oral Health Impact Profile (OHIP)	A comprehensive measure of self-reported dysfunction consisting of 49 questions
Kressin et al[26]	Male veterans aged > 47 y	1,242	Oral Health–Related Quality of Life	A brief global assessment of the impact of oral conditions, consisting of three items
Gift et al[27]	US citizens aged > 18 y	760 female, 555 male	1981 Health Resources and Services Administration study	Multidimensional concept using data from a large national sample
Gilbert et al[28]	Floridians aged > 45 y	491 female, 383 male	Oral Disadvantage Assessment	Eight self-reported measures of avoidance in daily activities because of decrements in oral health
Locker and Miller[29]	Canadians aged > 18 y	299 female, 244 male	Subjective Oral Health Status Indicators	Five oral health status indicators based on the WHO's International Classification of Impairments, Disabilities, and Handicaps
Locker and Slade[30]	Canadians aged > 50 y	168 female, 144 male	OHIP	See above
Slade and Spencer[31]	Australians aged > 60 y	660 female, 557 male	OHIP	See above
Leao and Sheiham[32]	Brazilians aged 35–44 y	303 female, 359 male	Dental Impact on Daily Living	36 questions that assess oral health impacts on daily living
Coates et al[33]	Australian dental patients	635 (+ 795 previously surveyed)	OHIP	See above

*Data from US Department of Health and Human Services.[22]

QOL, such as cleft lip/palate, malocclusion, oro-facial pain, oropharyngeal cancers, tooth loss, and early childhood caries. It also includes a useful summary table indicating many of the multi-dimensional oral health/QOL measures available (Table 17-2). The major conclusions presented in this report include the following:

1. Oral health is related to well-being and QOL as measured along functional, psychologic, and economic dimensions.
2. Cultural values influence oral and craniofacial health and well-being as well as health care utilization.
3. Oral and craniofacial diseases/treatments place a demonstrable burden on society in terms of work loss.
4. Reduced OHRQOL is associated with poor clinical status and reduced access to care.

The Surgeon General's report also points out that while there are promising measures of OHRQOL, more research is needed.[22]

Future Directions

Understanding the impact of impaired oral health, or excellent oral health status, and oral health care treatments on how well people live presents an array of research opportunities. While many specific research opportunities are discussed here, we would like to suggest a novel conceptual model for organizing different categories of research opportunities relevant to QOL assessment and oral health (Fig 17-1).[34]

This model draws upon one proposed by Gruman and Follick[35] that addresses the research agenda to accelerate translation of evidence-based behavioral interventions into health care practice. In presenting their model, these authors noted that behavioral interventions demonstrated to be effective—often as effective as biomedical innovations that had seen swift adoption—had shown relatively limited penetration in health care delivery. In parallel, oral health researchers might consider why

generic or disease-specific QOL measures have as yet seen relatively modest adoption into public health planning and health care delivery.

The original model as presented by Gruman and Follick[35] posits three key areas—technology push, delivery capacity, and market pull/demand—in which research and action can accelerate diffusion/adoption. Technology push encompasses all the research needed to develop, test, improve, and understand assessment measures to ensure that they work predictably, efficiently, and effectively in various populations. In the context of QOL assessment, it may be somewhat premature to expect immediate diffusion of QOL measures into practice or into health policy decisions, given the paucity of reliable, well-validated measures and of demonstrations of their applicability and acceptability in various settings and with different age and ethnic groups.

When measures become appropriate for wide diffusion, it then becomes important to build delivery capacity. Expanding delivery capacity requires analyzing and developing both the "who" and "how" of delivery of QOL assessments in settings in which public health policies are shaped, clinical research is conducted, and/or health care is delivered. Again, research agendas need to include deepening the understanding of the characteristics and determinants of how appropriate QOL assessments can be integrated into oral health research and care.

Finally, in the dimension of market pull/demand as it relates to QOL assessments in oral health, we need to question why policy makers, researchers, health care providers, health care consumers, or the public would seek out and commit to including appropriate QOL assessments as they deliver or receive health care, plan clinical trials, or formulate health policies. Possibly, strategies involving end users of QOL assessment measures early in the process of developing and testing these measures could help stimulate innovative approaches promoting wider diffusion of QOL assessment methods and concepts across different settings. Studies in each of these areas are needed, starting initially

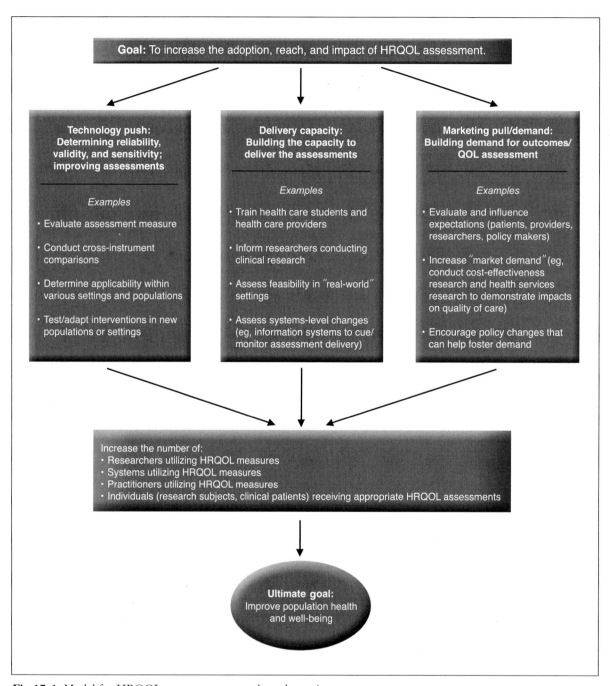

Fig 17-1 Model for HRQOL assessment, research, and practice.

with a stronger emphasis in the technology push domain, and will be critical to ensure real impacts of QOL research in clinical research, health policy, and health care delivery.

The organization of this volume reveals that both disease-specific and generic QOL measures are already contributing to the attainment of a number of important goals, including:

1. Assessing and comparing health status across various populations or health care delivery systems
2. Assessing and comparing health across subgroups and disease categories
3. Determining the side effects and benefits of specific preventive or therapeutic interventions and enhancing outcomes measurement in clinical trials
4. Strengthening the foundations for decisions that need to be made by policy makers, clinicians, and health care consumers

We look forward to seeing these efforts result in further interest and progress in research on oral health and QOL.

References

1. World Health Organization. Constitution of the World Health Organization. Geneva: World Health Organization, 1948.
2. US Department of Health and Human Services. Healthy People 2010, vol I. Available at: www.health.gov/healthy people/document/. Accessed April 24, 2002.
3. US Department of Health and Human Services. Healthy People 2010, vol II. Available at: www.health.gov/healthypeople/document/. Accessed April 24, 2002.
4. National Institutes of Health. ERA Commons: Computer Retrieval of Information on Scientific Projects. Available at: http://www-commons.cit.nih.gov/crisp. Accessed April 24, 2002.
5. National Institutes of Health. NIH Guide for Grants and Contracts. Available at: http://grants2.nih.gov/grants/guide/index.html. Accessed April 24, 2002.
6. National Institutes of Health. NIH Guide for Grants and Contracts. Available at: http://grants1.nih.gov/grants/guide/index.html. Accessed April 24, 2002.
7. Reisine S, Locker D. Social, psychological, and economic impacts of oral conditions and treatments. In: Cohen LK, Gift HC (eds). Disease Prevention and Oral Health Promotion: Socio-Dental Sciences in Action. Copenhagen: Blackwell Munksgaard, 1995:33–71.
8. Patrick D, Chiang YP. Measurement of health outcomes in treatment evaluations: Conceptual and methodological challenges. Med Care 2000;38(9, suppl II):14–25.
9. Feeny D, Barr RD, Furlong W, Hudson M, Mulhern RK. A postscript to the international workshop on assessing health-related quality of life in children with cancer. Int J Cancer Suppl 1999;12:154.
10. Slade G (ed). Measuring Oral Health and Quality of Life. Chapel Hill: Department of Dental Ecology, School of Dentistry, University of North Carolina, 1997.
11. Rettig RA, Sadler JH, Meyer KB, et al. Assessing health and quality of life outcomes in dialysis: A report on an Institute of Medicine workshop. Am J Kidney Dis 1997;30:140–155.
12. Barry MJ, Fowler FJ Jr, Mulley AG Jr, Henderson JV Jr, Wennberg JE. Patient reactions to a program designed to facilitate patient participation in treatment decisions for benign prostatic hyperplasia. Med Care 1995;33:771–782.
13. Lohr KN. Applications of health status assessment measures in clinical practice. Overview of the third conference on advances in health status assessment. Med Care 1992;30(5, suppl):1–14.
14. Furberg C, Shuttinga JA (eds). Quality of Life Assessment: Practice, Problems, and Promise. Washington, DC: National Institutes of Health, 1991.
15. Guyatt G, Feeny D, Patrick D. Issues in quality-of-life measurement in clinical trials. Control Clin Trials 1991;12(4, suppl):81S–90S.
16. Lohr KN. Advances in health status assessment. Overview of the conference. Med Care 1989;27(3, suppl):S1–S11.
17. Ware JE Jr. Standards for validating health measures: Definition and content. J Chronic Dis 1987;40:473–480.
18. Katz S. The science of quality of life. J Chronic Dis 1987;40:459–463.
19. Wenger NK, Mattson ME, Furberg CD, Elinson J (eds). Assessment of Quality of Life in Clinical Trials Cardiovascular Therapies. New York: LeJacq, 1984.
20. Berg R (ed). Health Status Indexes. Chicago: Hospital Research and Educational Trust, 1973.
21. Cohen LK, Gift HC (eds). Disease Prevention and Oral Health Promotion: Socio-Dental Sciences in Action. Copenhagen: Blackwell Munksgaard, 1995.
22. US Public Health Service, US Department of Health and Human Services. Oral Health in America: A Report of the Surgeon General—Executive Summary. Available at: www.nidcr.nih.gov/sgr/execsumm.pdf. Accessed April 24, 2002.

23. Gooch BF, Dolan TA, Bourque LB. Correlates of self-reported dental health status upon enrollment in the Rand Health Insurance Experiment. J Dent Educ 1989; 53:629–637.

24. Atchison KA, Dolan TA. Development of the Geriatric Oral Health Assessment Index. J Dent Educ 1990;54: 680–687.

25. Hunt RJ, Slade GD, Strauss P. Differences between racial groups in the impact of oral disorders among older adults in North Carolina. J Pub Health Dent 1995;55:205–209.

26. Kressin N, Spriro A, Bosse R, Garcia R, Kazis L. Assessing oral health-related quality of life: Findings from the normative aging study. Med Care 1996;34:416–427.

27. Gift HC, Atchison KA, Dayton CM. Conceptualizing oral health and oral health-related quality of life. Soc Sci Med 1997;44:601–608.

28. Gilbert GH, Duncan RP, Heft MW, Dolan TA, Vogel WB. Oral disadvantage among dentate adults. Community Dent Oral Epidemiol 1997;25:301–313.

29. Locker D, Miller Y. Subjectively reported oral health status in an adult population. Community Dent Oral Epidemiol 1994;22:425–430.

30. Locker D, Slade G. Association between clinical and subjective indicators of oral health status in an older adult population. Gerodontology 1994;11:108–114.

31. Slade G, Spencer AJ. Social impact of oral conditions among older adults. Aust Dent J 1994;39:358–364.

32. Leao A, Sheiham A. Relation between clinical dental status and subjective impacts on daily living. J Dent Res 1995;74:1408–1413.

33. Coates E, Slade GD, Goss AN, Gorkic E. Oral conditions and their social impact among HIV dental patients. Aust Dent J 1996;41:33–36.

34. Bryant PS. Summary of NIH-supported quality of life research projects: May 2000. Presented at the Workshop on Quality of Life and Oral and Craniofacial Conditions; Ann Arbor, MI, 7–13 May 2000.

35. Gruman, J, Follick M. Putting Evidence into Practice: Report of the Working Group on the Integration of Effective Behavioral Treatments into Clinical Care. Bethesda, MD: Office of Behavioral and Social Science Research, National Institutes of Health, 1998.

Index